Sustainability-oriented Innovation Systems in China and India

Global economic growth, recently fuelled by Asia's emerging economies, has greatly accelerated the accumulation of greenhouse gases in the atmosphere and boosted demand for scarce natural resources, including energy, food and mineral raw materials. These developments are pushing the planet close to its ecological boundaries.

Transforming the world economy towards sustainability, while ensuring decent levels of resource use for all global citizens, is the greatest challenge of our time. This book explores how innovation systems need to be adapted to successfully confront these challenges. The first chapter introduces the concept of sustainability-oriented innovation systems which highlights the systematic differences between systems that have developed along current resource-intensive technological trajectories and those that address the impending environmental mega-problems. The subsequent articles present case studies of sustainability-oriented innovations in a number of policy areas, including energy efficiency, electric mobility and generation of renewable energy, in China and India. These case studies confirm the specificities of innovation systems geared towards a green techno-economic paradigm.

This book was originally published as a special issue of *Innovation and Development*.

Tilman Altenburg is an economic geographer and Head of the Sustainable Economic and Social Development Department at the German Development Institute, Germany. Since 1986 he has carried out empirical research and published books and journal articles on issues of competitiveness, industrial and innovation policy, SME promotion and value chain development.

Sustainability-oriented Innovation Systems in China and India

Edited by
Tilman Altenburg

LONDON AND NEW YORK

First published 2016
by Routledge

2 Park Square, Milton Park, Abingdon, Oxfordshire OX14 4RN
52 Vanderbilt Avenue, New York, NY 10017

Routledge is an imprint of the Taylor & Francis Group, an informa business

First issued in paperback 2020

Copyright © 2016 Taylor & Francis

All rights reserved. No part of this book may be reprinted or reproduced or utilised in any form or by any electronic, mechanical, or other means, now known or hereafter invented, including photocopying and recording, or in any information storage or retrieval system, without permission in writing from the publishers.

Notice:
Product or corporate names may be trademarks or registered trademarks, and are used only for identification and explanation without intent to infringe.

British Library Cataloguing in Publication Data
A catalogue record for this book is available from the British Library

ISBN 13: 978-1-138-93769-7 (hbk)
ISBN 13: 978-0-367-59814-3 (pbk)

Typeset in Times New Roman
by RefineCatch Limited, Bungay, Suffolk

Publisher's Note
The publisher accepts responsibility for any inconsistencies that may have arisen during the conversion of this book from journal articles to book chapters, namely the possible inclusion of journal terminology.

Disclaimer
Every effort has been made to contact copyright holders for their permission to reprint material in this book. The publishers would be grateful to hear from any copyright holder who is not here acknowledged and will undertake to rectify any errors or omissions in future editions of this book.

Contents

Citation Information

The chapters in this book were originally published in *Innovation and Development*, volume 2, issue 1 (April 2012). When citing this material, please use the original page numbering for each article, as follows:

Chapter 7
Key actors and their motives for wind energy innovation in China
Frauke Urban, Johan Nordensvärd and Yuan Zhou
Innovation and Development, volume 2, issue 1 (April 2012) pp. 111–130

Chapter 8
Challenges of low carbon technology diffusion: insights from shifts in China's photovoltaic industry development
Doris Fischer
Innovation and Development, volume 2, issue 1 (April 2012) pp. 131–146

For any permission-related enquiries please visit:
http://www.tandfonline.com/page/help/permissions

Notes on Contributors

Tilman Altenburg is an economic geographer and Head of the Sustainable Economic and Social Development Department at the German Development Institute, Germany. Since 1986 he has carried out empirical research and published books and journal articles on issues of competitiveness, industrial and innovation policy, SME promotion and value chain development.

Shikha Bhasin is a Researcher in the Energy research Centre of the Netherlands (ECN).

Ankur Chaudhary is based in the Indian Institute of Technology, New Delhi, India.

Doris Fischer is Professor and Chair of the Department of Chinese Studies at Würzberg University, Germany. She was previously based at the German Development Institute, Bonn, Germany.

Adrian Lema is based in the Danish Ministry of Climate, Energy and Building.

Rasmus Lema is an Associate Professor in the Department of Business Studies at Aalborg University, Denmark.

Ajay Mathur is based in the Bureau of Energy Efficiency for the Indian Government.

Johan Nordensvärd is a Lecturer in Social Policy at the University of Southampton, UK. He was previously based at the London School of Economics, UK.

Jonathan Nowak Delgado works for Next Century Strategy + Innovation (UG).

Anna Pegels is an economist based in the Sustainable Economic and Social Development Department at the German Development Institute, Germany.

Ambuj Sagar is based in the Indian Institute of Technology, New Delhi, India.

Frauke Urban works as a Senior Lecturer in Environment and Development at the Centre for Development, Environment and Policy, SOAS, London, UK.

Rainer Walz is based in Competence Center Sustainability and Infrastructure Systems, Fraunhofer Institute for Systems and Innovation Research, Karlsruhe, Germany.

Yuan Zhou is an Assistant Professor in the School of Public Policy and Management at Tsinghua University, Beijing, China.

Preface

The chapters of this book are articles that originally appeared in one of the special issues of *Innovation and Development*, an inter-disciplinary international journal from Globelics network, published by Taylor & Francis. http://www.tandf.co.uk/journals/RIAD

Innovation and Development is a relatively young journal born at a particular juncture in the discourse on development. The closing decades of the last century witnessed unprecedented changes in different spheres of economies and societies. This was induced by, among others, technological innovations led mainly by information communication technology and institutional innovations, resulting in increased integration between countries under globalization. In the emerging context of heightened competition, international competitiveness became the only means of survival. With the expanding global production networks and global innovation networks, different sectors across countries got themselves located appropriately in the global value chains. Instances of high rates growth sustained even for decades tended to suggest that achieving faster economic growth is within the reach of developing world. Unfortunately, however, the episodes of high growth induced by innovation at different levels turned out to be not inclusive and sustainable. The challenge, therefore, is to accomplish development that is sustainable and inclusive.

The mandate of *Innovation and Development* has its roots in this new millennium challenge. Since the role of innovation in development is increasingly being recognized in both the developed and the developing world, an enhancement of our understanding on the interface between innovation and development might help to find ways of addressing many of the developmental issues and of making growth process inclusive and sustainable. Hence, understanding the link between innovation, capacity building and development has emerged as a critical issue of concern for the academia, practitioners and policy makers, including international organizations such the World Bank or United Nations.

But our understanding of the links between innovation and development remains at best rudimentary, notwithstanding an unprecedented increase in studies on development and innovation on the one hand and a heightened interest in development practice on the other. While the two disciplines (development studies and innovation studies) have been growing in parallel, as they are traditionally separated with limited linkages, in recent years there has been an upsurge of interest in innovation issues in development studies. At the same time, with an increasing engagement of civil society organizations in developmental issues, innovative development practices are becoming more visible and their impact felt more than ever before.

By adopting a broader approach to innovation (to include technological, institutional, organizational and others) the journal and this book series aims at providing a forum for discussion of various issues pertaining to innovation, development and their interaction, both in the developed and developing world, for achieving sustainable and inclusive growth.

It is matter of great satisfaction that *Innovation and Development* has been able to lay the strong foundations for integrating innovation studies and development studies through the high quality articles contributed by scholars across the world. These articles dealt with issues pertaining to diverse contexts ranging from primary agriculture to high-end services and from low technology sectors to high technology sectors operating in both the developing and developed world. In tune with the Globelics research agenda, *Innovation and Development* has also been promoting research and discourse on innovation at the national, regional, sectoral and societal level to facilitate building up of systems for learning, innovation and competence building. A unique feature of Innovation Developments is its supplementary sections that publish Ph D abstracts, web resources for research and innovations in practice.

The editorial board of *Innovation and Development* also takes pride in highlighting the significant contribution of this journal during the last five years of its existence through its special issues that focused on subjects of much relevance for theory and policy. The special issues brought out by the journal dealt with issues that include;

a) Sustainability–oriented innovation systems in China and India, guest editor Tilman Altenburg
b) Capability building and global innovation networks, guest editors Glenda Kruss and Michael Gastrow
c) Innovation and global competitiveness: case of India's manufacturing sector, guest editors N. S. Sidharthan and K. Narayanan;
d) Innovation for inclusive development, guest editor Fernando Santiago, and
e) New models of inclusive innovation for development, guest editors Richard Heeks, Christopher Foster and Yanuar Nugroho

We place on record our appreciation for all our guest editors for joining hands with us in our endeavor to take forward the agenda of *Innovation and Development*. We also take this occasion to acknowledge the liberal support that we received from the Editorial Advisory Board and the Scientific Committee. Our special appreciation for Taylor & Francis for bringing out this book series from the special issues of *Innovation and Development* and Ms Emily Ross for taking this project to its local conclusion.

It is our hope that this book series will be found useful by the academia at large, innovation scholars in particular and the policy makers concerned.

K. J. Joseph (Editor in Chief),
Cristina Chaminade, Susan Cozzens, Gabriela Dutrénit,
Mammo Muchie, Judith Sutz and Tim Turpin

Editors, Innovation and Development

Introduction

Global economic growth, recently fuelled by Asia's emerging economies, has greatly accelerated the accumulation of greenhouse gases in the atmosphere and boosted demand for scarce natural resources, including energy, food and mineral raw materials. These developments are pushing the planet close to its ecological boundaries. Transforming the world economy towards sustainability, while ensuring decent levels of resource use for all global citizens, is the greatest challenge of our time. This year, the Rio + 20 United Nations Conference on Sustainable Development marks a renewed effort to embark on ways of 'greening' the global economy in the context of sustainable development and poverty eradication. Greening the economy entails a techno-economic paradigm shift that needs to be:

- *radical*, as unsustainable technological trajectories need to be disrupted and replaced by new generations of technologies in order to decouple economic development from resource consumption and carbon emissions;
- *rapid*, because this decoupling has to take place within the next decade or two – a failure to take immediate action will overstrain the carrying capacity of critical global ecosystems and lead to much higher costs in the future; and
- *systemic*, as it implies changing technological regimes and combining industrial and institutional sub-systems in innovative ways.

This Special Issue explores how innovation systems need to be adapted to successfully confront these challenges. The first article introduces the concept of Sustainability-oriented Innovation Systems (SoIS) which highlights systematic differences between systems that have developed along current resource-intensive technological trajectories and those that address the impending environmental mega-problems. The subsequent articles present case studies of sustainability-oriented innovations in a number of policy areas, including energy efficiency, electric mobility and generation of renewable energy, in China and India.

The concept of SoIS is presented by Altenburg and Pegels. In trying to accelerate the development and deployment of environmentally sustainable technologies, SoIS are confronted with all-pervasive market failures that place high demands on governance. Governments need to find ways to internalise environmental costs, using a range of innovative policy instruments, such as cap-and-trade systems, feed-in tariffs for renewable energy, or environmental standards and labels that make markets more transparent. Also, they need to discourage the use of less sustainable alternatives and encourage promising 'clean' technologies, in some cases for decades before they emerge as cost-competitive under free market conditions. Which technological alternatives deserve support is often politically contested, as ongoing heated debates on biofuels, nuclear energy, or carbon capture and storage exemplify. Thus, governmental agencies need to establish a political consensus over technological roadmaps; and they need to be able to mobilise and eventually withdraw subsidies for selective technologies in ways that minimise misallocation and political capture. At the same time, the fact that roadmaps are highly policy-driven and dependent on societal preferences and political settlements suggests a considerable divergence of national technological trajectories.

The following case studies explore how China and India deal with these challenges of 'transitioning' towards developing into sustainable economies. Given the size and sustained growth of these two economies, their efforts to decouple economic development from carbon emissions and resource consumption are crucial to avoid overstretching of the global ecosystems' carrying capacities. Both countries have recently adopted ambitious plans to curb carbon emissions and advance sustainability-oriented innovations. China and India are latecomers to industrial development, with innovation systems heavily reliant on foreign companies, joint ventures and technology licensing; but in recent years have also managed to spawn industrial champions that are amongst the world leaders in low carbon technologies. China is the largest manufacturer of wind turbines, photovoltaic cells and electric two-wheelers and among the world's leaders in battery technology for cars. India is lagging behind China in most technologies and has more budget constraints, but has nevertheless been able to bring forth successful companies including one of the world's leading wind turbine manufacturers and one of the first exporters of electric cars. Given their differences in initial economic and environmental conditions, policy objectives and patterns of economic governance, both countries offer interesting comparisons.

Lema and Lema explore the relevance of different international transfer channels for low carbon technology acquisition in China and India. Looking at wind and solar power as well as electric and hybrid vehicle technologies, the authors find that conventional technology transfer mechanisms such as foreign direct investments, joint ventures and licensing were important for industry formation and take-off. However, over the last 10 years, China and India's cross-border technology relations have evolved significantly and unconventional mechanisms for technology acquisition, such as investment in international R&D collaboration and acquisition of foreign firms, are today very important in defining their technological trajectories.

Chaudhary, Sagar and Mathur focus on energy-efficiency programmes in India. The authors start from the key challenge of SoIS – that environmental public goods are typically under-provided by ordinary market activities and require a coordinating organisation that is able to identify innovation gaps and design programmes to address them. They analyse four programmes run by the Bureau of Energy Efficiency, including a standards and labelling programme to provide the consumer an informed choice about the energy saving potential of household equipment; a programme to accelerate the dissemination of compact fluorescent lamps; the introduction of the Energy Conservation Building Code; and a market-based mechanism to enhance energy efficiency in the industrial sector. The case studies reflect how large-scale deployment needs to draw on a combination of policy measures (including information campaigns, standards and labels, demonstration projects), economic incentives and a mix of voluntary and mandatory regulations. The combination of such elements depends on the specificities of each technology. The authors also highlight the importance of a commercial orientation in the programmes for technology dissemination.

Altenburg, Bhasin and Fischer have applied the SoIS concept to electromobility in China, France, Germany and India. They highlight the transition to e-mobility as a multidimensional challenge implying severe coordination failure. For example, mass production of electric vehicles is hampered by the lack of public infrastructure for recharging batteries, which in turn only attracts investments if a considerable fleet of electric vehicles ensures demand for charging services. Likewise, simultaneous investments need to be made in interdependent technologies, such as batteries, light materials and power trains. Policymakers therefore need to provide upfront incentives and ensure synchronisation of R&D and investments activities to mobilise the entire sector. Incentive packages depend on the underlying objectives of e-mobility promotion, e.g. whether only renewable energy sources are eligible or not, and on the interest of the incumbent automotive industry.

The authors show that all four countries adopt very different policy packages, and trace differences back to initial industry characteristics, specific political priorities and patterns of economic governance.

Two papers analyse the emergence of the wind turbine industry. Walz and Nowak Delgado show how China and India have successfully developed indigenous wind turbine industries. In both countries, leading domestic players started by obtaining production licenses, moved on to form joint ventures, and finally started to produce their own designs and in some cases took over their foreign joint venture partners. At the same time, both countries' technology acquisition strategies differ markedly. India pursues a private sector-led approach, with fairly open trade regimes and an open door policy for foreign investors. Technology has mainly been acquired through international R&D collaboration and firm acquisitions. China, on the other hand, has followed a more policy-driven strategy, with state-owned enterprises playing a prominent role. The Chinese government strongly fosters capability building and supported the emergence of big national wind turbine manufacturers.

Urban, Nordensvärd and Zhou complement this research by analysing the motives that have been driving wind turbine industry growth in China. They argue that specific configurations of interest groups influence the direction, speed, development and implementation of wind energy policies and technological trajectories. Having analysed the interests of national and provincial government authorities, state-owned-, private-, and foreign firms, as well as research institutions and NGOs, the authors find that the primary motives driving wind energy innovation in China seem to be related to energy security and competitiveness, despite a growing climate change discourse. Wind turbine manufacturing is seen as an opportunity for Chinese firms to build cutting-edge capabilities and compete with international players. While in the beginning the domestic wind turbine industry was built on technology transfer from foreign investors and local content requirements, reliance on both factors has recently decreased and a large number of domestic firms have emerged under strong state leadership and state financing.

Finally, Fischer discusses the deployment of solar energy technologies in China. Due to its competitive advantages in manufacturing, China has become the largest producer of solar photovoltaic (PV) cells and modules in the world. Production, until recently was almost completely export oriented since the government was not willing to provide the necessary subsidies for promoting PV deployment in its home market: firstly, to keep energy prices low, and secondly, to avoid dependency on imported purified silicon. However, in 2009 this situation changed and the local market for PV installations is now growing rapidly. The author argues that this change was not mainly driven by climate change concerns. Instead, the fear that export markets would plummet due to the economic crisis in industrialised countries and China's own increased ability to produce purified silicon and therefore become technologically self-reliant, were decisive factors for embarking on an ambitious solar energy deployment programme.

In sum, the case studies confirm the specificities of innovation systems geared towards a green techno-economic paradigm. The Governments in China and India have taken a pro-active role in incentivising and coordinating sustainability innovations, and are experimenting with a range of innovative policy approaches. The approaches taken by the two governments to tackle the problem of multiple market failures and balance economic and environmental policy objectives differ considerably. While the development of low carbon technologies is in most cases still at an early stage, different patterns of competitive specialisation are already becoming evident.

Most papers in this Special Issue have been developed under a collaborative research project on 'Technological trajectories for climate change mitigation in China, Europe and India'. The researchers involved in this network are grateful for funding from a consortium of three European research foundations: The Swedish Riksbankens Jubileumsfond, the German Volkswagen Foundation and the Italian Compagnia di San Paolo. Furthermore, the Altenburg/Pegels and Lema/Lema papers benefited from generous funding from the German Federal Ministry for Economic Cooperation and Development (BMZ), and the Lema/Lema and Fischer papers from the European Commission's CO-REACH programme.

Tilman Altenburg
German Development Institute

Sustainability-oriented innovation systems – managing the green transformation

Tilman Altenburg and Anna Pegels

German Development Institute / Deutsches Institut für Entwicklungspolitik, Bonn, Germany

Global warming and other impending environmental mega-problems call for a new technological paradigm. The urgency of the development and deployment of technological solutions is such that governments will need to make widespread use of 'carrots and sticks' to ensure that next-generation technologies are developed and deployed, more demanding standards and regulations are applied and stricter enforcement is guaranteed. To capture the main elements of this paradigm shift, we introduce the concept of Sustainability-oriented Innovation Systems (SoIS). SoIS make particularly high demands on governance, because governments need to disrupt unsustainable technological pathways and encourage alternative technologies long before they reach the stage of commercial viability. This implies picking winners in situations of technological uncertainty and highly disparate stakeholder preferences. SoIS also build on new types of policies that help to internalise environmental costs. The policy-driven nature of technological development may possibly result in a wide divergence of national technological trajectories.

Introduction: a new approach to innovation systems research

In the past, economic growth has been achieved at the expense of natural resource depletion, without stocks being allowed to regenerate. Ecosystems have been widely degraded and biodiversity has been lost at an unprecedented pace (Millennium Ecosystem Assessment, 2005). If current resource-intensity continues, environmental tipping points may create ecosystem disequilibria that will threaten human livelihoods.[1] While climate change is the most pressing challenge, many other environmental imbalances are expected to become unsustainable in the near future. A group of Resilience Alliance researchers has identified nine 'planetary boundaries' that must not be crossed if major risks to humanity are to be avoided. They include limits to freshwater use, ocean acidification, loss of biodiversity and chemical pollution (Rockström et al., 2009).

At the same time, the global economy is experiencing a phase of unprecedented growth which is putting an enormous strain on global and local ecosystems. Humankind is approaching the planetary boundaries at high speed.

Changing to sustainable patterns of development while ensuring decent levels of resource access for all the world's citizens is the greatest challenge of our time. It calls for what Freeman (1992) termed a *green techno-economic paradigm shift*: while the need for new generations of resource-efficient technologies is undisputed, a paradigm shift will also entail a change in societal norms and values, motivating new life styles, different ways of accounting for development and economic incentive schemes that systematically internalise environmental costs. In the same vein, the German Advisory Council on Global Change (WBGU) calls for a 'new global social contract for a low carbon and sustainable global economic system' to achieve a transformation similar in scope to the Neolithic and industrial revolutions (WBGU, 2011, p.1).

This paper sets out to develop a conceptual framework for the analysis of the innovation efforts required to embark on such a sustainable development path. Building on groundwork done by Stamm et al. (2009), we develop the conceptual foundations for Sustainability-oriented Innovation Systems (SoIS). This concept is based on evolutionary innovation systems research, but places far greater emphasis on governance and introduces relevant additional dimensions.

The starting point is the need to accelerate the development and deployment of environmentally sustainable technologies. In pursuing this objective, SoIS are confronted with particularly serious market failures. Innovation systems research traditionally concentrates on the market failure of non-appropriability: as the social benefits of science, technology and innovation tend to exceed privately appropriable benefits, the services concerned are frequently undersupplied. While this also applies to SoIS, the current rules of market economies are even less effective when new generations of environmentally sustainable technologies are to be developed: firstly, because they allow economic agents to externalise many environmental costs, which then have to be borne by society as a whole now and in the future. Secondly, SoIS need to disrupt unsustainable technological trajectories and foster the development of sustainable substitutes, some of which may require more than a decade or two to become competitive. Supporting these clean technologies of the future is fraught with coordination and information failures.

This has important ramifications for policy and future technological trajectories. As will be shown later, the multiple market failure calls for governments to play a more active guiding role and for a very distinctive range of policy instruments and may result in diverging national technological trajectories, reflecting specific societal preferences, power constellations and policy frameworks.

This paper is divided into three sections. Section 1 stresses the urgency of changing innovation efforts to the search for environmentally sustainable solutions and considers the extent to which innovation systems research has already taken up the challenge. Section 2 advances the existing literature further by developing the concept of SoIS. It highlights important differences between 'business as usual' innovation systems and those aimed at disrupting unsustainable trajectories and accelerating the development and deployment of 'clean' technologies. The three sub-sections of Section 2 are devoted to these differences: increasing demands on governance; different sets of policies; and potentially diverging technological trajectories. Section 3 concludes by identifying relevant topics for future research.

1.   Innovations for environmental sustainability: relevance and conceptual debates

1.1   *An evolutionary perspective on innovation*

The concept of innovation systems (Freeman, 1995; Lundvall, 1992) seeks to explain the systemic nature of innovation. More specifically, it helps us to understand how technologies, industries and institutions co-evolve and shows how technological paradigms are created and how they give rise to specific technological trajectories. Thus the concept provides in principle a suitable analytical framework for understanding the implications of a paradigm change from a fossil fuel-based economic system to one of resource-efficient sustainable production.

The core principle of the innovation systems approach is that innovation is a relational, inter-active and cumulative process that occurs between producers and users of goods and services, including private industries, universities, providers of knowledge-intensive business services, trade organisations and public support institutions. This relational nature means that technological knowledge cannot be fully codified and traded like any other good. Innovation is described as a process whereby institutions and technologies co-evolve in particular ways (Nelson, 1994): as initial institutional conditions differ – in terms of how markets operate or of societal values and product preferences, for example – different technologies necessarily evolve differently, which in turn leads to particular adaptations of the institutional framework.

Central to this evolutionary understanding of innovation are the notions of technological paradigms and technological trajectories. According to Dosi (1982), a technological paradigm is a kind of directed research programme aimed at discovering solutions to a specific set of perceived problems. Importantly, a paradigm implies 'strong prescriptions on the directions of technical change to pursue and those to neglect' (Dosi, 1982, p. 152). Once a technological paradigm has gained hegemony, the development of new technologies follows a certain direction of advance within its boundaries: a *technological trajectory*. As progress on a technological trajectory is cumulative, the search for new technologies reinforces its initial direction. As we argue later, this in-built path-dependency and inertia of technological trajectories constitutes the main challenge for sustainability-oriented innovation systems that try to disrupt firmly established, but environmentally unsustainable trajectories.

Traditionally, policy frameworks for technological innovation have been defined mainly at the level of nation states. This has given rise to the notion of *national* innovation systems. While these are mostly understood as a 'permeable territorial formation, the borders of which are crossed by numerous linkages within global-local production networks' (Coe et al., 2004), the focus on national systems and country-specific patterns of technological specialisation nevertheless means that home-country determinants, such as linkages between national firms and research institutions, are deemed more important than cross-border linkages. The popular debate on the 'competitiveness of nations' (for example, Porter, 1990) builds on the same premises.

With increasing globalisation, however, the number of international regulations has proliferated. Global and regional bodies have gained considerably in importance as sources of norms and standards to which national actors must adhere. Similarly, international sources of knowledge and transfer mechanisms are becoming increasingly important for technological learning. Among these new international conduits of technology acquisition are the integration of firms into global value chains, joint ventures, mergers and acquisitions, the formation of international research networks in both the public and the private sphere and international labour migration (Altenburg et al., 2008; see also Lema and Lema in this volume).

Innovation systems are therefore characterised by increasingly complex forms of multi-level governance. Nation states still have an important role to play in setting regulatory frameworks, defining national research priorities and promoting networks among national firms and supporting organisations. However, a growing body of rules and regulations is negotiated at international level and then further specified at lower levels – regional, national and sub-national. As we will show in Section 2, multi-level governance is particularly challenging when it comes to innovations in the field of global public goods.

1.2 *The need for a paradigm change towards environmental sustainability*

For more than two decades, the global economy has experienced a phase of unprecedented growth, fuelled mainly by the dynamism of Asia's emerging economies. Since the 1990s, the annual growth rate of the global economy has averaged about 3% (World Bank, 2011). This growth has led to rising demand for scarce natural resources, including food, energy and mineral raw materials, which has in turn contributed to accelerated growth in regions that are net exporters of these resources. A particularly noteworthy phenomenon is the rise across the globe of urban middle classes emulating the resource-intensive life styles of the West (Kharas, 2010; Ravallion, 2009), which is exerting additional pressure on scarce natural resources. Energy supplies, for example, would have to double by 2050 to meet the growing demand of all households worldwide (World Energy Council, 2007).

The economic activities of the past have already pushed the planet close to its ecological boundaries. Climate change poses one of the most urgent challenges. Owing to the accumulation of greenhouse gases in the atmosphere, the global mean temperature is rising. The Fourth Assessment Report of the Intergovernmental Panel on Climate Change calculates that total greenhouse gas emissions should peak around 2015 and then gradually fall to 50% of 1990 levels by 2050 (IPCC, 2007). Taking current economic growth rates into account, the 2°C limit can be respected only if the carbon intensity (that is CO_2 emissions per unit of economic output) of the world economy is drastically reduced. Technological innovation for climate change mitigation is therefore becoming crucial and needs to be accelerated substantially.

While greenhouse gas emissions are currently the most urgent topic, the traditional pattern of economic growth is depleting other environmental resources, too, particularly water, fertile soils, forests and biodiversity.[2] To focus solely on *low carbon* innovations would therefore be to take too narrow a view: interdependencies between different resource scarcities need to be taken into account. As an example, producing bio-ethanol as a substitute for fossil fuels may have negative effects on food production, water resources and soil fertility.

Market economies are already developing innovations that reduce resource consumption per unit of output. In OECD countries, energy and non-energy material consumption, CO_2 emissions and municipal waste generation are rising more slowly than GDP (OECD, 2011, p. 19). However, the current speed of decoupling is far too low, and the resource-saving effects of new technologies are at least partly offset by growing consumption ('rebound effect': Schipper, 2000).

The manifold threats to the earth system reflect the fact that economic incentives globally are geared to accumulating physical, financial and human capital without regard for environmental sustainability (UNEP, 2011). Investors can still externalise environmental costs to a large degree. Hence, what is needed is the consistent internalisation of environmental costs in economic decision-making. Ultimately, the way welfare is measured must change. Conventional indicators, such as GDP, are distorted measures of economic performance since they fail to capture the extent to which economic activities deplete natural capital (WBGU, 2011). As long as the ultimate aim of economic activities is not measured appropriately, the result will be wrong policies.[3]

The financial efforts required to manage the transformation are considerable, but bearable. According to UNEP (2011), the shift to a low carbon, resource-efficient path in 10 central sectors of the economy would require 2% of global GDP annually.

We do not yet know how soon this paradigm change will occur. After the no more than incremental successes of the Durban Summit there is little likelihood of the reforms needed to limit global warming to 2°C being undertaken in time. However, according to McKinsey (2009, p. 8), 'a 10-year delay in taking abatement action would make it virtually impossible to keep global warming below 2°C'. We do know that most resources currently in use are finite. Failure to take immediate action will overstrain the atmosphere's absorptive capacity, induce worse global warming and lead to much higher abatement costs in the future. The question is thus not whether the global economy will adopt resource-efficient (and particularly low carbon) production or not: it will have to. The question is whether this transition will be organised before major environmental and economic crises occur or whether abatement action will be taken only under the pressure of acute crises and at a far higher cost.

1.3 *Earlier attempts to incorporate environmental sustainability into innovation systems research*

The goal of internalised environmental costs is not new. Even in the early 1970s, growing concern about the environmental impact of sustained economic growth led to an increase in interest in environmental sustainability. In 1972, the Club of Rome initiated a study on the 'Limits to Growth', which is regarded as one of the foundation stones of sustainability research (Meadows et al., 1972). In this study, a team of researchers built a comprehensive model of the world, in which several complex systems interacted. Among other things, the model simulated interrelations between population density, food resources, energy and environmental damage. The various scenarios developed on the basis of different policy options all led to similar outcomes: if the current trends were to continue, the world would see a catastrophic decline in population and standards of living within a century.

In the later 1970s, environmental economists such as Herman Daly took up this concern and began to criticise the externalisation of environmental costs in growth accounting. Daly attributed the systematic underpricing of natural resources to the societal dominance of the other production factors, capital and labour. Without an effective 'lobby', natural resources were seen as prone to overexploitation. He therefore promoted the concept of steady-state economics, implying that the economy does not grow beyond a certain level of wealth to preserve limited natural resources (Daly, 1977).

Another milestone was reached in 1987, when the World Commission on Environment and Development presented the Brundlandt report to the United Nations. This report advanced the understanding of sustainability by stating that 'environment' and 'development' are inseparable. It defined sustainable development as meeting 'the needs of the present without comprising the ability of future generations to meet their own needs'. As the authors of the report saw it, the limits that sustainable development implies are not absolute, but set both by the ability of the biosphere to absorb the effects of human activities and by the state of technology and social organisation. The enhancement of both technology and social organisation thus opens up avenues for future growth.

Despite this pioneering work, mainstream neoclassical economics has failed to incorporate the environmental dimension systematically both in its concepts (for example, economic growth accounting) and in its incentive systems. This, unfortunately, is also true of most approaches in evolutionary economics and innovation systems research. The main thrust of innovation systems research has been the attempt to increase allocative efficiency and profitability in terms of *monetary* value. Based on Schumpeter (1942), an innovation system was regarded as successful when it created 'new combinations' that could not easily be copied by competitors, thus allowing the innovator to reap above-average profits for a certain period of time. As environmental goods 'without price tags' had no impact on innovation rents, they were not considered relevant variables.

It was not until the 1990s that some innovation scholars began to incorporate sustainability concerns into their research. Following the concept of techno-economic paradigms, Freeman (1992) introduced the notion of the 'green techno-economic paradigm' as a new structural era of economic development. The 'green' era potentially follows the eras of steam power, electric power, mass production, information and communication technologies. It is seen as a precondition for sustained economic growth in the twenty-first century. However, it will not occur automatically. As necessary preconditions, Freeman refers to a combination of such institutional changes as the effective regulation of pollution and major modifications to the pattern of inputs.

Segura-Bonilla (1999) takes up this concept and applies it to an analysis of the Central American forestry sector. Drawing on the systems of innovation approach and ecological economics, he introduces the 'sustainable systems of innovation' approach. This concept considers the possibility of including nature-human relationships in the 'systems of innovation' approach. Lundvall's (1992) definition of innovation systems is expanded through the explicit inclusion of natural elements: 'A sustainable system of innovation is constituted by human and natural elements and relationships which interact in the production, diffusion and use of new, and economically useful, knowledge' (Segura-Bonilla 1999, p. 79).

More recently, a related strand of discussion has emerged under the heading of 'sustainability transitions' (Grin et al., 2010). The sustainability transitions school originates from environmental research. It builds on the idea that the challenges of sustainability and sustainable development cannot be addressed with end-of-pipe solutions for mitigating environmental impacts or with incremental environmental improvements. Instead, this school of thought analyses the evolution of 'systems innovations' that would enable larger jumps in environmental efficiency (Elzen et al., 2004, p. 1). Its ultimate goal is to develop points of reference and promising tools for 'transition management'. Transition management is conceptualised as a multi-phase and multi-level concept based on the conviction that, although transitions cannot be entirely planned and managed, the direction and pace of the transition of socio-technical regimes can still be influenced. Transition management therefore aims at better organising and coordinating transition processes as well as influencing the speed of transitions, while steering them into a sustainable direction (Loorbach and Rotmans, 2006)

In sum, a number of attempts have been made to incorporate environmental sustainability into innovation systems research. In addition to the aforementioned conceptual papers, a growing body of literature discusses the emergence of specific technological trajectories in 'green' technologies (for example, Jacobsson andBergek, 2004; Foxon et al., 2008). All these authors agree that the objective must be to internalise environmental costs into economic decision-making. Few authors, however, explicitly address the implications for governance. Among them are Hübner et al. (2000), who argue that eco-innovations 'usually need state assistance and/or a strong and consistent long-term policy framework for economic actors,' but do not generalise the concept beyond their case study of the German automobile industry.

The literature thus still lacks a systematic overview of all the implications that the sustainability paradigm has for the structures and functions of innovation systems: how it affects the design of policy packages; how governance systems need to be adapted to be able to organise a major paradigm change; and how changing governance structures and policies impact on technological trajectories. The following section seeks to fill this gap.

2. The specificities of sustainability-oriented innovation systems

Building on previous work by Stamm et al. (2009), this section operationalises the concept of 'sustainability-oriented innovation systems' (SoIS), highlighting what is fundamentally different when innovation systems are developed with a view to 'greening the economy'.

We define SoIS as *networks of institutions which create, import, modify and diffuse new technologies that help to reduce environmental impacts and resource intensity to a level commensurate with the earth's carrying capacity.*[4] The argument centres on the need to decouple economic growth from resource consumption through technological innovation, which has three fundamental implications for the way innovation systems will unfold in the future:

1. *Demands on governance are particularly high*, because innovation systems need to disrupt environmentally unsustainable technological pathways and encourage alternative technologies, in many cases long before these reach the stage of commercial viability. This presupposes choosing and subsidising specific technologies on the basis of uncertain

assumptions about future cost-benefit ratios – with all the risks that such interventions entail.

2. *Fundamentally new policies are needed* to internalise environmental costs into economic decision-making and accelerate the deployment of 'green' technologies.

3. The fact that future technological pathways are highly policy-driven and dependent on societal preferences suggests a considerable *divergence of national technological trajectories.*

The following sections explore these distinctive features in greater detail.

2.1   *High demands on governance*

In facilitating the transition to sustainable 'socio-technical systems' (Geels, 2004), governments have a particularly important and challenging role to play. Given the growing pressure on global ecosystems, policymakers cannot sit back and wait for market actors to develop clean technologies on their own. Even if environmental costs were fully reflected in market prices (which, owing to strong political resistance, is unlikely to happen in the near future – see, for example, the failure to establish a global emissions-trading system), new technologies would most probably not emerge at the pace dictated by the need to avoid ecological tipping points. New generations of technology usually require many years of research, development and pilot-testing before they become commercially viable.

The sustainability transition thus calls for pro-active and targeted policies to accelerate the development and deployment of 'green' technologies. Under conditions of considerable uncertainty about future prices and technological options, this makes particularly high demands on governance:

- first, there is the need to *overcome the multiple market failures* in developing new technologies well ahead of their commercial viability, which presupposes the ability to pick the right future technologies and to manage subsidies in such a way that these technologies can be developed with a minimum of misallocation and political capture;
- second, the choice of technologies implies difficult trade-offs and affects stakeholders in different ways. Hence *the need for consensus on the overall direction of change and for political settlements* to compensate the losers in reforms;
- third, change must be brought about under considerable *time pressure*. Especially where greenhouse gas emissions are concerned, fundamental policy changes must be made within the next 10 years;
- fourth, there is a serious need to *harmonise national and international policy frameworks* so that there may be a response to, and benefit may be derived from, the international environmental governance regimes that are currently evolving.

Market failure and technology selection

In market economies, technological innovations are mostly driven by market prices and developed by private actors. Such market-based search processes, however, have their limitations when it comes to developing fundamentally new technologies for coping with environmental problems. This is due to a combination of multiple market failures plus the pressure to develop solutions in the time remaining before ecological tipping points are reached.

The urgency of environmental problems calls for the development of some new technologies that are indisputably necessary for any pattern of human development that is in line with the earth's carrying capacity. Renewable energy sources with sufficient supply potential, such as solar energy, are one example; low-emissions transport systems are another. Similarly, developing carbon capture and storage technologies may become inevitable if the world fails to decouple economic growth swiftly from the use of fossil fuels for energy generation.

This may require substantial technology-specific public support, especially when new technologies take years or even decades to become commercially viable. A combination of market failures make it fairly unlikely that market-driven search processes will suffice for the development of timely solutions:

- *Externalities*: There is a lack of incentives to *internalise environmental costs* in private investment decisions. While market-based incentives may be used to incorporate such costs, full internalisation is impossible for ethical and political reasons.[5]
- *Coordination failure*: Many new technologies require simultaneous investment in correlated activities, and individual investors will not make major commitments unless someone guarantees that the associated investment on which he or she depends will be undertaken at the same time. Such *coordination failure* is particularly serious when entire socio-technical systems (Ropohl, 1999) rather than specific artefacts are to be changed – as is often the case in sustainability transformations. The successful establishment of offshore wind-farms, for example, calls for synchronised outlays on wind turbines, underwater steel structures and grids. A technology-specific and coordinated 'mission-type' approach may be required to initiate such systemic innovations.[6]
- *Non-appropriability:* Innovators need to bear search costs individually, whereas the innovation rents that can be obtained in successful cases rapidly dissipate as followers copy the innovation. Thus the pioneer's individual benefits are lower than the social value of their innovation (Hausmann and Rodrik, 2003). Again, this market failure is particularly serious when established technological trajectories are abandoned.

An additional obstacle to the development of new 'green' technologies is path-dependency, which is linked to, but goes beyond, coordination failure. Once a technological path has been embarked on, economies of scale and network externalities lead to reinforcing patterns which give incumbents a competitive advantage that makes switching to alternatives difficult. Many technological patterns have been established at times when fossil fuels were abundant and climate effects largely unknown. Now that circumstances have changed, high switching costs discourage the development of alternatives. Overcoming this 'carbon lock-in' (Unruh, 2000) requires deliberate action to disrupt established trajectories and promote alternatives in such a way that they, too, are able to develop the necessary economies of scale in production and to lower production costs. As a successful example, subsidised feed-in tariffs for solar energy created a market for mass-produced solar photovoltaic panels, which reduced prices by almost 80% between 1990 and 2010, bringing solar energy ever closer to grid parity (NREL, 2011, p. 60). Similarly, the French and Chinese governments subsidise the purchase of electric vehicles to kick-start production, assuming that, once certain minimum scales of production are reached, the price gap between these vehicles and conventional cars will narrow considerably.

In sum, the transition to 'green' technology needs pro-active government support if multiple market failures are to be overcome. Given the public goods nature of environmental goods and the need to change entire socio-technical systems, these market failures are more pervasive than those in incremental, 'business-as-usual' innovations. The support needed is *technology-specific* to the extent that more sustainable technologies are preferred to less sustainable ones. Identifying the best technology among a range of sustainable options can be left partly to market forces, thus enabling competition and creativity to be unleashed. Governments can, for example, define renewable energy targets and leave it to market forces to choose the best technology to achieve them. But even then there is a case for offering technology-specific subsidies: it may be appropriate to provide higher subsidies for the development of technologies that make use of abundant resources than for those with a small resource base. While markets would opt for technologies close to commercial viability (for example, first-generation bio-fuels or wind turbines), governments might prefer to encourage more expensive long-term solutions (such as second-generation bio-fuels or solar energy). Similarly, Kalkuhl et al. (2012) make the case for technology-specific quotas in order to 'learn' the best technology and avoid lock-in into an inferior technology.

Selective interventions entail considerable risks (Pack and Saggi, 2006), which increase with distance from commercial viability and size of the subsidy component. On the one hand, governments may bet on the wrong technologies. The development of sustainable technologies is often uncharted territory and requires experimenting with different options. When governments began supporting solar energy technologies, they could not know how much it would cost until these technologies reached grid parity, or whether it would have been better to invest in other sources of renewable energy. In their current decision-making on investment in low carbon mobility, they cannot know whether fuel cells, lithium-ion batteries, hybrid engines or other technologies will become the dominant design. Wrong choices may be very costly for taxpayers as well as for private investors who follow national policy signals. In India, for example, many poor smallholders lost money when governments encouraged them to cultivate biofuel plants which never became a viable business (Altenburg et al., 2009).

On the other hand, providing long-term subsidies under conditions of technological uncertainty is particularly prone to result in rent-seeking and fraud. Governments need to decide on subsidy allocation on the basis of scarce information. Similarly, they must be able to reduce or withdraw subsidies when new technologies approach commercial viability and to redirect them when more promising alternatives emerge. Of course, lobbyists will try to gain as much support as possible for their respective technologies, exaggerating both their future prospects and the need for subsidies. Quite often subsidies for 'green' technologies have been criticised as being too generous. Also, complicated schemes for managing environmental goods have led to cases of corruption, as in the case of the European Emissions Trading System.[7] SoIS therefore presuppose substantial government capabilities to 'manage rents' productively, meaning that governments need to interact closely with industry, identify the right degree of support required, establish good monitoring and evaluation systems, assess the performance of the industries supported and decide when subsidies can be withdrawn, either because they are failing to achieve the expected results or because they are no longer needed (Khan, 2004).

Building societal consensus on technology choices

In an incremental, 'business-as-usual' scenario of technology development, the choice of technology is largely determined by market forces. Countries specialise in goods that match their factor prices, technological capabilities and demand conditions. Our main argument here is that, in innovation for sustainable development, *political settlements* play an increasingly important role in determining the choice of technologies.

The transition to sustainable production makes it necessary to disrupt established technological trajectories and to support replacement technologies: coal-based power stations are gradually being replaced by renewables-based power stations, traditional light bulbs by light-emitting diodes and combustion engines by electric motors. These substitutions devalue existing assets and increase the value of others. Furthermore, polluting products and industries are taxed, 'clean' substitutes subsidised. Rents are thus taken away from incumbents and transferred to emerging industries. This process, of course, provokes resistance from those who stand to lose and encourages new industries to lobby for subsidies.

It is not only the interests of industries that are affected. The transformation also has many impacts on other stakeholders: how strictly environmental goods are regulated, how heavily resource use is taxed and how subsidies are used may have major repercussions for people's life styles. Societies are therefore often deeply divided on issues of sustainability transformation, as regards nuclear power, genetically modified organisms and carbon capture and storage technologies, for example. Even technologies that are accepted in principle – such as wind farms and new electricity transmission lines – often face strong resistance from local communities who do not want them built in their vicinity.

The choice of technologies and practicability in given political circumstances thus very much depend on *societal preferences* and the *power resources* of interest groups. On the one hand, technological preferences reflect deep-rooted national and local societal norms and values. Attitudes towards 'nature' and 'technology' vary significantly between nations, depending on differences in history, culture and living standards: societies with a marked preference for food safety are more likely to push for strict food standards and to accept the higher cost of organic food production; risk-averse societies are more likely to oppose the use of nuclear energy, carbon capture and storage, and other potentially dangerous technologies. The fact that French citizens are less concerned about nuclear risks than Germans and that Japanese consumers buy more eco-efficient cars than Americans is a clear expression of different norms and values.

On the other hand, interests differ within societies and lobby groups struggle to gain hegemony and influence national policies accordingly. Outcomes depend on the distribution of the power resources that can be used to influence interpretations of reality ('ideational power') and to ensure the implementation of specific options by providing, for example, financial resources and political backing ('material power').[8] The type of political regime also matters: authoritarian regimes typically find it easier to introduce risky technologies than open societies, in which stakeholders have many political channels through which to voice their concerns.

The choice of technologies thus depends heavily on political settlements, which – owing to differing preferences and power constellations – tend to be country-specific. This entails a major departure from the principle of the market-driven search which prevails in most other fields of innovation, where market failure is less pervasive and policymakers leave the choice of technologies largely to market actors. Understanding the power struggle between sustainability-oriented reform coalitions and veto players and how it affects technological trajectories is an important element of SoIS analysis.

Time dimensions: long gestation periods and the urgency of action

Policy decisions incorporating environmental restrictions need to have a particularly long time-horizon. Moving technologies through all stages of maturity, from laboratory through pilot scale to full commercial operability, takes time. As Kramer and Haigh (2009, p. 568) show for a range of environmental technologies, it can take up to a decade after the invention stage to build a demonstration plant, overcome its initial setbacks and achieve satisfactory operability. Only then are investors confident enough to build the first full-scale commercial plant and it can take another decade to build a dozen. Governments therefore need to be able to make long-term commitments if they are to create credible investment incentives. Bringing solar energy to grid parity, for example, may require more than two decades of subsidisation. Companies need to be able to rely on these incentives and on their endurance. If they adapt early, they gain early-mover advantages. But they put their competitiveness at risk if they adapt and find that policies, though announced, are not being implemented.

Furthermore, many industrial-scale technologies have depreciation periods of several decades. Coal-fired power stations, for example, have a life span of 30 to 40 years. Consequently, the emissions from those built today will be locked in until 2050, unless policymakers insist on an earlier decommissioning date. That, however, will reduce their profitability and meet with opposition from the respective lobbies.

The necessary long-term orientation of policy frameworks conflicts with the short-term nature of electoral cycles and calls for new accountability mechanisms that force politicians to take the interests of future generations into account. It also challenges the conviction of most industrial policymakers that governments should avoid engaging in the development of technological opportunities available only in the very distant future.[9]

At the same time, the paradigm change needs to be rapid and comprehensive. The time available for embarking on the new paradigm without overstretching the earth's carrying capacity is short. The clearest example is the atmosphere's shrinking capacity to absorb greenhouse gases: the longer the global economy remains on a high emissions track, the greater the irreversible ecosystem damage and the more costly the corrective and adaptive measures needed in the future. The same logic applies to other finite resources.

Harmonising national and international policy frameworks

As stated in Section 1, innovation systems generally tend to 'go global': the actors competing or collaborating to develop innovations are increasingly international, and regulatory frameworks and supporting institutions are formed at different levels of intervention – global, regional, national or sub-national. Hence the analytical focus must shift from national innovation systems to a multi-level governance perspective.

In SoIS, the degree to which framework conditions are negotiated internationally tends to be particularly high, mainly because governments cannot manage global public goods effectively at a national level. To name just a few of the issues, governments need to

- manage transboundary risks and environmental damage. The EU's efforts to agree on safety standards for nuclear power stations and to have Member States commit themselves to binding road maps in the search for sites for nuclear waste repositories are one example;
- distribute equitably rights to use finite resources, as in the case of carbon emissions and fish stocks;
- tax international air and sea traffic to reflect their environmental costs better and to raise revenues for necessary investments in climate change mitigation and adaptation;
- agree on new forms of multilateral cooperation on science, technology and innovation; and
- resolve legal and sharing issues when it comes to investment in energy grids and other cross-border infrastructure.

Such agreements are difficult to achieve, not least because causality chains are not easy to establish in global ecosystems and environmental costs cannot therefore be clearly attributed to specific actors. The debate on 'embedded carbon' demonstrates the difficulties encountered in attributing environmental effects in an interconnected world (see for example, SEI, University of Sydney, 2008). Here, the question is whether the environmental cost of carbon emissions from industrial production should be borne by the producing or the consuming country. As long as such questions remain disputed, the 'polluter pays' principle will not be applicable. There are, moreover, major international disparities in terms of historical responsibility: to what extent were the 'early polluters', such as the forerunners of industrialisation in Europe, responsible for the depletion of natural resources in the past? Hence a need for agreement on baselines against which resource consumption can be measured and usage rights defined. While the basic idea that rich and poor countries have 'common, but differentiated responsibilities' (UNFCCC, Art. 3 and 4) is now widely accepted, agreement on a concrete burden sharing formula has yet to be reached.

As well as considering historical responsibilities, international agreements must take account of the international asymmetries in (absolute and per capita) rates of resource consumption and environmental degradation and of the political and financial ability of countries to cope with environmental challenges. As a rule, international transfers of finance and technology are therefore included in political deals between developed and developing countries. Examples in the environmental sphere include the Global Environmental Facility and the recently proposed Green Climate Fund; the implementation of projects under the Clean Development Mechanism (CDM); and the Climate Technology Mechanism, on which further progress was made during the UNFCCC negotiations in Durban in late 2011.

However, the need to harmonise national and international policy frameworks is not only a challenge, but also an opportunity. International cooperation, in research and development, for example, can produce spillovers and mutual benefits for the cooperating parties. Furthermore, it helps to share the public costs of sustainable innovation and fosters technology transfer across countries (OECD, 2011). Joint research by developed and developing countries can also help to focus minds on the specific needs of the latter. Where research is financed by private investors, it is usually focused on areas with the highest potential for profits and so overlooks countries with low market potential, but a high environmental risk profile. Research partnerships involving developing countries can address this by explicitly targeting local needs.

At national level, progress in the field of green technologies increasingly depends on the ability of governments to exploit the opportunities emerging from international environmental politics. The CDM is a good example of how widely developing countries differ in their ability to benefit from a market-based international transfer scheme. Hosting 43 and 25% of the world's CDM projects respectively, China and India are the two countries that have been able to benefit most from the CDM (UNEP Risoe, 2011). In contrast, less than 3% of all CDM projects were implemented in Africa. Jung (2006) ascribes this to the various host countries' institutional capacities and general investment climates, among other factors.

2.2 *Different sets of policies*

The many challenges associated with establishing SoIS call for a radical shift in policies. While existing environmental policies are a start, they need to be developed further, disseminated and complemented by new policies. Policymakers also need to make a careful choice out of the most efficient and effective measures for their specific country backgrounds.

To address the market failures in developing sustainable technologies, policymakers need first and foremost to internalise environmental costs in economic decision-making. Suitable measures may include cap and trade systems for carbon emissions and taxes on pollution. Such price signals foster innovations in and deployment of sustainable technologies. Their advantage is their technology neutrality: market actors rather than policymakers determine which technological solution is best suited to achieving the desired resource efficiency. It must be admitted that governments around the globe are still some way from correctly pricing environmental externalities, such as those caused by carbon emissions. On the contrary, price and production subsidies for fossil fuels are still widespread: they collectively exceeded US$650 billion in 2008 (UNEP, 2011, p. 6). Reducing these subsidies is a vital task for the coming years.

While pricing mechanisms form an essential part of sustainability policies, they also have their limitations. Many environmental costs cannot be calculated in monetary terms. In some cases, costs will become calculable only in the distant future. An international consensus on prices of environmental goods is also hard to achieve. If some countries do not join a trading system, or if some industries are exempted, factor allocation will be distorted and free riding encouraged.

Command-and-control measures[10] thus need to complement pricing instruments. It has been argued that, compared to pricing mechanisms, such measures may be less likely to encourage innovations. The incentive for further modernisation vanishes once the given limit value is reached (BMU, 2008, 14). However, this problem can be overcome by gradually imposing ever stricter environmental standards in a transparent and foreseeable manner. The appropriate mix of market-based instruments, and command and control measures depends on the type of public good to be protected and on country characteristics, for example, the maturity of markets and the enforcement capacity of governments.

Naturally, policymakers need a certain degree of societal support to be able to enforce sustainability policies, be they market-based or command-and-control. The degree of such support may differ from one country to another, and even from one group to another within countries. However, the support of societies and governments alike in the case of such long term issues as environmental degradation tends to melt away as soon as a pressing economic problem appears on the agenda. An example is the recent European debt and currency crisis, which largely crowded climate change out of minds and media in 2011 (Horn, 2011). The enforcement of sustainability policies is certainly easier when they can be linked to the achievement of other societal benefits, such as economic growth or the electrification of rural areas. In the 'Hartwell Paper', a group of 14 natural and social scientists go even further in arguing that 'decarbonisation will only be achieved successfully as a benefit contingent upon other goals which are politically attractive and relentlessly pragmatic' (Prins et al., 2010). However, this approach may not suffice to prevent global ecosystems from collapsing, with potentially catastrophic consequences for humankind. This knowledge, derived from the complexities of climate science, needs to be translated and communicated to the broader public and included in school and university curricula.

To trigger technological change at the required pace, policymakers must also be prepared to intervene boldly in markets in order to depart from unsustainable 'business as usual' development pathways. The traditional aim of innovation policies has been to foster new activities expected to be more productive and/or to create important knowledge spillovers into different parts of the national economy. 'Creative destruction' (Schumpeter, 1942), meaning the diffusion of newly developed technologies and the crowding out of less efficient ones, was normally left to market forces. However, socio-technical systems are characterised by considerable inertia – because alternative technologies may not yet be available, because of lock-in effects of established technology systems or because consumers do not change their habits immediately. As the tipping points in global ecosystems are rapidly approaching, governments need to complement the above policies with a range of additional measures, such as public support for basic and applied research; the removal of entry barriers to sustainable technologies; sustained support for new 'green' technologies until they become cost competitive; and consumer education and information. Supporting the *deployment* of technologies is justified when it saves scarce environmental resources – in stark contrast to standard technologies, where governments should, and mostly do, not become involved in technology diffusion.

The mix of policy instruments must change as a technology moves along the deployment curve. Market incentives make sense only when a technology is relatively mature, and public research is inefficient when a technology is mature enough to attract private research activities. Once the technology is proven on a commercial scale, policymakers can make its use compulsory or subsidise its dissemination. These subsidies can, in turn, be phased out when the technology is fully competitive with less sustainable alternatives. For renewable energy technologies, Foxon et al. (2005) provide an overview of policies adapted to particular stages in the life cycle of products.

2.3 *Diverging technological trajectories*

Innovation systems research stresses that technologies and institutions co-evolve in interdependent ways, thus leading to country-specific trajectories (Nelson, 1994; Dosi, 1982). Similarly, Porter (1990) has shown that, even when factor costs converge, intra-industry specialisation may diverge owing to specific national factors, such as pools of experienced labour or particular demand conditions. Globalisation, however, has a balancing effect, as standards and business models are diffused through international competition and value chain integration. Whether national technological trajectories converge or diverge thus depends on the relative importance of country-specific factors.

Innovation policies geared to environmental sustainability are likely to lead to *diverging patterns of specialisation*, because technology choices are strongly driven by national policies, which in turn differ widely from one country to another, reflecting specific national preferences and political settlements.[11] We expect national technological trajectories of policy-driven industrial subsystems, such as electric vehicle manufacturing, to diverge far more than those of more mature and market-driven industries, such as the traditional car industry.

There is empirical evidence of diverging trajectories. An analysis of patent applications filed between 2003 and 2008 under the Patent Cooperation Treaty reveals that Japan specialises mostly in electric and hybrid vehicles (in terms of specific patents as a percentage of the country's total patent applications); The Netherlands shows strong specialisation in patents for energy efficiency in buildings and lighting; Germany specialises in the abatement of air pollution; and Australia focuses on technologies related to water pollution. More than 4% of Danish and more than 3% of Spanish applications concern renewable energies, compared to an OECD average of less than 0.7% (OECD, 2011).

The same patent analysis shows that sustainability innovations are concentrated in a fairly small group of countries, the USA, Japan and Germany accounting for the largest shares. Sector analyses indicate that country-specific policy packages were instrumental in the development of these patterns of specialisation: Denmark's decision to opt out of nuclear energy and subsidise the development of wind energy technologies as an alternative is a case in point (Lipp, 2007). In 2000 Germany became the first country to adopt a highly subsidised feed-in tariff for solar energy and went on to become a leader in solar energy technologies.[12] The world's strictest emission standards for cars led Toyota in Japan to set up an ambitious research programme for hybrid engines, a field in which it subsequently became a global leader. These cases confirm the views presented by Porter and van der Linde (1995), who showed that stricter environmental regulations increase the competitiveness of national firms vis à vis rivals operating in less demanding policy environments.

The transition to sustainable development is a major paradigm shift and therefore often presented as an opportunity for technological leapfrogging (Goldemberg, 1998; Ho, 2006). Newly industrialising countries may bypass fossil fuel-based development and base their development directly on the latest generation of sustainable technologies. This may even give them a competitive edge over incumbents, whose accumulated investments and relationships may become a burden when radical technological change renders them useless.

Mastering (rather than just using) new technologies, however, requires multiple capabilities. In this regard, industrial latecomers are at a disadvantage. It may in fact be easier for old industrialised countries to mobilise spillovers from their established industries for the development of new 'green' competencies than for newcomers to create them from a weak technological base. In fact, there is (so far) little evidence of leapfrogging into sustainability technologies. The few promising cases relate to large, fast-growing economies, foremost among them China, Brazil and India. Here, the rapid expansion of markets and replacement of capital stocks, combined with substantial R&D budgets, may indeed facilitate leapfrogging. Electric vehicles, for example, may become a major breakthrough for China (see Altenburg, Bhasin and Fischer in this volume).

3. Conclusions and outlook

This paper has highlighted fundamental differences between 'business as usual' and sustainability-oriented innovation systems (SoIS). The former mainly support incremental innovations along established technological trajectories, while the latter seek a policy-induced paradigm change and therefore need to navigate their way through uncertainty, long time horizons and multiple market failures.

Empirically, the shift to SoIS is comparatively recent. While the density of environmental regulations and the diversity of policies have increased over the last decade, and the share of 'green' technologies in patented inventions has grown rapidly,[13] this shift is still largely incremental in nature. So far, most of the improvements have been confined to established technologies, with few substantial changes to core technologies and institutions.

However, rapidly growing concern about planetary boundaries in general and climate change in particular calls for more radical and systemic changes in the near future. The expected resource scarcities are likely to increase the pressure on policymakers. The – still slow – progress of carbon pricing in several regions of the world and the establishment of pilot schemes that provide payment for ecosystem services may herald forthcoming institutional arrangements that oblige investors to internalise environmental costs more thoroughly.

As the importance of sustainability-oriented policies grows, more research into the changing nature of innovation systems is needed. Three particularly relevant future research issues are highlighted in the following:

First, comparative analysis of sustainability-oriented policies is needed. As this paper has shown, these policies entail particular risks of misallocation and political capture, since they are applied under conditions of uncertainty and with long time-horizons. Many countries are currently experimenting with such policies. Assessing the wealth of empirical experiments will help to identify policies that are effective in accelerating the necessary paradigm change while keeping the risks manageable.

Second, we have shown that country-specific political settlements are reflected in particular policy packages, which in turn lead to diverging technological trajectories. It is not clear, however, whether this divergence will endure beyond the point where technologies become mature and initial support is phased out. Only empirical research will show whether the levelling forces of competition will dissipate the pioneers' initial gains and technologies will migrate to locations with lower production costs, or whether early-mover advantages have self-reinforcing effects that lead to further divergence.

Third, the issue of leapfrogging is of particular relevance to latecomer development. Will the shift towards sustainable production revolutionise the international division of labour? How substantial are the opportunities for leapfrogging, and how serious is the carbon lock-in in today's industrialised countries? Comparative analysis of SoIS and technological trajectories in old industrialised and emerging economies may help to answer these questions.

Acknowledgements

The authors would like to thank Doris Fischer, Andreas Stamm, Georgeta Vidican, Shikha Bhasin and the anonymous reviewers for their helpful advice and comments on earlier versions of this paper.

Notes

1. 'Tipping points' are critical thresholds of complex systems at which the system changes abruptly from one state to another (Scheffer et al., 2009, p. 53).
2. See Rockström et al. (2009) for a discussion of the various 'planetary boundaries'.
3. Efforts to build environmental sustainability into economic accounting are currently being made on several fronts, for example the UN Statistical Division's System of Environmental and Economic Accounting and the adjusted net national savings methods developed by the World Bank (WBGU, 2011, 79).
4. The definition is based on Freeman (1987), with the addition of the environmental dimension.
5. From an ethical perspective, it is difficult to define the monetary value of a species, for example. Politically, it has proved difficult to agree on the international prices of environmental public goods, not least because there are no generally accepted principles for the allocation of usage rights. If countries set prices individually, incentives for free-riding and trade distortions are created.
6. Industry consortia – such as the Desertec Industrial Initiative formed to exploit the renewable energy potential of desert regions (http://www.dii-eumena.com/dii-answers/in-partnership-with-north-africa-and-the-middle-east.htmlmay) – may also alleviate coordination failure, but they are difficult to manage owing to high transaction costs and the considerable risks involved in contractual arrangements for interdependent long-term investment.
7. http://www.co2-handel.de/article58_15715.html, accessed 1 January 2012.
8. For material and ideational power see, for example, Fuchs and Glaab (2011, 730ff.).
9. Most prominently, Lin and Monga (2010) call for 'latent comparative advantages' to be made the focus, meaning that support should be given only to industries that have already been successfully developed by countries with a similar endowment structure and a somewhat higher per capita income.
10. According to the OECD, 'command-and-control policy refers to environmental policy that relies on regulation (permission, prohibition, standard setting and enforcement) as opposed to financial incentives, that is, economic instruments of cost internalisation' (OECD, 2001).
11. This argument may also apply to other policy-driven fields of technology development, including military and space technologies.
12. http://www.wind-works.org/FeedLaws/Germany/WhoInventedtheSolarFIT.html
13. Between 1999 and 2008, the number of patented inventions grew by 24% annually in renewable energy, 20% in electric and hybrid vehicles and 11% in energy efficiency in building and lighting, compared to an average annual patent increase of 6% (OECD, 2011, 28f.).

References

Altenburg, T., Dietz, H., Hahl, M., Nikolidakis, N., Rosendahl, C., and Seelige, K. (2009) Biodiesel in India: Value chain organisation and policy options for rural development. *Studies 43* (Bonn: Deutsches Institut für Entwicklungspolitik / German Development Institute (DIE)).

Altenburg, T., Schmitz, H., and Stamm, A. (2008) Breakthrough? China's and India's transition from production to innovation. *World Development*, 36(2), pp. 325–344.

BMU (2008) Ecological industrial policy: Sustainable policy for innovation, growth and employment, available at: http://www.umweltbundesmat.de/green-it/bmu_oeip.pdf, accessed on 22 March 2012.

Coe, N., Hess, M., Yeung, H.W-C., Dicken, P., and Henderson, J. (2004) 'Globalizing' regional development: A global production network perspective. *Transactions of the Institute of British Geographers*, 29(4), pp. 468–484.

Daly, H. (1977) *Steady-state Economics: The political economy of bio-physical equilibrium and moral growth* (San Francisco: W.H. Freeman and Co).

Dosi, G. (1982) Technological paradigms and technological trajectories: A suggested interpretation of the determinants and directions of technical change. *Research Policy*, 11(3), pp. 147–162.

Elzen, B., Geels, F.W., and Green, K. (2004) (eds) *System Innovation and the Transition to Sustainability: Theory, evidence and policy* (Cheltenham/ Northampton: Edward Elgar).

Foxon, T., Köhler, J., and Oughton, C. (2008) *Innovation for a Low Carbon Economy: Economic, institutional and management approaches* (Cheltenham/Northampton: Edward Elgar).

Foxon, T., Pearson, P., Makuch, Z., and Mata, M. (2005) Informing policy processes that promote sustainable innovation: An analytical framework and empirical methodology. *Working Paper Series 2004/4, Sustainable technologies Programme* (London: Imperial College).

Freeman, C. (1987) *Technology Policy and Economic Performance: Lessons from Japan* (London: Pinter Publishers).

Freeman, C. (1992) A green techno-economic paradigm for the world economy, in: C. Freeman (ed.) *The Economics of Hope: Essays on technological change, economic growth and the environment*, pp. 190–211 (London: Pinter).

Freeman, C. (1995) The 'National System of Innovation' in historical perspective. *Cambridge Journal of Economics*, 19(1), pp. 5–24.

Fuchs, D., Glaab, K. (2011) Material power and normative conflict in global and local food governance: The lessons of 'GoldenRice' in India. *Food Policy*, 36(6), pp. 729–735.

Geels, F.W. (2004) From sectoral systems of innovation to socio-technical systems: Insights about dynamics and change from sociology and institutional theory. *Research Policy*, 33(6–7), pp. 897–920.

Goldemberg, J. (1998) Leapfrogging energy technologies. *Energy Policy*, 2(10), pp. 729–741.

Grin, J., Rotmans, J., and Schot, J. (2010) *Transitions to Sustainable Development: New directions in the study of long term transformative change* (London: Routledge).

Hausmann, R., and Rodrik, D. (2003) Economic development as self-discovery. *Journal of Development Economics*, 72(2), pp. 603–633.

Ho, P. (ed.) (2006) *Greening Industries in Newly Industrializing Countries: Asian-style leapfrogging?* (London: Routledge).

Horn, H. (2011) As Euro crisis worsens, global climate efforts lose biggest leader. The Atlantic, 6 December 2011, available at: http://www.theatlantic.com/international/archive/2011/12/as-euro-crisis-worsens-global-climate-efforts-lose-biggest-leader/249481/, accessed on 3 January 2012.

Hübner, K., Nill, J., and Rickert, C. (2000) Greening of the innovation system? Opportunities and obstacles for a path change towards sustainability: The case of Germany. *Discussion paper 47/00* (Berlin: Institut für Ökologische Wirtschaftsforschung (IÖW)).

IPCC (2007) Climate change 2007 synthesis report: 4th assessment report of the intergovernmental panel on climate change. Intergovernmental Panel on Climate Change (IPCC), Geneva.

Jacobsson, S., and Bergek, A. (2004) Transforming the energy sector: The evolution of technological systems in renewable energy technology. *Industrial and Corporate Change*, 13(5), pp. 815–849.

Jung, M. (2006) Host country attractiveness for CDM non-sink projects. *Energy Policy*, 34(15), pp. 2173–2184.

Kalkuhl, M., Edenhofer, O., and Lessmann, K. (2012) Learning or lock-in: Optimal technology policies to support mitigation. *Resource and Energy Economics*, 34(1), pp. 1–23.

Khan, M.H. (2004) Strategies for state-led social transformation: Rent management, technology acquisition and long-term growth. Paper presented at the ADB Workshop on Making Markets Work Better for the Poor, Hanoi, April 2004.

Kharas, H. (2010) The emerging middle class in developing countries (Paris: OECD Development Centre).

Kramer, G.J., and Haigh, M. (2009) No quick switch to low-carbon energy. *Nature*, 462(7273), pp. 568–569.

Lin, J., and Monga, C. (2010) Growth identification and facilitation: the role of the state in the dynamics of structural change. *Policy Research Working Paper 5313* World Bank, Washington, DC.

Lipp, J. (2007) Lessons for effective renewable electricity policy from Denmark, Germany and the United Kingdom. *Energy Policy*, 35(11), pp. 5481–5495.

Loorbach, D., and Rotmans, J. (2006) Managing transitions for sustainable development, in: X. Olsthoorn and A.J. Wieczorek (eds) *Industrial Transformation – Disciplinary approaches towards transformation research* Dordrecht: Springer, pp. 187–206.

Lundvall, B.-A. (1992) *National innovation systems: Towards a theory of innovation and interactive learning* (London: Pinter).

McKinsey (2009) Pathways to a low-carbon economy: Version 2 of the global greenhouse gas abatement cost curve, McKinsey and Company.

Meadows, D., Randers, J., Meadows, D., and Behrens, W. (1972) *The Limits to Growth* (London: Potomac Associates).

Millennium Ecosystem Assessment (2005) *Ecosystems and HumanWwell-being: Synthesis* (Washington, DC: Island Press).

Nelson, R. (1994) The Co-evolution of technology, industrial structure, and supporting institutions. *Industrial and Corporate Change*, 3(1), pp. 47–63.

NREL (2011) 2010 Solar technologies market report, available at: http://www.nrel.gov/docs/fy12osti/51847.pdf, accessed on 5 January 2012.

OECD (2001) Glossary of statistical terms: Command-and-control policy: Studies in methods, Series F, No. 67. United Nations, New York, available at: http://stats.oecd.org/glossary/detail.asp?ID=383, accessed on 4 January 2012.

OECD (2011) Fostering innovation for green growth. OECD Green Growth Studies, OECD Publishing.

Pack, H., and Saggi, K. (2006) The case for industrial policy: A critical survey. *Policy Research Working Paper 3839* (Washington, DC: World Bank).

Porter, M. (1990) *The Competitive Advantage of Nations* (New York: Free Press).

Porter, M., and van der Linde, C. (1995) Green and competitive: Breaking the stalemate. *Harvard Business Review,* Sept./Oct, pp. 120–134.

Prins, G., Galiana, I., Green, C., Grundmann, R., Korhola, A., Laird, F., Nordhaus, T., Pielke, R., Rayner, S., Sarewitz, D., Shellenberger, M., Stehr, N. and Tezuko, H. (2010) The Hartwell Paper: A new direction for climate policy after the crash of 2009. Institute for Science, Innovation & Society, University of Oxford; LSE Mackinder Programme, London School of Economics and Political Science, London, UK

Ravallion, M. (2009) *The Developing World's Bulging (but Vulnerable) "Middle Class"* (Washington, DC: World Bank).

Rockström, J., Johan, R., Steffen, W., Noone, K., Persson, Å, Stuart, F., Lambin, E., Lenton, T.M., Scheffer, M., Folke, C., Schellnhuber, H.J., Nykvist, B., de Wit, C.A., Hughes, T., van der Leeuw, S., Rodhe, H., Sörlin, S., Snyder, P.K., Costanza, R., Svedin, U., Falkenmark, M., Karlberg, L., Corell, R.W., Fabry, V.J., Hansen, J., Walker, B., Liverman, D., Richardson, K., Crutzen, P., and Foley, J. (2009) Planetary boundaries: Exploring the safe operating space for humanity. *Ecology and Society,* 14(2), pp. 32, available at: http://www.ecologyandsociety.org/vol14/iss2/art32/, accessed 22 March 2012.

Ropohl, G. (1999) Philosophy of socio-technical systems. *Society for Philosophy and Technology,* 4(3), pp. 59–71.

Scheffer, M., Bascompte, J., Brock, W., Brovkin, V., Carpenter, S., Dakos, V., Held, H., van Nes, E., Rietkerk, M., and Sugihara, G. (2009) Early-warning signals for critical transitions. *Nature,* 461(7260), pp. 53–59.

Schipper, L.(ed.) (2000) On the rebound: The interaction of energy efficiency, energy use and economic activity *Energy Policy,* 28(6–7), pp. 351–353.

Schumpeter, J.A. (1942) *Capitalism, Socialism and Democracy* (New York/London: Harper and Row).

Segura-Bonilla, O. (1999) Sustainable systems of innovation: The forest sector in Central America. Ph.D. Thesis, Department of Business Studies, Aalborg University, Aalborg, available at: http://www.business.aau.dk/ike/upcoming/osb.pdf, accessed on 25 November 2011.

SEI, University of Sydney (2008) Development of an embedded carbon emissions indicator: A research report to the Department for Environment, Food and Rural Affairs. The Stockholm Environment Institute and the University of Sydney, (London: Department for Environment, Food and Rural Affairs).

Stamm, A., Dantas, E., Fischer, D., Ganguly, S., and Rennkamp, B. (2009) Sustainability-oriented innovation systems: Towards decoupling economic growth from environmental pressures? *Discussion Paper 20/2009* (Bonn: Deutsches Institut für Entwicklungspolitik / German Development Institute (DIE)).

UNEP (2011) Towards a green economy: Pathways to sustainable development and poverty eradication, available at: www.unep.org/greeneconomy, accessed on 3 January 2012.

UNEP Risoe (2011) CDM projects by host region, available at: http://cdmpipeline.org/cdm-projects-region.htm#7, accessed on 22 December 2011.

UNFCCC (1992) United Nations Framework Convention on Climate Change, available at: http://unfccc.int/essential_background/convention/background/items/1355.php, accessed on 22 March 2012.

Unruh, G.C. (2000) Understanding carbon lock-in. *Energy Policy,* 28(12), pp. 817–830.

WBGU (2011) World in transition: A social contract for sustainability. Special Report. German Advisory Council on Global Change, Berlin.

World Bank (2011) World development indicators, GDP growth (annual %), available at: http://data.worldbank.org/indicator/NY.GDP.MKTP.KD.ZG?display=graph, accessed on 3 January 2012.

World Energy Council (2007) Deciding the future: Energy policy scenarios to 2050. (London: World Energy Council).

Technology transfer? The rise of China and India in green technology sectors

Rasmus Lema[a] and Adrian Lema[b]

[a]Department of Business Studies, Aalborg University; [b]Ministry of Climate, Energy and Building, Denmark

International technology transfer is central to the debate about how to curb the carbon emissions from rapid economic growth in China and India. But given China and India's great progress in building innovation capabilities and green industries, how relevant is technology transfer for these countries? This paper seeks insights from three green technology sectors in both countries: wind power, solar energy and electric and hybrid vehicles. We find that, conventional technology transfer mechanisms such as foreign direct investments and licensing, were important for industry formation and take-off. However, as these sectors are catching up, new 'unconventional technology transfer mechanisms' such as R&D partnerships and acquisition of foreign firms have become increasingly important. We argue that there is limited practical and analytical mileage left in the conventional approach to technology transfer in these sectors in China and India. We argue that the emphasis should shift from transfer of mitigation technology to international collaboration and local innovation.

1. Introduction

Rapid economic growth in both China and India has now been sustained for more than a decade and it is set to continue in the foreseeable future. These two countries now account for a substantial amount of the production of the world's goods and services. There is therefore increasing agreement that a global shift in economic power is under way: from the West to the East. However, the build-up of capabilities in China and India is not only occurring in the sphere of production, it is also in the sphere of innovation and technological development (Altenburg et al., 2008).

While commentators and the scholarly literature are still trying to catch up with the changing global distribution of innovation capabilities (Ely and Scoones, 2009; Leadbeater, 2007), climate change is emerging on the top of the economic and political agenda (Stern, 2007). Policymakers, scholars and the wider public increasingly agree that economic growth needs to change direction, not least in China and India. The change that is needed is one in which new technological paradigms decouple growth from environmental problems – particularly greenhouse gas emissions – through the development and use of new technologies (Altenburg and Pegels, 2012).

The views and opinions expressed in this article are those of the authors and do not necessarily reflect the official policy of the Ministry of Climate, Energy and Building.

Technology transfer is seen as a cornerstone in reaching a global solution to climate change. China and India are particularly important, not only due to the substantial climate change effects associated with the rapid industrial transformation in these large and populous countries but also because of their weight in the negotiations within the United Nations Framework Convention on Climate Change (UNFCCC).

In this paper, we seek to connect the mounting shift from production to innovation capabilities in China and India with the debate over the global transfer of green technology. If China and India are making the transition from users to producers of technology, what does that mean for the green technology transfer debate?

In order to discuss this question we proceed in three main steps. First, we discuss the theoretical notion of technology transfer and provide a new conceptual framework devised to capture conventional and unconventional types of technology transfer as well as localised innovation (Section 2).

Second, we explore the extent of catch-up and the role of technology transfer in building technological capacity in three key green technology sectors in China and India (Section 3). It is necessary to step back and examine: (i) whether and to what extent the 'breakthrough' in the transition from production and innovation has occurred in low carbon technology and (ii) the extent and nature of technology transfer in this process. We review the insights from three key 'low carbon' sectors with high mitigation potential: wind power, photovoltaic (PV) solar energy and electric and hybrid electric vehicles.[1]

Third, we discuss the implications of the findings. We show that when it comes to key green technology sectors in China and India – two very important countries in the climate change equation – the conventional approach of technology transfer is increasingly surpassed by reality (section 4). Two main reasons lie behind this: (i) the technological gap is now small and decreasing in these key low carbon sectors and (ii) when technology transfer occurs, it is no longer conventional transfer that is most important. We discuss this by contrasting a broad and a narrow perspective on technology transfer.

We end the paper by discussing how much mileage is left in the concept of green technology transfer and the implications of our findings for the technology policy debate in and around the UNFCCC. We also discuss the limits of this research and propose questions for further research (section 5).

2. Conceptual framework

This section provides the key analytical concepts which will aid our subsequent analysis of technology transfer in the chosen green technology sectors in China and India. It defines what technology transfer is and it makes a simple distinction between (i) conventional transfer mechanisms, (ii) unconventional transfer mechanisms and (iii) localised innovation.

2.1 *Defining technology transfer*

A widely used definition describes technology transfer as a broad set of processes covering flows of equipment, know-how and experience between various types of actors (IPCC, 2000, p. 3). Our focus in this paper is mainly on the private sector because it 'is the main source for the worldwide diffusion of technology' (Schneider et al., 2008, p. 2930; see also Stern, 2007). We are not concerned with transfer within countries, but with the potential flows across the divide between OECD countries and emerging economies (China and India). We are concerned with the potential flows that may be involved in or lie behind effective mitigation of climate change (Ockwell et al., 2008; Stamm et al., 2009).

According to Bell (1990), technology is transferred via distinct flows of transferable technology between suppliers and importers (recipients):

- Flow 1: *Capital goods, equipment designs and other artefacts*. This flow consists of tangible assets such as equipment, as well as paper-embodied knowledge for processes and products such as blueprints and written specifications.
- Flow 2: *Skills and know-how for operation and maintenance*. This flow consists of intangible assets that may also be thought of as 'disembodied technology'. The skills and competences to operate technical systems arrive as human and knowledge capital.
- Flow 3: *Knowledge and experience for technological change*. This flow also consists mainly of intangible human capital but in contrast to flow 2 it also includes organisational assets. It can be further specified as 'delivering' and creating people embodied technology.

The first two flows are useful to deliver new and increased *production capacity* to technology importing firms or countries. But alone they add little or nothing to their *innovation capacity* (Bell, 1990, 2009). The latter depends on all three flows, but it is the third flow that is most critical. The third flow is most relevant to breaking out of 'carbon lock-in' in emerging economies – following the premise that local technological capability and related innovation is crucial for countries to leapfrog to low-carbon pathways. We proceed by outlining different organisational *mechanisms* that may facilitate these *flows* of transferable technology.

2.2 *Distinguishing transfer mechanisms*

Our analysis in later sections is based on the distinction between 'conventional' and 'unconventional' technology transfer mechanisms. The starting point is the early economic literature in which there was a strong distinction between innovation and diffusion. It was assumed that once technology was developed in advanced countries, it could flow freely (diffuse) without significant interaction between technology producer and importer and without substantial investment in absorption and related capability building in importing organisations. It assumed that new technology, once created, could be used immediately by all actors. Economic and technological catch-up would therefore be rapid (as reflected in Grossman and Helpman, 1995; Romer, 1994).

However, a range of studies in the technology and innovation literature has now pointed out the limitations of this assumption (Shamsavari, 2007; Kulkarni, 2003; Reddy and Zhao, 1990). We draw on Reddy and Zhao's (1990) distinction between the 'transaction perspective' and the 'host perspective' of technology transfer. This line of thinking suggests that diffusion is an active and creative process (see section 4.2) and that two key dimensions are central. First, transfer can occur with varying degrees of interaction across geographical and cultural distance between suppliers and importers of technology. Second, it can involve varying degrees of internal effort and investment in so-called 'recipient' firms and countries. These factors – (i) the degree of cross-border interaction and (ii) the degree of internal effort and investment – are key variables in our conceptual framework. We use them to distinguish between conventional and unconventional mechanisms in a two dimensional space as shown in Figure 1.[2]

2.3 *Conventional technology transfer mechanisms*

Conventional technology transfer mechanisms involve comparably low levels of cross-border interaction (one-way inward flow) and all else being equal they require less recipient effort and investment in capability. As observed by Stamm et al. (2009, p. 19): 'There are a number of technological artefacts for the transition towards more sustainable development patterns, and these are

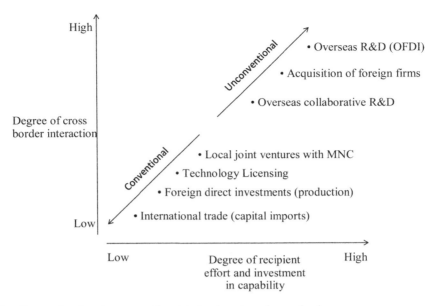

Figure 1. Conventional and unconventional technology transfer mechanisms.
Note: This figure is meant as a heuristic device and the notions of conventional and unconventional mechanisms are 'ideal types'. In reality there is not a proportional relationship between the two axes and the specific order of the different mechanisms along this continuum depends on the relative weight of the underlying factors.

available "off the shelf"'. The import of off-the-shelf equipment or blueprints is the classical example of conventional transfer.

Recipient effort and investment is always required but may be limited to purchase and installation or minor tweaking of existing solutions. Typical joint ventures – with local production based on foreign technology – have higher interaction and investment requirements, but still involve one-way technology flows from distant MNC headquarters to the joint enterprise (Lall, 1993). Our focus is on such firm-level modes of importing technology in 'local' firms. However, we also include the role of foreign direct investment since it is central to the policy and academic debate (Ueno, 2009). Most of the literature concerned with 'technology transfer' is focused on such conventional mechanisms (Popp, 2011; Schneider et al., 2008; Ueno, 2009; Less and McMillan, 2005)

As mentioned, these conventional mechanisms are unlikely – in and by themselves – to facilitate flows of knowledge, experience and expertise for generating and managing technological change (flow iii). Whether they do so depends on how they are used within 'recipient' organisations. Furthermore, as shall be discussed, these mechanisms may be dynamic and change over time.

2.4 *Unconventional technology transfer mechanisms*

Unconventional transfer mechanisms – overseas R&D, foreign acquisitions and collaborative R&D with foreign organisations – require substantial interaction and depend on substantial 'recipient' effort and investment.

Unconventional mechanisms are typically difficult to manage. For example, it is not easy to internalise knowledge embodied in people and organisational routines in an acquired firm; it requires absorptive capacity (Rui and Yip, 2008). In addition, they are likely to depend on significant expenditure outlays. While these mechanisms are difficult and costly, the literature on technological learning and catching up (e.g. Fu et al., 2011; Lall, 1993) suggests that they are critical to the creation of knowledge and experience for creating new technology. They have been particularly important in 'national champion firms' in emerging economies (Zeng and Williamson, 2007; Altenburg et al., 2008; Fu et al., 2011).[3]

As noted by Stamm and colleagues (2009, p. 2), large developing countries are 'less and less willing to accept traditional modes of transfer that imply continued dependence on international technology providers'. Our hypothesis is that unconventional mechanisms are key in green technology sectors.

It is central to our hypothesis that, in general, these mechanisms are becoming increasingly central in the way globalisation unfolds. For instance, large MNCs from the developed world are increasingly locating R&D activities in China, India and Brazil due to the increasing technological capacity, access to human resources and proximity to growing markets (Lema et al., 2012). So the term 'unconventional' is used with particular reference to the way technology transfer is discussed in the climate technology debate; unconventional mechanisms tend to receive insufficient attention.

2.5 *The learning process and localised innovation*

In addition to discussing the role of conventional and unconventional technology transfer mechanisms we also discuss a closely related issue, namely how important technology transfer is in relation to – and in combination with – 'localised innovation' – that is, indigenous knowledge and technology creation by domestic organisations. Foreign technology transfer and local innovation are largely complementary and only partly substitutable (Fu et al., 2011; Lall, 1993).

At the micro-level (the firm), the accumulation of capabilities – technological learning – is likely to involve a sequence of activities that combines firm-internal generation of skills and capabilities with outside knowledge (Bell, 2009). It combines internal and external learning. Although parts of the technology transfer literature describes the process as a simple matter of choosing off-the-shelf technology, the importing firms need to raise absorptive capacity and actively integrate the acquired technology (Ernst and Kim, 2002). It is beyond the scope of this study to examine this process in-depth. However, we can assess the role of firm-internal effort by examining the extent to which firms conduct local in-house R&D as a part of their technology development effort. They key issue is how firms combine internal and external learning.[4]

'External learning' is not necessarily international. On the contrary, there is a huge literature that stresses the importance of interactive learning in systems within the bounds of nation states (Lundvall, 1992). As argued by Altenburg and Pegels (2012), in the context of climate change, effective mitigation will involve the creation of 'sustainability-oriented innovation systems' (SoIS). To address this, we therefore examine local technology linkages such as collaborative R&D between firms and research institutes.

3. The rise of green technology sectors in China and India

How far have India and China come in catching up in green technology sectors and what mechanisms led to progress? Did these mechanisms differ in formative and catch-up phases? To examine this we review three sectors in both countries: (i) wind turbines, (ii) solar PV energy and (iii) electric and hybrid electric vehicles.

The purpose of this section is twofold. First, it seeks to examine the technological development of the industries and addresses the question of whether the green technology gap between emerging economies and OECD countries has diminished. Second, it seeks to identify the key technology transfer mechanisms. This is done primarily with the firm-level as a useful focusing devise, but the understanding of individual firms needs to be situated in the sectoral context.[5]

The micro-level analysis centres on 'national champions' defined as the firms with technological leadership and dominant market or export shares in their home economies. These firms are therefore key actors in climate change mitigation through diffusion of green technologies in China and India (Table 1).

Table 1.   The key national green technology champions.

	Wind	Solar	Electric and Hybrid Vehicles
China	Goldwind Science and Technology (1998), a publicly traded company emerged as a subsidiary of the Xingjian Wind Energy Company established in 1986. Sinovel Wind (2006), a state-owned company; spin-off from giant Dalian Heavy Industry, established in the 1920s. Dongfang Electric (1984), a subsidiary of a state-owned power station contractor and manufacturer of power equipment, which dates back to the 1950s.	Suntech Power (2001), a private start-up by a Chinese entrepreneur who headed thin film research at the University of New South Wales, Australia. Yingli Solar (1998), a publicly traded vertically integrated photovoltaic manufacturer. Trina Solar (1997), a start-up by a group of scientists with an initial focus on systems installations and later a manufacturer of mono and multicrystalline modules.	BYD (2003), a private automobile company based in Shenzhen; spin-off from BYD Company (1995), an energy storage producer that started making rechargeable batteries for cell phones. Chery Auto (1997), a state owned enterprise (by local government of Wuhu) produces sedans and is China's largest auto exporter. Shanghai Automotive Industry Corporation, SAIC (1955), a major state-owned automobile company.
India	Suzlon Energy (1995) from Pune, Maharashtra, spin-off from a family-owned textile firm, which was ridden with power cuts and increasing electricity prices in early 1990s.	Moser Baer Photo Voltaic (2005), a subsidiary of Moser Baer, founded in 1983, a firm focused on optical storage media products such as DVDs and Blu-ray Discs. TATA BP Solar (1989), a joint venture between energy giant BP's solar spin-off and Tata Power; Tata Power is India's largest power utility company, a part of Tata Group, India's largest private conglomerate, which dates back to 1868. HHV Solar (2008), a subsidiary of Bangalore based Hind High Vacuum Company, a long time engineering company in vacuum and solar technologies.	Mahindra REVA (1994), originally an Indian majority share joint venture between the Maini Group and US company, AEV but is now majority owned by Indian Mahindra & Mahindra (1945), which also has hybrid-electric autos. TATA Motors (1945), a private held and Indian leading automobile company with numerous alliances and joint ventures; part of Tata Group. Bharat Heavy Electricals Limited (1952), a large state-owned power sector industrial company.

3.1 *Wind power sector*

Chinese wind power began in the mid-1980s with imports of turbines from Europe, but today it boasts more than 40 domestic manufacturers catering for what has become the world's largest wind power market with 62 gigawatt installed capacity by 2012. The national champion firms have become some of the world's largest in a very short period: in 2006, no Chinese companies were in the global top 10 but by 2009, Sinovel, Goldwind and Dongfang became global top 10 players (BTM, 2010).

In the formative phase, responding to the high-growth market and mandatory 70% local content requirements, almost all major global wind power firms established production in China, a minority through joint ventures (Lema and Ruby, 2007). Leading national players, Sinovel, Goldwind and Dongfang all initiated production through licensing foreign technology from European design houses in the early 2000s. As the companies' in-house design capabilities have matured, the relationships to foreign licensors developed into co-design relationships (Lema et al., 2011). Unconventional transfer strategies by Chinese national champions seeking to engage in the development and design process were successful because foreign technology partners were not manufacturing competitors but rather specialised technology design houses achieving new business ventures through co-design relationships.

Unconventional mechanisms helped to achieve turbines of comparable size (and sometimes sophistication) as those currently under development by global competitors (Lema et al., 2011). Goldwind achieved strong overseas R&D capabilities through its acquisitions of German Vensys (as well as key suppliers), and both Donfang and Sinovel cooperated with foreign technology companies. A number of smaller Chinese companies have independent design of wind technology and all major Chinese wind turbine manufacturers have undertaken considerable in-house R&D for own solutions with the support of government R&D grants (Tan, 2010). For instance, Sinovel has a newly established 'National Offshore Wind Power Technology and Equipment R&D Center' and is approaching the frontier with Sinovel's new own-designed 5 MW offshore turbine.

Local technology agreements with local centres of excellence have not played a strong role for national champions, but other national companies have local technology linkages to centres of excellence, such as Shenyang University of Technology.[6]

With a slow take off in the 1980s, the Indian market has now become the fifth largest in the world (BTM, 2010). The domestic industry developed through conventional and unconventional transfer of technology. Production facilities have been set up by foreign wind turbine and key component manufacturers both as joint ventures and wholly owned subsidiaries (Mizuno, 2007). While there are more than 30 Indian wind turbine manufacturers, the uncontested national wind power champion is Suzlon and is responsible for almost half of the installed capacity in India (C-WET, 2009). Suzlon entered the business through license agreements to manufacture turbines and blades from Aerpac and Enron Wind. However, Suzlon moved away from the license strategy and acquired AE-Rotor (blades), Hansen Transmissions (gearboxes) and REpower (offshore turbines and R&D). It also established a joint venture with Austrian Elin to co-design wind turbine generators. Suzlon now has state-of-the-art technology and R&D facilities in Germany and has become the world's fifth largest turbine manufacturer (BTM, 2010). In addition to conventional (licensing) and unconventional (foreign acquisition, joint R&D and overseas in-house R&D) technology transfers, Suzlon is also embarking heavily on in-house R&D in India (Lewis, 2007).

Substantial contributors to the development of the Indian wind energy industry are interactive learning in the local innovation system, for instance with quality testing and standard setting provided by the Centre for Wind Energy Technology. Although there is still a gap to the world

Table 2. Technology transfer and localised innovation in wind power (summary).

Technology transfer		Other mechanisms
Conventional mechanisms	Unconventional mechanisms	Localised innovation
Trade (capital imports): Was of considerable importance in early stages. Now relatively unimportant as most turbines are based on high degrees of locally produced components	*Joint R&D:* has become very important as initial technology licensing arrangements have evolved into co-design partnerships (Goldwind, Sinovel, Dongfang, Suzlon)	*In-house R&D*: is now undertaken by all national champions, including for offshore deployment (Goldwind, Sinovel, Dongfang, Suzlon)
Inward FDI: Was of high importance for industry formation. Spillover effects to local industry are not documented.	*Foreign acquisitions*: are now central to the technological learning and innovation strategies of key national champions (Goldwind, Suzlon).	*Local technology linkages*: have become increasingly important, as national industries and institutional support structures have matured (Suzlon)
Joint ventures: Were of some importance at the industry level during formative phase and continue to play a role, but mostly in the supply base. Few champions engaged in local joint ventures (Suzlon).	*Overseas R&D (OFDI)*: is now undertaken on a significant scale in champion firms (Goldwind, Suzlon)	
Licensing: Was very important for 'take off' for local turbine manufacturing and continues to play a role (Goldwind, Sinovel, Dongfang, Suzlon)		

technological frontier, Kristinsson and Rao (2008) argue that the 'innovation system' performs an important supportive role in the catch-up process (see also Rajsekhar et al., 1999; Mizuno, 2007).

China and India have both developed globally leading national wind power champions. In both countries, the industry formation phases from the 1980s were characterised by capital imports and the industries emerged as a combination of FDI and licensing strategies by local companies. However, as the national champions have entered a catch-up phase they began to mix transfer strategies and localised innovation and shifted towards unconventional technology transfer (Table 2).

3.2 *Solar PV sector*

Both China and India have rapidly built national solar PV industries with notable catching up, but China is taking the lead with major global-scale companies and technological capabilities (Fu and Zhang, 2011).

China's PV industry has moved from component supply to production of complete panels and has become the world's largest producer of solar PV cells (Liu et al., 2009; Fischer, 2012; Kirke-gaard et al., 2010). With a 98% export share, foreign markets drive Chinese companies and the success is one of export-oriented technological upgrading (Fu and Zhang, 2011). However, the home market is picking up through subsidies of 50–70% of total solar PV investments (Climate Group, 2009; Howell et al., 2010).

By 2009, three Chinese national champions reached global sales top 10 (Hirshman, 2010; Climate Group, 2009). The Chinese leader, Suntech Power, emerged with a mix of local technology and international technology transfer and managed to become second in the world. World-class technological expertise was developed with in-house R&D combined with various mechanisms – licensing, a joint venture, overseas FDI and acquisitions, and collaboration with the University of New South Wales (BCG, 2010). Suntech also has local technology cooperation linkages with research institutions, such as Sun Yat-sen University and Shanghai University of Technology.

Trina Solar have established a government supported R&D 'State Key Laboratory' and cooperates with key suppliers as well as local universities and research institutions. The company has reported to invest 10 billion Yuan in R&D over five years, corresponding to about 5% of expected revenue. In addition to local innovation, Trina has strong international technology linkages including R&D cooperation with MIT in the US, Australia National University and Singapore's national institute for applied solar energy research.

Yingli Solar's trajectory is similar. On the one hand Yingly has in-house R&D, local R&D cooperation and acquisitions backwards in the supply chain. On the other hand, it has research agreements with centres of excellence and technology companies in The Netherlands and has opened a facility in Singapore to do overseas in-house R&D.

India's solar PV sector has transformed from mainly public supply and demand in the 1970s to private technology and production capacity by the late 1980s (Bhargava, 2009; Kathuria, 2002). When demand from state-owned enterprises ceased in the 1990s, solar producers sought export markets which now take about 75% of PV output (Srinivasan, 2005; Mallett et al., 2009).

Moser Baer is one major player that has used unconventional technology transfer strategies such as strategic and equity alliances with foreign solar technology companies, in addition to conventional licensing of thin film photovoltaic technology. Moser Baer also undertakes significant overseas in-house R&D in The Netherlands as well as jointly with various overseas research institutions. Within India, Moser Baer has close linkages to research institutions, including the National Chemical Lab, the National Physical Laboratory and the Indian Institute of Technology Kanpur.

HHV Solar use in-house R&D as the primary source of technology and also engage in crystalline and thin film solar cell and module technology, of which the majority is locally developed (ISA, 2008). TATA Power has followed a more conventional technology transfer route. Since 1989, it has engaged in a joint venture with British BP Solar for marketing a wide range of solar photovoltaic solutions in India.

Indian manufacturers have used licensing or external, expired patents for mono- and multi-crystalline silicon cells (Mallett et al., 2009). However, Indian companies have also used a wider range of mechanisms including joint ventures, R&D cooperation, foreign acquisitions and in-house R&D. Links to foreign technology-firms are strong, but Mallett et al. (2009, p. 73) argue that 'Indian firms actively drive the process and so play more a leadership role in the technology transfer process'. Collaboration with national research institutions and in-house R&D has proved important to pick up and refine technologies, produce at a low cost and engage in own patenting.

Both countries have experienced a mix of conventional and unconventional technology transfer with an emphasis on the latter in recent years (Table 3). Localised innovation has been a very strong contributor to technological capabilities in this sector in India and China (Fu and Zhang, 2011). Most firms are predominantly export oriented, have played an important role in global supply chains driving down costs and contributed to climate change mitigation at a global level (Fischer, 2012).

3.3 *Electric and hybrid electric vehicles sector*

With a number of preferential policies, China aims to become the leading producer of plug-in hybrid and electric passenger vehicles with about 5% of China's new vehicle sales by 2015.

Table 3.   Technology transfer and localised innovation in Solar PV (summary).

Technology transfer		Other mechanisms
Conventional mechanisms	Unconventional mechanisms	Localised innovation
Trade (capital imports): has played a limited role as these industries focus on exports for global markets. *Inward FDI:* has not been important to industry formation but is beginning to occur in the catch-up phase, especially in China. *Joint ventures*: are not significant in the industrial structure but have played a major role in the Indian take-of (TATA BP Solar). Some companies are using overseas joint ventures to access technology and foreign markets (Moser Baer). *Licensing*: was very important for the take off and continues to play some role during to access advanced PV technologies such as thin film (Suntech; Moser Baer).	*Joint R&D:* has played a role in the overall industry formation although with a practical impact for few champion firms (Moser Baer). *Foreign acquisitions*: has become important to access advanced foreign technology by leading champion firms (Suntech; Moser Baer) *Overseas R&D (OFDI)*: was of limited importance during the take of, but champion firms are increasing overseas R&D and cooperation with research institutions (Suntech; Moser Baer).	*In-house R&D*: has been and continues to be very important in almost all champion firms in combination with conventional and unconventional technology transfer strategies (Suntech, Yingli, Trina Solar; Moser Baer, HHV Solar). *Local technology linkages*: had a limited practical impact during take off, but has now become important to complement in-house R&D (Suntech, Trina, Yingli; Moser Baer).

The government has within a decade provided about 2 billion Yuan in R&D and demonstration support and a tenfold increase in public R&D and demand side support for the coming decade has been reported (Watson et al. 2011). China is already the leading producer of rechargeable batteries – a key technology, in the electric vehicle value chain (IEA, 2009; MOF and MOST, 2009).

There are important examples of conventional technology transfer in this sector. Joint ventures emerged largely as a response to the combination of two circumstances. First a 'market pull' was driven by mandatory emissions standards – currently stricter than those in the US. Second, government legislation dictates that entry by foreign auto companies requires Chinese majority share joint ventures.

China's largest auto manufacturer, state-owned SAIC has established electric car joint ventures with an US lithium-ion battery company and with Volkswagen. Also, SAIC established a joint development facility in China assisting in designing General Motors's hybrid and all electric vehicle technology. Another international linkage is SAIC's overseas R&D through its acquisition of a UK company. SAIC is also developing an electronic drive system through in-house R&D (Wang, 2009).

Several companies have relied on in-house R&D rather than technology transfer to develop electric and hybrid vehicles, especially small-car versions (People's Daily Online, 2009; IEA, 2009). Chery Auto have developed and commercialised a small electric car based on own technological resources.

BYD acquired a small Chinese car manufacturer and started intensive in-house R&D to combine its lithium-ion battery technology with car making. BYD's all localised innovation approach introduced the first plug-in hybrid electric vehicle in 2008. BYD has now established a R&D joint venture in which it will bring together Daimler's car platform and BYD's battery and electric motor technology to co-design electric vehicles under a joint brand (BYD, 2010). Thus for BYD, technology transfer has intensified *after* the building up of an in-house innovation platform.

A number of Indian electric and hybrid vehicle manufacturers have road-ready or demonstration models, including three leading car companies: REVA, TATA Motors and Bharat Heavy Electricals Limited. These companies are not at the technological frontier of the global market but are evolving through a mix of mechanisms, including in-house R&D, licensing, joint ventures and joint development with foreign firms.

An example of a non-transfer route is Bharat Heavy Electricals Limited which has developed electric buses, vans and special purpose vehicles for the government sector through in-house R&D (Awasthi, 2009). On the other hand, Tata Motors has used an unconventional technology transfer strategy by acquiring a majority stake of a Norwegian lithium-ion battery technology developer to utilise this foreign technology in Tata's car platform to design an electric car (Mallett et al., 2009).

REVA, an Indo-US R&D joint venture, brought together electric vehicle expertise from both organisations, but was established to conduct in-house R&D in combination with external R&D collaboration (Bajaj, 2009; Menon, 2009). REVA now markets own-brand electric vehicles and reportedly has more electrical vehicles on the global market than any other player in the industry. REVA started as a R&D joint venture, a strategic *licensee* of patents coupled with an intensive in-house R&D (about 7% of annual turnover) with the result of building strong technology with which it now carries out R&D collaboration and has become a *licensor* (Maini, 2005).

China and India's electric and hybrid auto industries are younger than wind power and solar PV and reflect that the global market is less developed. The sector is also special in that local technology linkages are less developed, but companies have very strong in-house R&D. The Chinese case has some foreign technology linkages (especially joint R&D) but is less a 'transfer' case than a 'localised innovation' case. India's trajectory emerged closer to conventional technology transfer with joint ventures and licensing, although unconventional transfer mechanisms such as joint R&D, foreign acquisitions and overseas R&D are also, if not more, important during catch-up (Table 4).

Table 4. Technology transfer and localised innovation in Electric and Hybrid vehicles (summary).

Technology transfer		Other mechanisms
Conventional mechanisms	Unconventional mechanisms	Localised innovation
Trade (capital imports): has played a limited role because manufacturing is highly localised. *Inward FDI:* has played some role although the core technology tend to be nested in and around the headquarters of large car manufacturers *Joint ventures*: are important to link smaller companies to foreign technology companies (SAIC; REVA) *Licensing*: Does occur but is not very important for champion firms across the board (REVA)	*Joint R&D:* has become very significant for some companies and it seems that top companies especially in this sector are partners with equal or superior technological capabilities in partnerships (BYD; REVA) *Foreign acquisitions*: is not a common strategy across the board but has served as an entry strategy in some cases (TATA) *Overseas R&D (OFDI)*: is rather limited but is sometimes used in combination with foreign acquisitions (TATA)	*In-house R&D*: is carried out by all identified national champions and appears to be the central strategy of most champions firms (BYD, Chery Auto, SAIC, REVA, TATA, BHEL) *Local technology linkages*: have played fairly a limited role in this sector with no apparent evidenced of R&D relationships between firms and local institutions

Table 5.   Assessment of the importance of different technology transfer mechanisms over time.

Group	Specific organisational arrangement	Formative phase	Catch-up phase
Conventional mechanisms	Trade(imports)	****	*
	FDI/Joint ventures	****	***
	Technology licensing	****	****
Unconventional mechanisms	Joint R&D with MNC	**	****
	Overseas R&D lab	**	****
	Cross-border M&A	**	****
Localised innovation	Local technology linkages	**	****
	In-house R&D	****	*****

Source: Drawing on tables 2-4 in this section. Note: This table is meant as a summary assessment and does not reflect the full complexity and sectoral variety. We have used the following classification system to describe the importance of the different organisational arrangements:

*	=	low
**	=	low and medium
***	=	medium
****	=	medium and high
*****	=	high

3.4   *Summary of the insights*

Three main conclusions arise from the analysis in this section: First, these three key green technology sectors in India and China are managing the transition from simple production to innovation capability. While there are differences between sectors, the technological gap between China and India and so-called advanced economies is now relatively small and decreasing.[7]

Second, unconventional technology transfer mechanisms were very important in most cases and this importance tended to increase over time. The crucial ingredients were rarely knowledge embodied in 'hardware'. In recent years, the crucial ingredients were people-embodied knowledge, acquired through R&D networks and overseas investments in firms and technology alliances. However, the unconventional mechanisms played a more important role in the catch-up phase than in the take-off phase. Licensing was often a stepping stone. The cases reveal that it is a matter of sequence. This is what we seek to illustrate in Table 5, showing our assessment of the relative importance of different mechanisms in the formative and catch-up phases.

Third, technology transfer was only one element in the development of these green technology champions. Endogenous technology creation was crucially important as (i) a prerequisite (in creating absorptive capacity), (ii) a complement and (iii) an alternative to technology transfer. There is also evidence which suggests that localised innovation has increased in importance. It has interacted with learning in global innovation networks (for example cooperation with design houses) and it has partly substituted such networks (for example, creation of own designs). The next section draws out some of the central implications of these three conclusions.

4.   **The relevance of technology transfer**

In this section we discuss the relevance of our empirical findings with respect to the notion of technology transfer in the low carbon policy debate. We argue that this debate has taken its point of departure in a 'narrow view' of technology transfer. This view derives from the early technology transfer literature and conventional economics (Krugman, 1979; Grossman and Helpman, 1995; Romer, 1994; Jian-Ye, 1990) and is discernible in numerous climate change reports and studies (e.g. Ueno, 2009; Commission on Growth and Development, 2008; IPCC, 2007; World Bank, 2010). In Table 6, the narrow view is contrasted with a 'broad view' which derives from innovation studies (Lundvall et al., 2002; Nelson, 2011) and the literature on technological learning and catching up (Fu et al., 2011; Lall, 1993; Ernst and Kim, 2002).

Table 6.   Contrasting perspectives on technology transfer.

		Narrow View	Broad View
1:	Developed and developing countries	• The global economy is divided between innovating (developed) and non-innovating (developing) economies.	• The simple distinctions between innovating and non-innovating economies is misleading
2:	Technological innovation and diffusion	• The notion of technological innovation refers to global novelties (new to the world innovations);these are usually derived from science, research and experimental development • Innovation and diffusion are separate and distinguishable processes	• Innovation consists not only of global novelties but also of incremental improvements (e.g. new to the firm or country); these are often made in the organisations that undertake production. • The distinction between innovation and diffusion is blurred and often misleading
3:	Cross border interaction	• The content of technology transfer consists mainly of tangible assets and skills and know-how for operation and maintenance • Technology transfer is essentially a process of one-way flows between exporters and importers of technology • The organisational arrangements for technology transfer are largely confined to 'conventional mechanism'.	• Effective 'transfer' of technology is likely to include not only artefacts but also people-embodied knowledge as well as organisational assets • Effective transfer is an interactive process • Different organisational arrangements are needed for different types and degrees of knowledge and capability acquisition
4:	Localised innovation – recipient efforts and investment in capability	• Technology transfer (importing) involves merely choosing adopting, and occasionally adapting technologies • Technology transfer and localised innovation are alternatives	• Technology transfer is usually much more creative and complex than simply choosing, purchasing and adopting technology • Effective transfer rests on recipient efforts and investments in capability within firms and in innovation systems. • Technology transfer and localised innovation are complementary activities; these are combined in the process of technological learning

Sources: Drawing on Bell (2009, 39–42) and references cited in sections 2 and 5.

The argument is not that elements of the broad view are absent in the climate technology debate. As will also be discussed, the broad view is slowly gaining ground. However, the different conceptions of developed vs. developing countries (row 1) and innovation vs. diffusion (row 2) has important implications for the thinking of cross-border interaction (row 3) and localised innovation (row 4). The remainder of this section discusses the dimensions of Table 6 in relation to our analysis.

4.1   *The distinction between developed and developing countries*

There is overall acknowledgment of the crucial role of technology in climate change mitigation and the increasing importance of mitigation in emerging economies. However, we argue that the dominance of the 'narrow view' of technology transfer in the policy debate means that core 'discourses' become overly simplified. The World Bank's report on 'Development and Climate Change' illustrates this tendency:

> *Developed countries* have produced most of the emissions of the past and have high per capita emissions. These countries *should lead the way* by significantly reducing their carbon footprints and stimulating *research into green alternatives*. Yet most of the world's future emissions will be generated in the *developing world*. These countries will *need adequate funds* and *technology transfer* so they can pursue lower carbon paths—without jeopardizing their development prospects. (World Bank, 2010, pp. 13–14, emphasis added)

This passage illustrates how the narrow view draws on a stark distinction between those who 'lead the way' and those who need 'technology transfer'. This rests on the notion that 'most technologies are still mainly developed and first deployed in the industrialised world' (Schneider et al., 2008, p. 2931; see also IPCC, 2007; Ueno, 2009; Tomlinson et al., 2008, p. 56). Such a binary worldview of innovating and non-innovating economies is evident in much of the influential literature on technology transfer (Commission on Growth and Development, 2008; World Bank, 2008, 2010).

However, as was shown in the previous section, China and India – countries that still have relatively low per capita incomes compared to OECD countries – have now acquired considerable technological capacity (Stamm et al., 2009, p. 22). This means that the distinction between innovating (developed) and non-innovating (developing) countries is deceptive for the technology debate. While this is particularly true in the context of emerging economies, it applies more broadly. To bring this out, it is necessary to consider critically the meaning of the terms 'innovation' and 'diffusion'.

4.2 *Technological innovation and diffusion*

The narrow view tends to equate innovation with novelties. The World Bank (2010) quote above highlights the important role of formal 'research into green alternatives'. Drawing implicitly on the linear model of innovation, the narrow view tends to see research as the key route to create 'new to the world' innovations required to tackle global warming (World Bank, 2008). It further distinguishes the innovation process (in developed countries) – undertaking research and creating new products – and the subsequent diffusion activity of *transferring* the results to developing countries. In short, innovation and diffusion are two separable processes.

Our analysis questions this view. The national champion firms in India and China drew heavily on flows of transferable technology which were 'diffused' from developed countries, but this was in itself an innovative process. It created technological solutions that were 'new to the firm' and it involved creative interaction and reshaping of external knowledge. This means that the process of adopting and adapting technologies was not a simple process of 'diffusion' in the way this process is sometimes conceptualised. Acquiring capabilities involved a pervasive occurrence of creative change in recipient organisation which is best described as a process of innovation. In short, innovation and diffusion was not separate processes.[8]

The analysis also suggests that while 'research into green alternatives' may play an important role in advancing the frontier, the research lab is not the only locus of innovation. 'Innovation' is more than 'science'. This analysis has suggested that in building green technology capabilities, scientific research was only one element among a number of mechanisms involved. In fact, research within the science sector was not central to the catch- up process in these sectors and countries, but they are likely to become more important in the future (see section 4.4).

It is worth noting the differences in policy emphasis that follow the contrasting views. Because of the capability gap, proponents of the narrow view believe it is most efficient if OECD countries with stronger capabilities engage in technological innovation, and developing countries merely use the 'results'. This implies, in the narrow view, that innovation in developing countries is costly and inefficient so technology transfer (diffusion) is preferable until developed country status is reached. It tends to underemphasise the importance of supporting innovation in developing countries because 'actual installation of mitigation technologies can reduce emissions, regardless of their origin' (Ueno, 2009, p. 3).

By contrast, the broad view maintains that support for innovation is important because efficient 'diffusion' involves creative shaping of technologies also in developing countries. The formation of green technology sectors in China and India relied much less on simply purchasing equipment and simple know-how than on a creative process of knowledge absorption that is essentially a learning and innovation process. The resulting policy focus is one that is primarily concerned with supporting technological learning.

The typical conceptualisation of innovation and diffusion in the climate change technology debate has important follow-on implications with regard to the thinking about cross-border inter-action and localised innovation and we discuss them in the remainder of this section.

4.3   *Cross-border interaction*

Some of the technology transfer discussion seems to be mainly about shipping ready-to-use equipment to developing countries and combining this with knowledge for operation and main-tenance – not with the deeper capabilities which is fundamental to technologic change.

The report on technology transfer by the Intergovernmental Panel on Climate Change (IPCC) states that climate change mitigation: 'will require rapid and widespread transfer and implementation of technologies, including know-how for mitigation of greenhouse gas emis-sions' (IPCC, 2000, p. 3, emphasis added). The IPCC emphasises the transfer of *know-how* as opposed to *know-why* which is arguably required for effective innovation (Lundvall and Johnson, 1994).

Also in line with the narrow view is the UNFCCC's (1992, Article 4.5) emphasis on facilitat-ing 'transfer of, or access to, environmentally sound' technology and know-how. The discourse of the UNFCCC largely emphasises flows to developing countries of embodied technology and skills required to operate imported technology (Ockwell et al., 2010), i.e. flows i and ii as defined in Section 2.

Developing economies seem to be viewed mainly as *consumers* of technology which is developed in the North (UNFCCC, 1992, 2002; World Bank, 2010). As discussed, this policy approach draws on a concept of diffusion, which is distinct from innovation, and therefore on the mechanisms thought central to the envisaged one-way technology 'hand-off'.

This relates closely to the 'mechanisms' discussed in this paper. A large number of studies see conventional mechanisms as the main vehicles of technology transfer (e.g. Less and McMillan, 2005; Ueno, 2009; World Bank, 2008; Popp, 2011). As stated by Schneider et al. (2008): 'The main channels of private sector technology transfer are trade, licensing, and foreign direct investment' (Schneider et al., 2008, p. 2931).

All of these one-way mechanisms have been involved in the development process in the green technology sectors in China and India. However, they have primarily been important to industry formation. They have been less significant in contributing to core skills and capabilities that have been essential to the technological prowess and the cost innovation (Zeng and Williamson, 2007) which lies behind technological upgrading and fast deployment of wind power and green vehicles (electric two-wheelers in China), and export of solar PV panels.

Firm centred cross-border interaction is under-emphasised in the technology transfer debate but has been of central importance in the cases reviewed. The critical factor was flows of knowledge, experience and expertise for generating and managing technological change (flow iii). Such knowledge is inherently difficult to 'move' across space because it is often tacit and built up in an interactive, cumulative and path dependent way (Ernst and Kim, 2002). However, 'thick' linkages that facilitate two-way flows (interaction) make 'transfer' possible.

It is interesting to note the dynamic nature of cross-border interaction. For instance, relationships that started out as one-way licensing arrangements have changed into co-design arrangements. FDI investments that were originally focused solely on producing and selling technology developed in OECD countries are now platforms for technology R&D relevant for the global market. Overall the cases suggested that conventional forms of cross-border interaction were important in early stages of formation. In later stages, a combination of conventional and unconventional forms was utilised. The core insight in this respect is that different organisational arrangements are needed during different stages of technological learning. Networks and mechanisms become more complex and demanding over time as sectors mature (Dantas and Bell, 2011; Fu and Zhang, 2011).

4.4 *Localised innovation*

This subsection continues the discussion of our findings in relation to the narrow view, but we turn the attention to the role of internal effort and investment and localised innovation in firms ('in-house R&D') and innovation systems ('local technology linkages').

The analysis suggested that China and India did not rely solely (or even mainly) on external green technology. In the three sectors, in-house effort and investment in innovation was a key determinant of the speed and depth of technological learning. The trajectories of national champion firms have integrated internal technology development efforts with the acquisition of skills and knowledge from outside in a cumulative process. Leading firms are increasingly global and they perform a key function in pulling together local and global knowledge flows for creating and putting green technology in use. The important role of localised innovation is unsurprising, but it is not always given sufficient attention.

A substantial body of literature (Ernst and Kim, 2002; Lall, 1993; Bell, 2009) has shown the limitations of the idea that 'technology importers' only need to choose and absorb technology that is available elsewhere. As stressed earlier, the innovation literature has shown that this process is not at all trivial and involves significant investments in knowledge, experimentation and organisational routines.

But rapid development also depended on implementation of green technology support mechanisms such as feed-in tariffs (creating demand) and public investment in training and R&D (helping supply). Over time, local technology linkages such as collaborative R&D between firms and research institutes became important elements of the upgrading model, particularly in wind and solar but also, to some extent, in electric and hybrid electric vehicles.

The analysis provides two main insights. First, global linkages ('technology transfer') and local innovation systems were not alternatives as is sometimes implied. Local and global flows were supplementary 'mechanism' in both the formation and catch-up phases. Second, capability building in firms was a prerequisite for local linkage formation – not the other way around. Champion firms benefited from linkages with national research institutions but as with international technology transfer, the key point is about sequencing and evolution. R&D linkages – local and global – only became important once the sectors were beyond the formation phase.

Technology 'transfer' can hardly be understood in isolation because the use of external technologies and local learning were *complementary* elements that were combined in the technological upgrading process. These points may seem trivial to innovation scholars. However, they are of great importance in relation to climate policy and will be discussed further in the concluding section.

5. Conclusion

The starting point for this paper was the connection between the mounting shift from production to innovation capability in China and India (Altenburg et al., 2008; Ely and Scoones, 2009) and the debate over the global transfer of green technology (Ockwell et al., 2008; Schneider et al., 2008; IPCC, 2007). It is sometimes argued that the rise of China and India in green technology is overstated (Watson 2011). We agree that there is a gap to the frontier and that the catch-up process is uneven among sectors and countries. However, the gap is now relatively small and decreasing. As China and India transcend from users to producers and innovators of green technology, this has increasingly important implications for the global low carbon technology transfer debate and policy process.

5.1 *How much mileage is left in technology transfer?*

The implication of the analysis in this paper is that there is limited *practical mileage* left in the conventional approach to technology transfer in the chosen sectors in India and China. The conventional narrow technology transfer focus on trade in capital equipment, traditional FDI and licensing (e.g. Schneider et al., 2008) is increasingly obsolete in these countries. The notion of technology transfer was introduced by economists more than 50 years ago, a time when it was difficult to see beyond trade, FDI and licensing. While these channels are still important they are used in new ways and they are increasingly being supplemented and surpassed by new mechanisms.

China and India's cross-border technology relations have evolved significantly over the last ten years with the effect that unconventional mechanisms such as investment in internal R&D, global R&D collaboration and outward knowledge-seeking FDI are increasingly important. While the notion of technology transfer is inherently problematic, the limitations of the concept are accumulating because of the way globalisation and economic development in China and India have changed how technological capability accumulation now takes place in these countries.[9] Both countries seek to take full advantage of these changes by making their own investments.

But our analysis is relevant beyond China and India because it suggests that there is also limited *analytical mileage* left in the conventional technology transfer concept. In reality, technology can be 'transferred' only in a very narrow sense and only provided that one adopts a narrow and outdated notion of technology development, learning and innovation. Capabilities are *built* and *acquired* rather than *transferred* (Bell, 2009; Lall, 1993). The emphasis on *transfer* of mitigation technology should be complemented or replaced by *international collaboration* and *local innovation*.

5.2 *Technology and climate change policy*

The findings of this analysis have important implications for the technology transfer debate, not least under the UNFCCC. The UNFCCC approach to technology transfer is mainly focused on the provision of information regarding available climate change mitigation and adaptation technology, rather than practical transfer mechanisms and learning (Thorne, 2008; Ockwell et al., 2010).[10] Although tackling climate change requires catching up and innovation in green technologies in the developing world, this receives inadequate attention in the technology transfer discussion. The analyses in this paper lead us to suggest that the international technology approach of the UNFCCC and other multilateral organisations needs reorientation in three important ways.

First, our main argument is that the international dimension of technological learning requires more than information about available technology alternatives and financial support to mitigation. However, core UNFCCC agreements (UNFCCC, 1992, 2002) largely reflect a narrow view of technology and its global mobility; overall the debates in the negotiation rooms are similarly narrow in scope. A discourse shift is slowly underway within the UNFCCC, but has not moved far into the sphere of policy formulation. There has been little and inadequate negotiation over the definition of 'technology collaboration', what it should achieve and the mechanisms to underpin it. Policies and initiatives need to go beyond the typical focus on framework conditions for trade, FDI and arms-length licensing (e.g. World Bank, 2010). New sources and organisational arrangements are becoming increasingly important for technological learning in many countries, in particular in China and India.

Second, the emerging focus on localised learning and innovation in UNFCCC policy (2007, 2010) could be strengthened and integrated into the framework with equal weight as international technology collaboration. So far the framework has had only little focus on local capability formation overall (Ockwell et al., 2010). Where capability formation and strengthening has been an explicit goal within bilateral and multilateral arrangements, it has tended to focus on support for public sector R&D institutions. By contrast, private sector organisations have been underemphasised because the targeted strengthening of firms remains controversial. In fact, the global climate technology discussion largely ignores the established insight that 'for countries aiming to catch up, developing the capabilities for learning and innovation *in firms* is the heart of the challenge' (Nelson, 2011, p. 48, emphasis added). Specialised R&D organisations can play a very important role, but firm capability remains a central prerequisite for interactive learning and innovation (Bell, 2009; Lall, 1990).

Third, the distinction within the UNFCCC framework (1992) between Annex 1 Countries (developed) and non-Annex 1 Countries (developing) does not seem conducive to progress with respect to technology arrangements for climate change mitigation. Policies that work for China and India may be very different for countries with other needs. Particularly in least developed countries more basic capability building remains important in many green technology sectors. So far, the BASIC countries (Brazil, South Africa, India and China) have only been an informal negotiation group within the UNFCCC process. However, the pressing question is whether it is now time to introduce new country classifications into the framework.

5.3 *Limitations and issues for further research*

In this paper we have questioned the relevance of the conventional approach to technology transfer in green technology sectors in China and India. In assessing the scope and weight of our key points, it is important to have in mind that we have focused mainly on national champions and that the focus on three 'new' sectors was narrow. For example, it remains an open question whether similar conclusions would be reached in studies of mainstream power generation such as higher efficiency coal fired power generation, carbon capture and storage or energy efficiency technologies in buildings and industrial production. Some of the greatest opportunities for low carbon innovation are perhaps in materials-intensive and energy-intensive sectors. In these areas, China and India still seem to be lagging considerably behind levels of efficiency in OECD countries (IEA, 2010).

These reservations need to be acknowledged but the insights of this paper do nevertheless have implications that should be explored in further research. There is a global trend in which innovation is decomposing and decentralising within and beyond multinational corporations and specialised technology firms (Lema et al., 2012). The question is how decomposed and open innovation (Lema, 2010; Srinivas, 2011) affect the building up of advanced green innovation capabilities in the developing world. This paper suggests implicitly that these trends have been a precondition for unconventional technology transfer, but further research should address this question directly.

Moreover, a key question for new research is whether technologies developed under national policy agendas and factor endowments specific to emerging economies will be more adequate for least developed countries in Africa and Asia than those developed in the OECD countries (Stamm et al., 2009, p. 22).

Research into these issues is needed because much of the previous debate has been over the *scale* of innovation capability building as opposed to the *direction* (Bell, 2009). The notion of technology transfer implies an adherence to given technological paths, but the key need is for new trajectories (Altenburg and Pegels, 2012). As China and India gradually move 'beyond' catch-up, these countries may already be pushing the green technological frontier in new directions.

Acknowledgements

We appreciate valuable comments on an earlier version of the paper from Tilman Altenburg, Erik Haites, Martin Bell and two anonymous reviewers. Rasmus Lema is grateful for funding from the Federal Ministry for Economic Cooperation and Development (BMZ), Germany.

Notes

1. We recognise that effective mitigation will require changes in a much wider range of sectors including conventional energy and transport systems, heavy industry, construction, etc., but it is not the focus of this paper.
2. It is important to emphasise that – even as ideal types – these mechanism classifications are not absolute categories. There is a continuum between conventional and unconventional mechanisms.
3. However, it needs to be stressed that there is also a large degree of variability – meaning that there is no straightforward relationship between the different mechanisms and the acquisition of different types of capability. It depends on strategic intent and the way the transfer mechanisms are organised and managed.
4. Firm-internal R&D is an imprecise proxy for firm-internal technological activity. The reason for focusing on R&D – rather than a broader array of technological activities (including non-R&D activities) – is merely operational. We did not conduct fieldwork specifically for this article but relied mainly on information in the press and on websites. Such written sources often mention R&D projects, but rarely other types of innovative activities.
5. The analyses in this section draw on existing literature and company sources in the public domain. The micro-level components of the analyses and the underlying information about individual companies are based on company websites and documents unless otherwise cited.
6. Some foreign companies also engage in local R&D. Vestas have established an R&D centre in Beijing, tapping into the wind competences being built in China and signalling commitment to technology development in China (Lema et al., 2011).
7. This corresponds with patent data. In renewable energy and electric and hybrid vehicles, China and India are increasing patenting activity and have shown a strong growth in patent applications from 1999 to 2008, although from low levels. What is also worth noting is that China and India have higher shares of renewable energy in overall patent applications than the OECD average (OECD 2011). However, the available data does not show a shift from patenting by foreign subsidiaries to national companies (Lee et al., 2009; UNEP, 2010).
8. This issue is not just definitional. The emphasis on the narrow view comes at the cost of neglecting the important role of incremental and other types of innovation that clearly mattered for climate change mitigation in these cases. The key process was not about adopting technological breakthroughs but

more about adopting (and increasingly contributing to) incremental innovations, such as those that improve key performance indicators in the wind or solar power technology industries.

9. Prospects of gaining increased access to enormous markets in India and China seem to have motivated foreign players to 'share' their knowledge collaborative relationships. They may be less motivated to do so in smaller countries with less bargaining power.

10. Recent Conference of the Parties (COPs) introduced the planned establishment of a Climate Technology Centre and Network and a Technology Executive Committee. However, the details of these initiatives have not yet been specified in detail.

References

Altenburg, T., and Pegels, A. (2012) Sustainability-oriented innovation systems – managing the green transformation. *Submitted to Innovation and Development*, forthcoming 2012.

Altenburg, T., Schmitz, H., and Stamm, A. (2008) Breakthrough China's and India's transition from production to innovation. *World Development*, 36(2), pp. 325–34.

Awasthi, S.R. (2009) Development of reneable energy technologies in India: The role of BHEL. *Akshay Urja Renewable Energy. A newsletter of Ministry of New and Renewable Energy*, 2, pp. 26–33.

Bajaj, V. (2009) The tiny leader of the pack. *New York Times*, October 28.

BCG (2010) Sunrise in the east: China's advance in solar PV-and the competitive implications for the industry. Boston Consulting Group.

Bell, M. (1990) Continuing industrialisation, climate change and international technology transfer (Brighton: Science Policy Research Unit, Sussex University).

Bell, M. (2009) Innovation capabilities and directions of development *STEPS Working Paper* (Brighton: STEPS Centre).

Bhargava, B. (2009) Overview of photovoltaic technologies in India. *Solar Energy Materials and Solar Cells*, 67(1–4), pp. 639–646.

BTM (2010), World market update 2009. BTM Consult Ringkøbing, Denmark.

BYD (2010), Green tech for tomorrow. Annual report 2009. BYD Company Limited.

C-WET (2009) *Manufacturers-wise wind electric generators installed in India (As on 31.03.2009)* available at: http://www.cwet.tn.nic.in, accessed May 2010.

Climate Group, T. (2009) China's clean revolution II: Opportunities for a low carbon future.

Commission on Growth and Development (2008) The growth report: Strategies for sustained growth and inclusive development. World Bank on behalf of the Commission on Growth and Development, Washington, DC.

Dantas, E., and Bell, M. (2011) The co-evolution of firm-centered knowledge networks and capabilities in late industrializing countries: The case of petrobras in the offshore oil innovation system in Brazil. *World Development*, 39(9), pp. 1570–1591.

Ely, A., and Scoones, I. (2009) The global redistribution of innovation: Lessons from China and India. *STEPS Working Paper* 22, STEPS Centre, Brighton.

Ernst, D., and Kim, L. (2002) Global production networks, knowledge diffusion and local capability formation. *Research Policy*, 31(8–9), pp. 1417–1429.

Fischer, D. (2012) Challenges of low carbon technology diffusion: Insights from shifts in China's photovoltaic industry development. *Innovation and Development*, forthcoming 2012.

Fu, X., Pietrobelli, C., and Soete, L. (2011) The role of foreign technology and indigenous innovation in the emerging economies: Technological change and catching-up. *World Development*, 39(7), pp. 1204–1212.

Fu, X., and Zhang, J. (2011) Technology transfer, indigenous innovation and leapfrogging in green technology: The solar-PV industry in China and India. *Journal of Chinese Economic and Business Studies*, 9(4), pp. 329–347.

Grossman, G.M., and Helpman, E. (1995) Technology and trade, in: M.G. Gene and R. Kenneth (eds) *Handbook of International Economics*. Vol III. Amsterdam (Elsevier).

Hirshman, W.P. (2010) Surprise, surprise (Cell Production 2009: survey). *Photon International*, March 2010, pp. 176–199.

Howell, T.R., Noellert, W.A., Hume, G., and Wolff, A.W. (2010) China's promotion of the renewable electric power equipment industry (Washington: Dewey & LeBoeuf LLP for the National Foreign Trade Council).

IEA (2009) Technology roadmaps electric and plug-in hybrid electric vehicles. International Energy Agency, Paris.

IEA (2010) Energy technology perspectives 2010: Scenarios & strategies to 2050. International Energy Agency, Paris.

IPCC (2000) Methodological and technological issues in technology transfer. Intergovernmental Panel on Climate Change. Working Group III, Cambridge.

IPCC (2007) *Mitigation of climate change* (Cambridge, NY: Cambridge University Press).

ISA (2008) Solar PV industry: Global and Indian scenario. India Semiconductor Association, New Delhi.

Jian-Ye, W. (1990) Growth, technology transfer, and the long-run theory of international capital movements. *Journal of International Economics*, 29(3–4), pp. 255–271.

Kathuria, V. (2002) Technology transfer for GHG reduction – A framework with application to India. *Technological Forecasting and Social Change*, 69(4), pp. 405–430.

Kirkegaard, J.F., Thilo, H., Lutz, W., and Matt, M. (2010) Toward a sunny future Global integration in the solar PV industry. Peterson Institute for International Economics.

Kristinsson, K., and Rao, R. (2008) Interactive learning or technology transfer as a way to catch-up? Analysing the wind energy industry in Denmark and India. *Industry and Innovation*, 15(3), pp. 297–320.

Krugman, P. (1979) Model of innovation, technology-transfer, and the world distribution of income. *Journal of Political Economy*, 87(2), pp. 253–266.

Kulkarni, J.S. (2003) A southern critique of the globalist assumptions about technology transfer in climate change treaty negotiations. *Bulletin of Science Technology Society*, 23(4), pp. 256–264.

Lall, S. (1990) *Building industrial competitiveness in developing countries* (Paris, France: Organisation for Economic Cooperation and Development).

Lall, S. (1993) Promoting technology development: The role of technology transfer and indigenous effort. *Third World Quarterly*, 14(1), pp. 95–108.

Leadbeater, C. (2007) *The atlas of ideas. Europe and Asia in the new geography of science and innovation* (London: Demos).

Lee, B., Iliev, I., Preston, F., and Royal Institute of International Affairs (2009) *Who Owns Our Low Carbon Future? : Intellectual property and energy technologies* (London: Chatham House).

Lema, R. (2010) Adoption of open business models in the west and innovation in India's software industry. *IDS Research Reports*, 2010, pp. 1–144.

Lema, R., Berger, A., Schmitz, H., and Song, H. (2011) Competition and cooperation between Europe and China in the wind power sector. in: *IDS Working Papers*, 2011, pp. 1–45.

Lema, R., Quadros, R., and Schmitz, H. (2012) Shifts in innovation power to Brazil and India, *IDS Research Report* (Brighton: Institute of Development Studies, University of Sussex).

Lema, A., and Ruby, K. (2007) Between fragmented authoritarianism and policy coordination: Creating a Chinese market for wind energy. *Energy Policy*, 35(7), pp. 3879–3890.

Less, C.T., and Mcmillan, S. (2005) , Achieving the successful transfer of environmentally sound technologies: Trade-related aspects. OECD Publishing.

Lewis, J.I. (2007) Technology acquisition and innovation in the developing world: Wind turbine development in China and India. *Studies in Comparative International Development*, 42(3–4), pp. 208–232.

Liu, L.-Q., Wang, Z.-X., Zhang, H.-Q., and Xue, Y.-C. (2009) Solar energy development in China – A review. *Renewable and Sustainable Energy Reviews*, 14(1), pp. 301–311.

Lundvall, B.-Å. (1992) *National systems of innovation: towards a theory of innovation and interactive learning* (London: Pinter).

Lundvall, B.-Å., and Johnson, B. (1994) The learning economy. *Journal of Industry Studies*, 1(2), pp. 23–42.

Lundvall, B.-Å., Johnson, B., Andersen, E.S., and Dalum, B. (2002) National systems of production, innovation and competence building. *Research Policy*, 31(2), pp. 213–31.

Maini, C.K. (2005) REVA electric car: A case study of innovation at RECC. *International Journal of Technology Management*, 32(1–2), pp. 199–212.

Mallett, A., Ockwell, D., Pal, P., Kumar, A., Abbi, Y., Haum, R., Watson, J., Mackerron, G., and Sethi, G. (2009) UK-India collaborative study on the transfer of low carbon technology. Phase II Final Report. SPRU and TERI.

Menon, N. (2009) Chetan Maini is charged about the prospects of electric car REVA. *The Economic Times*, 28 March 2009.

Mizuno, E. (2007) *Cross-border transfer of climate hange mitigation technologies: The case of wind energy from Denmark and Germany to India* (Ph.D. Dissertation). Massachusetts Institute of Technology.

MOF & MOST (2009) Information about the promotion experiments with models of energy efficient and new energy cars (in Chinese), Directive 2009/6. Ministry of Finance and Ministry of Science & Technology, available at: http://www.gov.cn/zwgk/2009-02/05/content_1222338.htm.

Nelson, R.R. (2011) Economic development as an evolutionary process. *Innovation and Development*, 1(1), pp. 39–49.

Ockwell, D., Watson, J., Mallett, A., Haum, R., Mackerron, G., and Verbeken, A.-M. (2010) Enhancing developing country access to eco-innovation: The case of technology transfer and climate change in a post-2012 policy framework. *OECD Environment Working Papers*, OECD.

Ockwell, D.G., Watson, J., Mackerron, G., Pal, P., and Yamin, F. (2008) Key policy considerations for facilitating low carbon technology transfer to developing countries. *Energy Policy*, 36(11), pp. 4104–4115.

People's Daily Online (2009) China's new energy vehicles head for the world. *People's Daily*, 11 February 2009.

Popp, D. (2011) International technology transfer, climate change, and the clean development mechanism. *Review of Environmental Economics and Policy*, 5(1), pp. 131–152.

Rajsekhar, B., Van Hulle, F., and Jansen, J.C. (1999) Indian wind energy programme: Performance and future directions. *Energy Policy*, 27(11), pp. 669–678.

Reddy, N.M., and Zhao, L. (1990) International technology transfer: A review. *Research Policy*, 19(4), pp. 285–307.

Romer, P.M. (1994) The origins of endogenous growth. *Journal of Economic Perspectives*, 8(1), pp. 3–22.

Rui, H., and Yip, G.S. (2008) Foreign acquisitions by Chinese firms: A strategic intent perspective. *Journal of World Business*, 43(2), pp. 213–226.

Schneider, M., Holzer, A., and Hoffmann, V.H. (2008) Understanding the CDM's contribution to technology transfer. *Energy Policy*, 36(8), pp. 2930–2938.

Shamsavari, A. (2007) , The technology transfer paradigm: A critique. Kingston upon Thames, UK Faculty of Arts and Social Sciences, Kingston University.

Srinivas, K.R. (2011) Role of open innovation models and IPR in technology transfer in the context of climate change mitigation, in: J. Haselip, I. Nygaard, U. Hansen and E. Ackom (eds) *Diffusion of Renewable Energy Technologies: Case studies of enabling frameworks in developing countries* (Denmark: UNEP Riso Centre).

Srinivasan, S. (2005) Segmentation of the Indian photovoltaic market. *Renewable and Sustainable Energy Reviews*, 9(2), pp. 215–227.

Stamm, A., Dantas, E., Fischer, D., Ganguly, S., and Rennkamp, B. (2009) Sustainability-oriented innovation systems: Towards decoupling economic growth from environmental pressures? *Discussion Paper – DIE Research Project 'Sustainable Solutions through Research'*, German Development Institute / Deutsches Institut für Entwicklungspolitik, Bonn.

Stern, N.H. (2007) *The Economics of Climate Change: The Stern review* (Cambridge, UK; New York: Cambridge University Press).

Tan, X.M. (2010) Clean technology R&D and innovation in emerging countries – Experience from China. *Energy Policy*, 38(6), pp. 2916–2926.

Thorne, Steve (2008) Towards a framework of clean energy technology receptivity, *Energy Policy* 36(8): pp. 2831–2838.

Tomlinson, S., Zorlu, P., and Langley, C. (2008) Innovation and Technology Transfer (London: E3G and Chatham House).

Ueno, T (2009) Technology transfer to China to address climate change mitigation Resources for the Future, Issue Brief 09-09, August 2009. Washington D.C.

UNEP, E. a. I (2010) Patents and clean energy: Bridging the gap between evidence and policy. United Nations Environment Programme (UNEP), European Patent Office (EPO), and International Centre for Trade and Sustainable Development (ICTSD), Munich.

UNFCCC (1992) United Nations framework convention on climate change. United Nations.

UNFCCC (2002) The Marrakesh accords. United Nations Framework Convention on Climate Change.

UNFCCC (2007) Bali action plan, decision 1/CP.13. United Nations Framework Convention on Climate Change.

UNFCCC (2010) Outcome of the work of the ad hoc working group on long-term cooperative action under the convention, 1/CP.16. *Cancun Agreements* (Bonn: United Nations Framework Convention on Climate Change).

Wang, G. (2009) Shanghai auto group on move in developing new energy cars. *Xinhua News*, 11 March 2009.

Watson, Jim (2011) China's low-carbon leadership headlines fail to capture the reality, *The Guardian*, 18 April 2011.

World Bank (2008) Technology diffusion in the developing world. International Bank for Reconstruction and Development, Washington, DC.

World Bank (2010) World development report 2010: Development and climate change. World Bank, Washington, DC.

Zeng, M., and Williamson, P.J. (2007) *Dragons at Your Door: How Chinese cost innovation is disrupting global competition* (Boston, MA: Harvard Business School Press).

Innovating for energy efficiency: a perspective from India

Ankur Chaudhary[a], Ambuj D. Sagar[a] and Ajay Mathur[b]

[a]Indian Institute of Technology, Delhi; [b]Bureau of Energy Efficiency, Government of India,

While it is well-understood that technological innovation offers much potential to meet sustainability challenges, realising this potential is not a trivial task. This is especially true in developing countries where resource and institutional limitations often impede innovation. This paper focuses on energy efficiency, increasingly recognised as a linchpin of a sustainable energy system, and through a set of case studies on energy-efficiency programmes in India, draws out lessons for innovation for sustainability, paying particular attention to the issue of 'scale-up,' which is key to a meaningful transition towards sustainability. We suggest that effective sustainability-oriented innovation must be rooted in the local context, prioritising local needs, identifying potential technological solutions, and then designing programmes that address the necessary elements of the innovation chain to ensure delivery at scale. Further, we suggest that such a process can be greatly facilitated by a coordinating agency (a 'system operator') with a bird's-eye view of the target system.

1. Sustainability and innovation

The Brundtland commission report in 1987 highlighted and stressed the need for 'sustainable development' defining it as '[. . .] development that meets the needs of the present without compromising the ability of future generations to meet their own needs' (Brundtland Commission, 1987). Since the report, the terms 'sustainability' and 'sustainable development' have entered the mainstream, beginning with the United Nations Conference on Environment and Development held at Rio de Janeiro in 1992. In fact, the transition towards sustainability is viewed as one of the central challenges of the twenty-first century (see, for example, National Research Council, 1999; United Nations, 2000; United Nations, 2002).

Even as the world marches on in economic, social, and human development terms (but with many developing countries still needing to go a long way), the inability of the local and global environment to sustain OECD-level per-capita resource consumption levels across all countries is widely accepted (National Research Council, 1999; Kates et al., 2001; Sachs, 2007). The disaggregation between 'throughput growth' and 'development' however, promises to enable qualitative improvement with a disproportionately smaller quantitative change in consumption (Goodland and Daly, 1996). Consequently, the vision of an environmentally sustainable development is contingent on our ability to harness science, technology and innovation towards this goal (Kates et al., 2001; Holdren, 2008), although such a move towards sustainability is complicated

---

AM notes that the views expressed in this paper are his alone and they do not reflect the views of the Bureau of Energy Efficiency.

by the wide range of technologies under purview as well as the disparate sector applications (Levin and Clark, 2010).

Efforts to enhance the science, technology and innovative capacity in the sustainability realm over the past few decades range, among others, from developing more efficient cook stoves for burning biomass (World Bank, 2011), to developing efficient coal power technologies (Chikkatur et al., 2011), to developing and improvising renewable-power-generation systems (Jacobsson and Bergek, 2004), and to research for sustainable agriculture (UNDP, 2001). However, despite these efforts, a thorough understanding of the critical attributes of a successful sustainability-oriented knowledge system is missing. Moreover, as the present technologies and policy regimes are deemed insufficient to attaining sustainable development (Stamm et al., 2009), it is critical that lessons are learnt quickly and employed intelligently to catalyse innovations as well as realise their impacts across the broadest possible regimes.

More recently, analysts have started examining the application of the Innovation Systems (IS) perspective to the sustainability *problematique* as a way to develop policy frameworks that could act as directional elements for leveraging innovation capabilities to tackle sustainability challenges (Bergh et al., 2006; Hekkert et al., 2007; Smith et al., 2010). Such thinking, of course, draws upon the broader IS literature that has had a major impact on innovation studies and practice through its approach of examining innovation processes from a 'systems' perspective to develop insights into the processes and determinants of innovation, and leveraging this knowledge to develop policies to facilitate and stimulate innovative activities (see, for example, Lundvall, 1992; Nelson, 1993). In a similar vein, sustainability-oriented innovation systems (SOIS) can be seen as instruments for mobilising innovation to facilitate the much needed move towards sustainable development. A much better understanding of the role of policy in the development and sustenance of SOIS as well as effective ways to adapt and deploy these SOIS across disparate geographies and sectors is much needed (Stamm et al., 2009; Altenburg and Pegels, 2012). However, the identification of market failures and the tailoring of appropriate policy instruments to address the needs of the SOIS to realise sustainable development is only now beginning to be explored. Towards this end, the experiences of present policy approaches and programmes intended to address market failures in sustainability-oriented areas should provide useful insights. This will help us better understand the operational as well as design attributes of a successful SOIS while keeping the local socio-technical milieu in the backdrop.

Research and development (R&D) plays a critical role as the source of new technologies to help meet sustainable development. Consequently R&D figures as a prominent objective of sustainability-oriented innovation (Margolis and Kammen, 1999; American Energy Innovation Council, 2011). At the same time, it is also recognised that paying attention to mechanisms that help introduce these new technologies into the marketplace and allow them to compete with established technologies is equally necessary. But it is equally obvious that these technologies need to be deployed at large to truly realise their potential as instruments of sustainable development. Often, innovation scholars focus on this last aspect in a limited way – in fact, the commercial introduction of a product into the marketplace traditionally is seen as the final step in the innovation process, with the expectation that market forces will ensure the uptake of the new technology if it offers a performance or cost benefit, which is indeed true for most technologies. But in many areas pertinent to sustainable development, the primary benefits are often 'public goods', such as an improved environment, and users (whether an individual or a firm) may have little motivation to take up these technologies (Stamm, et al., 2009). There also exist other challenges such as the risk perception of adopters, their understanding of the benefits of new technologies and the cost-benefit calculus, their financial and technical ability to deploy new technologies, to say nothing of the absence of policy frameworks to level the playing field for technologies (Brown, 2001).

Thus deployment efforts for sustainability-oriented technologies often face significant challenges. For example, the penetration of improved coal power generation technologies such as ultra-supercritical pulverised coal and, in some developing countries, even supercritical pulverised coal have been rather slow (Chikkatur et al., 2011). Similarly, efficient lighting solution such as compact fluorescent lamps (CFLs) and light-emitting diodes (LEDs) still account for only a small fraction of residential lighting worldwide; incandescent bulbs still account for almost half of the residential lighting (Nicholas Lefevre and Waide, 2006). Such delays, or even failures, in the scaling up of deployment efforts could prove detrimental in achieving the goal of sustainability and underpin the urgency of the needed efforts.

For the sustainability transition, this issue of large-scale deployment is a particularly important and thorny one. In the case of developing countries, where there is limited focus on, and capabilities for, development of new technologies, leveraging existing technologies becomes a key approach to transition towards sustainability – therefore, any perspective on SOISs must give appropriate attention to the issue of scaling up deployment. This paper will do so using lessons from a particular area, that of energy efficiency, in India.

2. Energy – the scope for innovation

Increasing the availability of sustainable, modern, affordable and reliable energy services is important to increase the standard of living across the globe, especially in rural areas. However, despite this centrality to development, nearly one-third of human population does not have access to modern energy services (IEA, 2010a). Moreover, there exists a strong agreement across all levels of deliberations on Millennium Development Goals (MDGs) that, despite improved access to energy being absent as an explicit part of MDGs, it is nevertheless a prerequisite to reach all of them (Modi et al., 2005; UNDP, 2005). Yet, the progress thus far on the energy access front has been severely lacking. If current trends continue, more people will be without access to modern energy services in 2030 than at present (IEA, 2010a), a clearly disconcerting projection.

For developing countries, expanding and modernising their energy sector makes particular sense since the limited availability of energy constrains human and economic development, and energy services enable a range of activities that underpin modern existence, such as sanitation and health services, food and water supplies, communication, and mobility, as well as economic activities across industries and services sectors (Sagar and van der Zwaan, 2006). Moreover, historically the pursuit for human development across the globe has resulted in a rise in energy consumption per capita to satisfy increasing demand for energy services that underlie the rising living standards and economic activities (Sagar et al., 2006b).

In 2008, with a global primary energy demand of 12,271 million tons of oil equivalent (Mtoe) primary energy demand, the global per-capita primary energy demand stood at 1.83 toe/annum. But the per-capita energy consumption average in 2008 of the member countries of the Organisation of Economic Cooperation and Development (OECD) of 4.57 toe/annum and the corresponding figure of 0.68 toe/annum for Africa reveals the stark inequalities in energy access that characterise the present energy-availability situation globally(IEA, 2010a). While it is often felt that the much higher per-capita energy-consumption precedent set by the OECD countries is not sustainable over the global population figures, the energy needs of the world nevertheless are projected to rise significantly over the coming decades. The International Energy Agency (IEA) under its New Policy Scenario projects a 36% higher global energy demand by 2035 over the 2008 levels, with over 90% of this increase being accounted for by the non-OECD countries (and China and India being among the major sources of this increased demand). However, even with these increases, the per capita energy consumption in this group of countries would still remain less than 40% of the corresponding OECD numbers (IEA, 2010a).

Along with the issues of energy access and the inevitable future energy-demand increase, energy services in the modern world are marked by pronounced externalities in the form of local and global impacts of the energy generation/extraction process (National Research Council, 2010). For example, coal-based power generation results in multiple, significant externalities with human health and potential climate change impacts being particularly important. Air pollutants in the flue gas–particulate matter (PM), sulfur oxides (SOx), nitrogen oxides (NOx) and other chemicals emitted from coal-fired power plants can have significant health impacts on the local and regional population (Chikkatur et al., 2011). Under the New Policies Scenario of the International Energy Agency (IEA), energy-related CO_2 emissions rise from 29.3 Giga-tonnes (Gt) in 2008 to 35.4 Gt in 2035(IEA, 2010a). As highlighted by the Intergovernmental Panel on Climate Change (IPCC) reports, the potential maximum damages can be quite large if the ultimate global mean temperature rise significantly exceeds $2°C$(IPCC, 2007). In fact, there now is significant scientific and political consensus that limiting to global average temperature increase to less than $2°C$ above pre-industrial levels is necessary to avoid dangerous climate change impacts (UNFCCC, 2010). Consequently, the large externalities of energy generation and consumption dictate that a move towards sustainability needs to reduce the energy consumption and production in conjunction with mitigating the externalities per unit of energy extracted, converted, and consumed.

The pursuit of sustainable development is thus, to a great extent, reliant on the ability to innovate to increase energy access for the energy poor in the developing countries as well as to mitigate the impacts from energy production and use. Accordingly, the development of renewable energy capacity to replace polluting and unsustainable fossil fuel energy base has received increasing emphasis in recent years (Kammen, 2006). This renewable-energy generation base, with fewer externalities than the fossil-fuel-based energy generation, is expected to lower the overall impacts of the energy-generation mix. Several major programmes in various parts of the world have been/are being targeted at developing and deploying renewable technologies (REDI; Reuters, 2009; JNNSM, 2010). However, even under the most optimistic projection scenarios of IEA fossil fuels like coal, gas and oil are expected to contribute significantly to the global energy mix even in 2035. For example, the combined share of these fossil fuels is projected to be 61% of the global primary energy demand under IEA's 450-ppm scenario(IEA, 2010a).Moreover, while technologies for ameliorating impacts from fossil fuels are at various stages of research, development and deployment, the extent of their deployment in the near future is not clear. Finally, it is quite probable that despite improvements in technologies, a large fraction of the energy generation infrastructure over the coming decades will continue to have substantial externalities, given the long lifetimes of such infrastructure, and may prove detrimental to the sustainable development efforts.

Given this backdrop, improving the efficiency of the energy system (both production and use) is an attractive option as 'a low hanging fruit' that can help conserve natural resources, reduce environmental pollution and CO_2 emissions, ease infrastructural bottlenecks as well as improve industrial competitiveness through reduced energy linked costs and others (IPCC, 2007; Linares and Perez-Arriaga, 2009; World Energy Council, 2010). In fact, energy efficiency improvements over the past three decades have provided for substantial energy savings over the 1970s levels (IEA, 2004). Looking ahead, as the single largest prospective deliverer of greenhouse gas (GHG) reductions, both in terms of the mitigation potential as well as the cost effectiveness of such mitigation, compared to other alternatives (IPCC, 2007), energy efficiency is seen as a crucial ingredient of the transition to a world with adequate and sustainable energy.

The European Commission, for example, considers it economically viable to leverage efficiency improvements for achieving reductions in energy consumption greater than 20% as compared to the 2020 business-as-usual projections (European Commission, 2005). Energy efficiency makes particular sense for developing countries that are projected to require enormous investments[1] in power generation infrastructure to meet their growing energy needs – improving energy efficiency can reduce these investment requirements. Moreover, the net financial impact of the energy-efficiency technologies could be negative, implying that the economic gains from lower energy consumption can potentially offset the costs involved in adopting these technologies (McKinsey, 2009a). Moreover, energy-efficiency improvements, through their reduction of the overall energy demand, ease the strain on renewable-energy deployment efforts that would require substantial investments to materialise at the requisite scales.

Despite the above considerations, and a generally accepted 'no-regrets' view of energy efficiency measures, it has often been pointed out that energy efficiency policy is not receiving sufficient emphasis compared with renewable energy policy, even though they have similar benefits in terms of energy security and climate change mitigation, and energy efficiency is often the more cost-effective of the two (PCAST, 1997; IEA, 2006; IEA, 2009a). While in some sense, it is perplexing as to why the 'low-hanging' fruit of energy efficiency has not yet been amply taken up, a number of factors – low energy price resulting from the lack of internalisation of environmental costs, market barriers such as lack of information, lack of technical expertise, rigid procurement practices (not considering life-cycle analysis, etc.) as well as the complexity of energy efficiency policy design – have been offered as the explanations for the limited adoption of energy efficiency technologies (Linares and Perez-Arriaga, 2009; World Energy Council, 2010). This market failure has deprived the energy efficiency technologies of their due impact.

With several mature end-use technologies offering considerable efficiency improvement potential, it is imperative that the regulation process to build acceptance and foster implementation is expedited. As pointed by a major World Bank study (Taylor et al., 2008), the major constraints on financing and implementing energy efficiency are institutional in nature, unlike some other sustainability-oriented sub-systems where research, development and demonstration are still quite important. Consequently, an appropriate SOIS to realise the potential of energy efficiency technologies is much needed, more so, due to earlier mentioned reasons, in the developing countries. Interestingly, the opportunities offered by the developing countries are quite commensurate with these challenges. As pointed out earlier, since a majority of the energy demand expansion in the coming decades is expected to occur in developing countries, these countries offer a chance for large-scale deployment of appropriate technologies and the realisation of huge efficiency enabled energy savings (IEA, 2010b).

One needs to understand the notion of sustainability-oriented innovation in the context of the dynamic technology paradigm, imperfect markets as well as the economics of the interventions. Consequently, the design of a successful SOIS needs to leverage lessons from the modalities of programmes in the past and their operational experiences. Close monitoring and evaluation of existing energy efficiency policies and measures are thus a prerequisite for devising successful programmes to further enhance energy efficiency by leveraging technological opportunities. In this context, we draw upon the almost-decade-long experience of the Indian Bureau of Energy Efficiency (BEE) programme to develop a better understanding of how SOISs can facilitate widespread deployment of socially and environmentally efficient technologies.

3. Energy efficiency programmes in India: case studies

Increasing industrialisation and the growing energy needs of a rapidly urbanising population have fuelled the growth in India's energy consumption over the past few decades. India consumed 600

Mtoe of primary energy in 2007, with the 0.53 toe per capita (tpc) being much lower than the world average of 1.82 tpc and even well below that of China (1.50 tpc) (IEA, 2011a). Moreover, the energy intensity of the Indian economy has been historically low and the energy use per-capita-GDP has been steadily declining since the 1990s. For example, between 1990 and 2005, while the GDP has increased by a factor of 2.3, the concomitant increase in energy consumption has been only 1.9 (de la Rue du Can, Letschert, McNeil, Zhou and Sathaye, 2009). Structural changes in the economy towards services as well as efficiency improvements in the industry and transportation sectors have contributed to this decoupling (de la Rue du Can, Letschert, McNeil, Zhou and Sathaye, 2009). According to IEA estimates, without the efficiency improvements since 2000, the total final energy consumption in 2007 would have been 10% higher (about 40 Mtoe) than it actually was (IEA, 2010b).

In 2005, the residential and industry sectors represented over 70% of the total primary energy consumption in India (Planning Commission, 2011). Within the industry sector, the sectoral variations in growth rates, consumption patterns as well as resource availability have led to wide variations in the energy consumption patterns across sectors. Energy intensive sectors like iron and steel and cement represent a large fraction of the overall energy use in industry while exhibiting a large bandwidth of energy consumption intensities within the sub-sectors (IEA, 2009b). All in all, factors such as the high energy prices due to fuel price reform, energy efficiency standards and requirements, etc. have made the overall industry sector more efficient since the 90s (Rao et al., 2009). That said, various assessments (IEA, 2009b; Rao et al., 2009; IEA, 2010b) of the Indian industry sector have highlighted the need for technology and policy interventions to further realise the energy savings potential of the sector.

The Indian buildings sector accounted for nearly one-third of the total energy usage in the country in 2005 with a strong growth rate of about 8% (EDS, 2010). However, despite the large energy consumption in the sector, the energy performance index of the Indian building stock remains poor with little consideration to energy efficiency planning in most constructions. Furthermore, household appliances that contribute significantly to the energy usage in a building (see Figure 1) need to be improved.

Considering the large energy usage in the industry and buildings sector as well as the limited penetration of the best available technologies in these sectors, energy-efficiency interventions in these areas promise substantial energy savings.

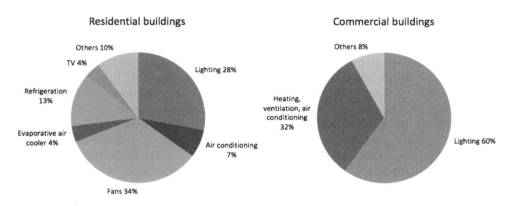

Source: Bassi, S. (n.d.), 'Bureau of Energy Efficiency and Energy Conservation Building Code: An Overview', available at http://www.eco3.org/news/BEE.pdf)

Figure 1.   Electricity use breakdown in commercial and residential buildings in India.

Given this range of opportunities for enhancing the efficiency of the Indian energy sector, the savings potential from energy efficient technologies is estimated to be quite large.[2] It was in recognition of such opportunities that the Government of India enacted the Energy Conservation Act of 2001. Under this act, the Government of India (GOI) set up the Bureau of Energy Efficiency (BEE) as a nodal statutory body at the central level in 2002. The mission of the Bureau of Energy Efficiency was mandated as:

[...] to assist in developing policies and strategies with a thrust on self-regulation and market principles, within the overall framework of the Energy Conservation Act, 2001 with the primary objective of reducing energy intensity of the Indian economy. This will be achieved with active participation of all stakeholders, resulting in accelerated and sustained adoption of energy efficiency in all sectors.

To achieve this mission, the BEE primarily coordinates through its regulatory and promotional functions with designated consumers, agencies and other organisations to leverage existing resources and infrastructure towards attaining better energy efficiency. The target intervention areas are selected based upon the availability and maturity of technologies to significantly improve efficiencies, their applicability in the local context, and potential of the intervention to impact the future energy trajectory through up scaling (BEE(I), 2011a). As a result, BEE and its programmes essentially target energy efficiencies across a broad range of sectors including household appliances, small and medium enterprises (SMEs), electricity use in agriculture, and buildings (www.beeindia.in).

Here we will focus on four case studies of BEE programmes that target household appliances, buildings, industries and CFLs. While the case study method, like all social sciences research methods, calls for methodological tradeoffs, it is useful in providing a good understanding of a complex issue while contributing to the experiential knowledge in the subject (Flyvbjerg, 2011). In this paper we have looked at inferences that are descriptive rather than causal while adopting an exploratory rather than confirmatory approach, thus adhering to the methodological considerations for case studies proposed by Gerring (2004). Moreover, we have chosen case studies that reflect a reasonably complete picture of the environment under study (in this case innovation for energy efficiency in India) both in terms of the intervention areas as well as intervention mechanisms. As a result, we believe that the lessons drawn from these case studies closely reflect the learning offered by the paradigm in consideration.

Table 1. A user-instrument matrix illustrating the target areas for the different case studies discussed above. The number in square brackets indicates the pertinent case as discussed below.

		Users		
		Residential	Commercial	Industrial
Instruments	Regulatory	Standards and Labels (minimum energy performance standards) [1]	Energy Conservation Building Code [3]	PAT (Standards and Targets) [4]
	Demand Creation	Standards and Labels (Label branding) [1]	Energy Conservation Building Code (Star Labels for Buildings) [3]	-
	Market Incentives	Bachat Lamp Yojana [2]	-	PAT (Energy Savings Certificates) [4]

As illustrated in Table 1 below, these case studies between them cover a wide range of consumers and organisations while offering perspective into supply side regulation as well as demand side incentives as intervention tools for market transformation and wide spread adoption. Further, the four case studies presented below represent interventions in varying degree of maturity as well as perceived success, thus affording a broader and more nuanced picture of BEE interventions.

Case 1: standards and labelling

The rapid increase in urbanisation in India has been accompanied by a concomitant increase in the use of electrical equipment (in particular home appliances). These appliances now account for a large share of consumption of Indian energy resources (see Figure 1). Without any substantial incentive to manufacture energy efficient appliances, the Indian market in the past decades was characterised by inefficient appliances, with no obligation on the part of manufacturers to reveal detailed power consumption and other performance characteristics of their products (Price, 2005). This lack of benchmarking (along with, in many cases, the presence of small and medium enterprises in the manufacturing ecosystem, either as component manufacturers and/or as assemblers) led to a wide variation in the operational characteristics of appliances in the Indian market. Furthermore, as a result of a rising middle class with greater disposable incomes, the consumer appliances market in India has experienced strong growth and is expected to grow in the future as well. As a result, the potential energy savings from an efficient consumer appliance stock are substantial (BEE, 2011b).

Despite the entry of several multinationals like Hitachi, LG, Philips, Whirlpool and others in the Indian market, little effort was undertaken by these consumer-appliance companies to introduce high-efficiency products in the market, a problem compounded by the lack of any performance benchmarks in the market (BEE(I), 2011a). Subsequently, the Standards and Labelling programme was initiated in 2006 to provide the consumer an informed choice about the energy saving, and thereby the cost-saving potential of the marketed household, and other equipment (BEE, 2011d). By extension, an incentive for the manufacturers to invest in the introduction of energy efficient products was also provided. Aggressive promotion and outreach programmes for the labelling scheme, projecting higher energy-efficiency performance as a superior product type, accompanied the initial voluntary introduction of labels in 2007 (Power Ministry). The categories of appliances targeted under the scheme were identified based on the overall energy use by the appliance product, expected future growth in the appliance numbers, failure of the market to use available energy-efficient technologies and categories where a significant energy-use bandwidth existed in the product offerings. Based on these criteria, voluntary labels (1 to 5 stars, with higher number of stars denoting better energy-efficiency performance) for a range of consumer appliances were introduced. During this initial phase, facilities to verify testing of appliances were also developed (BEE(I), 2011a). The labels were introduced on a voluntary basis as there was a strong presumption, especially among the industry players, that Indian consumers are price sensitive and consequently would not buy higher efficiency products, which would be more expensive (BEE(I), 2011a).

It is important to note that during the planning and design phase of the programme, extensive consultations with the manufacturers in the respective appliance category, government departments, electric utilities, standards bodies, industry associations as well as consumers were held. In the initial phases of the programme, the performance standards and labels were designed to include a large majority of the market with an understanding that the performance standards would be ratcheted up in subsequent years (BEE(I), 2011a). This phase was also accompanied with extensive consumer outreach to provide information about and build a credible brand for the labels as well as to monitor the effect of the labels on the market dynamics.

Subsequently, as consumers accepted labels – and more than 50% of the annual sales of refrigerators and air-conditioners were of labelled products – mandatory performance norms and labelling programmes were introduced for four product categories including air conditioners, frost-free refrigerators, tubular fluorescent lamps and distribution transformers. Voluntary labels are still in place for eight other appliance categories where the stage of market transformation is still not reached, with plans to introduce mandatory labels later. Interestingly, under the standards and labelling programme, BEE has empowered the manufacturers to self-certify the products by adopting approved testing procedure and making them responsible for the accuracy of these labels, thereby involving them as partners in the programme. At the same time, the BEE undertakes check-testing of the appliance (sample drawn from market) to verify the accuracy of labels (BEE, 2011b).

With the standards and labelling programme, the BEE effectively changed the incentive structure in the appliance sector by first providing information on technical performance in the public domain through advertising and building up the labels as a 'brand' thus ensuring customer demand for efficient appliances. This was accompanied by the introduction of labels for the manufacturers, initially voluntary and later mandated while maintaining a 'technology-neutral' view to achieving these performance standards, i.e. the manufacturers had the freedom to innovate with technologies to achieve the requisite energy efficiency performance. Furthermore, as a market-creation activity for the scheme, government procurement was mandated at the highest star ratings (BEE(I), 2011a).

As illustrated in the figures below, the standards and labelling effort has been able to bring about a market transformation towards more efficient appliances. According to BEE estimates, substantial energy savings have been reaped as a result of the labelling programme, effectively alleviating a capacity addition of over 2 Gigawatts (GW) in 2010–11, and over 7 GW for the 11th five year plan period (2007–12) (Mathur, 2011). To provide further impetus to the process of efficiency improvements, the labels and standards are due to be revised in 2012, further ratcheting up efficiency norms, thus providing incentives for manufacturers to invest in newer technologies.

Case 2: Bachat Lamp Yojana

A significant fraction, approximately 20%, of the Indian electricity demand is consumed for lighting services while constituting an important component of the peak load. Traditional incandescent

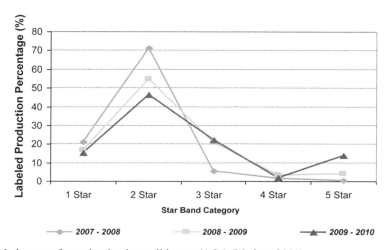

Figure 2.   Market transformation in air conditioners (ACs) (Mathur, 2011).

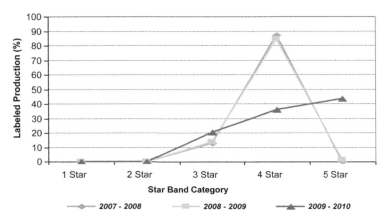

Figure 3. Market transformation for refrigerators (Mathur, 2011).

bulbs that still account for a major fraction of lighting devices are quite inefficient in converting electrical energy to light with almost 95% energy lost as heat. On the other hand, compact fluorescent lamps (CFLs) that provide the same amount of illumination with only one-fourth to one-fifth as much energy are yet to find widespread adoption mainly due to their significantly higher price (BEE, 2011c). According to BEE estimates, conversion to CFLs at the 400 million light points in the country could translate into electricity savings (measured at demand side) of up to 10 GWh. However, given the large price differential in the market prices of the above two lighting solutions, the penetration of the CFLs has been slow and limited.

To tap into this energy saving potential offered by the adoption of CFLs, the 'Bachat Lamp Yojana' was introduced[3]to realise a rapid dissemination of the CFLs by ensuring their availability at the price point of an incandescent bulb.[4] With the Bachat Lamp Yojana, the BEE is targeting households that cannot afford this conversion, with a deployment target of 100–150 million CFLs through the programme.[5] Each household can receive four CFLs if it hands in four functioning incandescent light bulbs and pays for the CFL what they would have to pay for incandescent ones (i.e. 15 Indian Rupees (INR)).The programme – formulated after a stakeholder consultation with CFL manufacturers, state-level Electricity Distribution Companies, government departments, potential investors and consumers – is designed as a public-private partnership between the GOI (represented by the BEE), project investors and the state-level Electricity Distribution Companies, with the project investors being responsible for CFL distribution in a designated project area (BEE, 2009). In order to realise the cost of distribution, the programme aimed to leverage the Clean Development Mechanism under the Kyoto Protocol, through which CFL suppliers would receive Certified Emissions Reductions (CERs) that can be traded in carbon-credit markets (Power Ministry, n.d.). To ensure requirement compliance, each CFL investor needed to be empanelled by BEE before undertaking any projects. The investor was left free to source his CFL supplies from any certified CFL supplier; BEE supported the supplier in implementing the Clean Development Mechanism (CDM) programme activities while also fulfilling the role of a monitoring body for the projects. Furthermore, the distribution programme also provides for the safe disposal of the collected incandescent bulbs as well as the CFLs as per the environmental norms. To better streamline the project approval process and facilitate the monitoring of various project implementation phases, BEE has formulated a programme of activities (PoA) to serve as an umbrella CDM project for the individual projects. Through the PoA, the BEE is better able to facilitate verification of CERs and recommend their allocation to the investors (BEE, 2009).

To better understand the stakeholder response and streamline the processes, BEE undertook pilot projects in the initial years of the Bachat Lamp Yojana programme. During these years, the scheme underwent changes in its design as well as the incentive mechanism. For example, until June 2009, the Bachat Lamp Yojana was being operated under the AMS IIC (Approved Methodology for Small-scale CDM project activities IIC) methodology as prescribed by the Executive Board of the CDM. Since this methodology required actual usage data of the CFLs to be monitored, BEE developed smart meters based on Global System for Mobile Communications (GSM) technology that are fitted between the socket and the CFL in sample households in each project area for monitoring the actual usage. While this innovation was helpful and was a part of the initial pilot tests, the monitoring requirements changed with the adoption of the AMS IIJ (Approved Methodology for Small-scale CDM project activities IIJ) methodology by the BEE for CDM projects linked to Bachat Lamp Yojana. Under the AMS IIJ methodology, which follows a deemed-saving approach, a fixed daily usage of 3.5 hours is assumed for emissions saving calculations, thus greatly simplifying the monitoring mechanism (BEE(I), 2011a).

BEE is also taking up awareness-building activities in association with the state-level electricity distribution companies. Thus, by creating consumer awareness of the energy-efficiency benefits as well as the lower upfront cost of the CFLs through Bachat Lamp Yojana, consumer demand and support for these projects have been created. Thus far, over 20 million CFLs have been distributed, through 35 CFL investors, as a part of the programme with over 16 Indian states under various stages of implementation with a push for completing more projects before December 2012 (the end of the first commitment period of the Kyoto Protocol) (BEE(I), 2011a; BEE, 2011c).

By integrating the Clean Development Mechanism (CDM) project with the CFL distribution programme and bringing the stakeholders together, the programme has aimed to leverage the benefits offered by already-existing institutional frameworks to facilitate the deployment of energy-efficient technologies. While this approach has enabled BEE to realise a large deployment of CFLs, the approach is not entirely devoid of risks and uncertainties. For example, recent raw material sourcing issues in India have put an upward pressure on the price of CFLs, thus increasing the financial risk for the CFL suppliers for the projects. At the same time, plunging carbon credit prices in the global markets have dampened the economic viability of the Bachat Lamp Yojana projects (BEE(I), 2011a).

Case 3: Energy Conservation Building Code (ECBC)

In 2005, with an overall constructed area of over 2.1 billion square meters, the building sector accounted for a significant share[6] of the total energy usage in India. With substantial growth projected for the sector over the next decade – projections for 2030 predict a fivefold increase in the overall built-up area in India (McKinsey, 2009; EDS, 2010) – with the residential and commercial sub-sectors expected to dominate (residential by itself is expected to account for almost 70% of the projected area in 2030), the GHG emissions and energy use in the sector are expected to grow rapidly (EDS, 2010). This tremendous growth coupled with the fact that most commercial buildings in India today have an energy performance index (EPI) of 200-400 KWh/sq m/year (contrasted against the 150 KWh/sq. m/ year in Europe and North America)[7] signals a area of huge energy-savings potential(Mathur, 2007).

Quite naturally, with a growth in the national building base, the concomitant energy consumption in the country is expected to rise significantly unless the EPI for the buildings is improved through energy-efficiency measures. For most of the building construction being undertaken in the country today, especially commercial buildings, the builder is not the future user of the building. As a result, there is little incentive for the builder to deploy energy efficiency measures in the buildings whose efficiency would benefit future users; at the same time, tenants/users do not want to pay higher upfront costs of construction (BEE(I), 2011a). As a result, there are rampant inefficiencies in the buildings stock of the country, with recent energy audits putting the potential energy efficiency savings at as high as 30–50% (Seth, 2011). While the inefficiencies exist in the commercial as well as the residential buildings in the country, savings in the commercial sector are a relatively 'low-hanging' fruit, with fewer monitoring, liaising and enforcement challenges as compared to the residential sector.

To facilitate the shift to energy efficient buildings, the GOI launched the Energy Conservation Building Code (ECBC) in May 2007 to set minimum energy standards for the design and construction of commercial buildings. The programme, finalised after extensive consultation with architects, industry associations, suppliers and government departments, has been introduced as a voluntary programme. The ECBC, adapted to the local climatic conditions at the state level, is intended for new commercial buildings having a connected load of 100 KW or 120 kVA and above[8] (BEE(I), 2011a).

The ECBC code addresses major energy usage/loss components such as walls, roofs and windows, lighting, heating, ventilation and airconditioning (HVAC), electrical distribution, as well as water heating and pumping systems of the building. While the BEE estimates that a mandatory compliance of the ECBC code would yield an annual saving of 1700GWh, the compliance at present is voluntary and is enforceable by the local governments (USAID, 2009). While introducing the voluntary programme, the codes have been developed initially for specific building types (day-use office buildings, Business Process Outsourcing (companies) (BPOs), and shopping malls), while looking at the introduction of codes for a broader range of buildings in the future.

Much like the standards and labelling programme, the ECBC is being developed as a 'brand', while disseminating information through advertising and building a 'demand pull' for energy efficient buildings. At present, the BEE has developed a star-rating programme for buildings that is based on the actual performance of a building in terms of its specific energy usage. This programme rates office buildings on a 1 to 5 star scale, with 5-star-labelled buildings being the most efficient (Seth, 2011). Thus, the programme provides public recognition to energy-efficient buildings and creates a 'demand side' pull for such buildings attracting users towards energy-efficient buildings, and thus creating a preferential market demand for such buildings. However, the presence of financial incentives for builders or building users, which could have provided a further demand impetus for energy efficient buildings, is missing at the present stage of the programme (BEE(I), 2011a). In the future, BEE aims to transition the current voluntary labelling programme under the ECBC into a mandatory programme.

A major challenge in the introduction of the ECBC has been the lack of technical competence at understanding the code and designing buildings compliant with the requirements. Since it is clear that any effort to achieve large-scale deployment of energy-efficient building codes would require sufficient expertise in the area, it is essential that this competence is rapidly built up (USAID, 2009). As a part of the ECBC programme, BEE has been organising workshops and training sessions for architects, construction consultants and other professionals involved, to familiarise and train them on the ECBC requirements as well as to provide information on the various tools (components, technology, etc.) for meeting the ECBC standards. Furthermore, information dissemination within the larger stakeholder community about business-model innovation as well as tools for meeting the ECBC code around the ECBC programme is also being undertaken through stakeholder liaising.

The ECBC programme has, at present, also been geared towards developing a critical base of Energy Services Companies (ESCOs). An ESCO engages in a performance-based contract with a client firm to implement measures, which reduce energy consumption and costs in a technically and financially viable manner. Thus, the BEE is seeking to leverage the voluntary period of the

ECBC programme to build capacity and gain implementation experience to fine-tune the mandatory rollout in the future (BEE(I), 2011a).

Case 4: Perform, Achieve and Trade (PAT)

Much of the Indian industry landscape is marked by some of the most efficient plants in the world that co-exist with a large number of inefficient plants. Being one of the major energy users in the country, with a consumption of 150 Mtoe in 2007, the sector offers opportunities for reductions in energy use as well as emissions through efficiency improvements (IEA, 2011b). While high electricity tariffs and rising costs of other energy inputs have provided an incentive for higher efficiency, the capital-intensive nature of several energy-efficiency interventions in the industry sector has been a deterrent for the industries to engage in these interventions. Thus, despite the availability of suitable technologies, the move towards energy efficiency has been a slow one. Moreover, the wide bandwidth of efficiency present in the industry sector makes it difficult to specify a single energy-consumption norm (IEA, 2010b). For example, as illustrated in the figure below, there is a wide variation in the Specific Energy Consumption (SEC) for clinker production across cement plants, making it a challenge to specify the SEC norm for the cement sector.

To address this challenge and realise the energy saving opportunity offered in the industrial sector, the GOI introduced the 'Perform, Achieve and Trade' (PAT) scheme, aimed at developing a market-based mechanism to enhance energy efficiency, in a cost effective manner, across industrial units (referred to as the 'designated consumers'), while specifying 'individual' SEC reduction criterion for every plant. These 'individual' reduction targets are 'almost unit-specific', with energy bands of differential targets being created within each sector (Kumar, 2010). The SEC reduction targets, given for a period of three years, for a plant are contingent upon its present energy intensity and set in accordance to the Energy Conservation Act of 2001 that calls for the efficiency targets to reflect fuel usage and the economic effort involved. In general, less efficient plants would be required to reduce their energy consumption by a higher percentage (NMEEE, 2008). Thus, through the PAT scheme, BEE aims to provide a market mechanism that is methodology driven and transparent to address the challenge of providing an incentive for SEC reduction while being responsive to the industry structure. Moreover, through a 'technology-neutral' approach, the BEE has also provided for ample flexibility for the designated consumers to achieve the energy-efficiency targets through the approach that they deem most appropriate. At the same time, to address concerns of baseline manipulation by firms, the baseline assessment and methodology development for the scheme were undertaken in parallel.

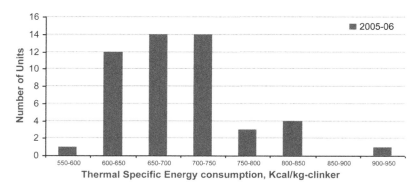

Figure 4. Thermal specific energy consumption distribution for Indian cement plants (Mathur, 2011).

The first cycle of PAT, to be implemented through 2011–2012 to 2013–2014, will involve mandatory participation by the 468 designated consumers across eight industrial sectors. The BEE was designated as the overall regulator and dispute resolution agency while the Energy Efficiency Service Limited (EESL), a joint venture of four GOI public sector units[9], functions as an implementation and monitoring agency. Plants, placed under different SEC bands within their sector, would be mandated to reduce their SEC by a specific percentage based on their current position within the sectoral SEC bandwidth. At the end of the target period of the first cycle, Energy Savings Certificates (ESCs) would be issued to plants that achieve better than target SECs and penalties would be imposed on those who fell short of the target SEC, with the ESCs and penalties reflecting the difference between the achieved and the target SEC. Plants would further have an option to purchase SECs through a ESC market that is being established with BEE help to attain compliance. Through the first phase of PAT, according to BEE estimates, a collective 5% reduction[10] in the SEC of the designated consumers should be possible (Mathur, 2011).

As with the introduction of building codes, in the PAT scheme, the availability of trained resources to support the technical assessment and monitoring requirements of the programme is a possible constraint. To address this concern, the training of Energy Managers and Energy Auditors by BEE and ESCO support by EESL and BEE are being undertaken.

4. Lessons for, and pathways towards, sustainability

Innovation systems are characterised by a set of actors with inter-relationships embedded in an institutional context that all together determine the performance of the system (Fagerberg, 2004). In the case of developing countries, all these three elements – actors, their inter-relationships, and institutions – are generally weaker than in industrialised countries that possess well-functioning innovation systems (Chaminade et al., 2009). Limitations in human and financial resources, capabilities of various actors (firms, academia, government agencies, etc.) and often weak institutions constrain the scale and scope of innovation activities in developing countries. In addition, sustainable development requires progress in areas that are characterised by provision of 'public goods', with little investment interest among firms and consequently, under provision by ordinary market activities (Brown, 2001). While this market failure is a challenge even in the developed countries, the problem is further exacerbated by the weak innovation capabilities in the developing world. Sustainability-oriented innovation in developing countries has therefore to overcome these dual limitations.

Sectors that operate in well-functioning markets and have a strong set of actors often see the appearance of an innovation system without any overarching coordination. Actors identify opportunities and orient their activities to exploit them – for example, venture capitalists in industrialised countries have recently started investing in clean technologies since they see potential payoffs in this area, just as they did in biotechnology and information technology in the past few decades (Greenwood, 2007). However, the combination of the above two limitations makes the self-assembly of SOISs in developing countries that much more difficult. In fact, leveraging innovation to advance sustainability in developing countries while offering great potential, is a challenging proposition.

With this backdrop, the experience of the energy-efficiency programmes highlighted above offer some important lessons for advancing sustainability-oriented innovation.

Given the enormous range of potential areas of intervention, a first key step should be the identification and prioritisation of areas that offer the highest impact. This, of course, requires a sophisticated understanding of local needs, the market and institutional context, as well as the suite of available relevant technologies' performance and cost envelopes. At the same time, it also requires consultations with a range of stakeholders to ensure the selection process which is robust and that there is buy-in by a wide group of actors who would eventually be key players in the innovation process. In fact, the areas selected by the BEE, including the cases discussed above, were the result of precisely such an analytical and consultative process as highlighted in the case studies.

As and when areas of interventions are selected, identification of the innovation gaps in each particular area and the development of appropriate steps to target these lacunae is of great use. It is through such a strategic approach, based on a bird's-eye view of the full innovation process and the existing activities, that programmes, policies and partnerships can be tailored to bridge most effectively existing innovation gaps.

This, then, is one possible approach to enhancing sustainability-oriented innovation, that is based on the understanding that there is no 'one shoe fits all' approach to SOI, that different countries will have different sustainability needs and opportunities, that the limited resources in developing countries necessitate prioritising areas of action, and lastly that the specifics of the innovation processes (and therefore the relevant innovation systems) can vary substantially across technologies and across countries (Sagar, 2011). For example, innovation in grid-connected solar power requires a very different constellation of actors, resources and policies as compared to innovation in energy-efficient lighting. Thus there is no universal SOIS – advancing sustainability in different areas requires the presence (or establishment) of an innovation ecosystem that is suited for that particular area.

The BEE's experience suggests that sustainability-oriented innovation could be greatly facilitated by a coordinating organisation – a 'system operator' so to speak – that is able to help prioritise high-potential areas, identify the innovation gaps that exist and help design programmes to address them. For example in each of the case studies discussed, the innovation-system lacunae were due to disparate reasons and thus, the interventions had to be designed appropriately by BEE to address them.

Not only could such a system operator strengthen and improve the existing actors, it can encourage new players in the areas innovation chain that are marked by absence of actors. The BEE, for example, facilitated a market transformation through programmes like the Bachat Lamp Yojana, while bringing on board key actors such as finance providers, technology vendors, and energy service companies (ESCOs) by building a better understanding within these actors of the opportunities offered by energy efficiency and promote networks among by facilitating early projects. As these strengthened actors try to build markets for their own services and products, they themselves become 'agents of change' and drivers of the technological transformation. The resulting dynamics in the market, while driving the scale-up activities, also provides for learning and course correction opportunities for the system operator.

It may be possible to have system operators that spans multiple areas (as has been suggested with the model of Climate Innovation Centers) (Sagar et al., 2009; Sagar, 2011), or by organisations that are focused on specific areas, as illustrated by the example of BEE in India.

In the best possible scenario, the system operator would identify and facilitate the effective functioning (and, if needed, even the development) of the relevant SOIS, with the understanding that the actors, policies and programmes needed to achieve successful outcomes are specific to the targeted sustainability challenges/opportunities. For example, the programme for achieving deployment of renewables could look quite different from a programme for deployment of energy-efficiency technologies, owing to the differences in the overall innovation requirements. Within a particular SOIS, the coordinating agency needs to deliver mechanisms to make the constellation of actors into a functional system, while bridging the existing innovation gaps, while addressing the needs of each part of the innovation chain. We discuss below the functions of the coordinating agency, drawing lessons using the BEE case studies as illustrations.

BEE identified energy-efficient appliances as an early and key area for intervention. In a layered, multi-pronged, approach, it began by introducing voluntary energy-performance labels on appliances, which provided information for consumers and manufacturers about the relative performance of appliances in the market – therefore the gap being targeted was on the deployment piece of the innovation cycle with the intention of enhancing the decision-making on both the supply-side and the demand-side. This is to be followed by the introduction of standards that raise the minimum performance for these appliances. The next step is the Super Efficient Equipment Program (SEEP), which aims to make available in the market place household appliances with greatly enhanced efficiency.[11] Here a central focus of the effort is technical in nature, where manufacturers are being encouraged to invest in developing equipment substantially[12] more efficient than the existing best available technologies. The ceiling fan is being targeted as the first appliance, reflecting its role as an appliance having a large Indian market and a relatively small market abroad (and consequently with little on-going R&D efforts). The programme also proposes incentives to manufacturers for each super-efficient appliance sold, thereby complimenting the technical efforts by helping create a market for super-energy-efficient appliances. To introduce competitiveness into the R&D process and ensure the cost effectiveness of the programme, the incentive amount would be decided through a bidding process and would be paid for 2–3 years on the basis of monitored sales and performance. Furthermore, as achieved in the case of the standards and labelling programme, the SEEP equipment would also be marketed through a customer outreach campaign. While such programmes are important, the provision of improved communication, collaboration and interactions between the actors of the innovation system is equally important with the ensuant innovation system linkages.

Importantly, while exploring the technology options, it is crucial to explore the supporting technologies that could contribute to the better functioning of the programme. For example, for the Bachat Lamp Yojana of the BEE, while the CFL technology deployment delivers the energy savings, the introduction of the GSM-based usage-monitoring technology was critical to the CDM programme design, which required an assessment of the carbon emissions avoided through the switch from incandescent bulbs to CFLs. However, once an alternate mechanism was available, one that afforded CDM benefits with lesser monitoring requirements (AMS IIJ methodology of the Executive Board of the CDM), it was integrated into the programme design. Thus, along with technology options it is important to keep changing institutional mechanisms in mind to better implement the programme. Thus, flexibility in the programme design is quite important in providing much needed course correction in terms of the institutional framework and incentive structure.

One of the key observations from the Indian experience has been the importance of a commercial orientation in the programmes for the dissemination of sustainability-oriented technologies. Demand-driven programmes that are not overtly reliant on the government for financial support for wide-scale deployment are more likely to achieve their objectives. That said, regulatory incentives for innovation and adoption of sustainability-oriented technologies could be effective mechanisms for achieving wide-scale deployment, as demonstrated by the PAT programme.

The risk associated with new technologies being introduced in the market, often coupled with lack of robust information on technical and cost performance, serves as a major barrier for sustainability-oriented technology adoption. While the technology may have been successfully deployed in other countries, uncertainties exist about the technology uptake in the market despite the changed incentive structure. Therefore an effective SOIS needs to be able to facilitate technology uptake through demonstration programmes or voluntary adoption phases that help improve technologies through a better understanding of operation under real-world conditions and also build user confidence. Another area of focus is overcoming the risk faced (or perceived) by early adopters, for example, by developing programmes that help underwrite performance

Table 2. Key functions of a SOIS, drawing on lessons from India's energy-efficiency programmes (adapted from Sagar, A., 2011).

	INNOVATION STAGES			
	Pre-Innovation Analysis	Technology Development and Adaptation	Early Deployment and Learning	Scale-up/ Wide-scale Commercialisation
FUNCTIONS/ ACTIVITIES	Technology needs assessment/options analysis to understand which technologies are best suited to advance sustainable development in the local context	Direct provision of grants for targeted research to promote technology development/ adaptation	Technology demonstration programs with support from the government	Technology standards and certification schemes to build consumer confidence in new technologies;
	Exploration of appropriate process/ program for advancing relevant technology dissemination (including better understanding of supporting technologies needed for scale-up (eg GSM technology in the Bachat Lamp Yojana))	Networking and collaborations between domestic actors and with international actors	Overcome risk of adoption of new technologies for early adopters, for example, by developing programs that help underwrite performance guarantees	Identify and overcome barriers to deployment (for example, lack of consumer awareness tackled through the Standards and Labeling program, making available financing options for firms that do not have resources to invest in energy-efficient options that have high initial investments but low payback periods)
	Market analysis and user surveys to help better understand the characteristics of the demand and markets for specific technologies;		Enterprise creation by linking technical researchers with entrepreneurs, venture capitalists, and businesspeople; coordinate funding avenues	Financial support for the scale-up of production, distribution, and marketing activities (e.g. Bachat Lamp Yojana)
	Communication, interactions, and collaboration among actors; Information provision to relevant actors about new technologies		Facilitate learning inputs from early deployment into pre-innovation analysis as well as technology development and adaptation (eg, learning from the voluntary phases of standards and labeling and the ECBC)	Regulatory measures and other policies to incentivise large-scale technology deployment (e.g. PAT)
			Technical as well as entrepreneurial training as well as technical support (eg the Energy managers training program and the support for ESCOs)	

guarantees. In fact, the perception of performance risk faced by early adopters need special attention and therefore mitigating this risk has to be an important function of SOIS.

As highlighted by the BEE case studies, more particularly by the standards and labelling programme, the achievement of large-scale deployment is substantially aided by well-designed outreach efforts that seek to inform and influence public/consumer opinion about the technologies or the programme itself. Moreover, 'branding' in itself is an important tool for gaining traction in the market as illustrated by the Star Ratings programme of the BEE. In conjunction with information provision, for facilitating early introduction of technologies, efforts for 'market creation' have proved to be valuable tools. A gradual nature of intervention (with voluntary schemes being ratcheted to binding standards) provides the consumer with a power of informed choice while signalling to the manufacturers to invest and improve upon appropriate technologies, thus building requisite technological and manufacturing capabilities. This simultaneous focus on supply-side and demand-side elements has been a key to success in BEE's programmes.

Moreover, given the desirable scale of sustainability-oriented technology deployment, the technical-support needs of any such SOIS are bound to be substantial. As a result, the SOIS needs an intensive technical support and training effort to tackle any emerging technical barriers and to provide for the human resource need of the overall SOIS. For the BEE programmes, technical support in the form of ESCOs for the ECBC and PAT, Energy Managers/Auditors Training programmes, etc. are oriented to serve this need. Further, BEE is playing a facilitating as well as a technical advisory role for the Bachat Lamp Yojana as well as the standards and labelling programme. Apart from aiding the present deployment efforts, the presence of and interaction between training and technical support actors enables the experiential learning to feed into the training efforts, thus streamlining the programme and strengthening its technical expertise.

One of the underlying rationales of BEE's programmes mentioned above is the effectiveness of public policy nudges in contrast to large policy pushes to create markets for sustainability-oriented technologies (Thaler and Sunstein, 2008). Highlighting the importance of experiential learning and effective training in the SOIS, this approach leverages limited-scale or voluntary programmes to establish better policies and other interventions through repeated course correction. Overall, the BEE experience highlights the importance of understanding and aligning stakeholder interests with the broader objective of the SOIS through incentives, information dissemination, branding as well as regulatory intervention, advocating a regulatory push as well as a market pull to successfully deploy appropriate technologies at a large scale.

Based on these observations, Table 2 below catalogues what we see as key functions of an innovation system for advancing the sustainability-oriented technologies.

To conclude, sustainability-oriented innovation, in order to be successful in creating significant impact, requires paying attention to the full innovation chain, including large-scale deployment, and developing targeted programmes and activities that address gaps or leverage particular opportunities to help advance innovation. This, in turns, requires the involvement of a number of actors, with different actors playing key roles in different parts of the innovation cycle. In many cases, a 'system operator' can play a particularly key role by taking a bird's-eye view and facilitating the establishment of a successful innovation system by supporting actors, creating networks and strengthening institutions in a systematic and strategic manner. A tall order, perhaps, but the results can be well worth it.

Acknowledgement

The authors would like to thank Ms Vandana Thakur, Mr Sanjay Seth and Mr Sandeep Garg from the Bureau of Energy Efficiency for their valuable insights on the case studies reported in this paper. The authors would also like to thank the anonymous reviewers who provided thoughtful and insightful comments that helped to make this a more meaningful paper.

Notes

1. The IEA estimates that globally some $26 trillion would be required as supply infrastructure investments between 2006 and 2030 with 87% of this growth expected in developing countries (IEA, 2010a).
2. LBNL estimates a macroeconomic cumulative benefit bonus of $500 billion from improved productivity as a result of energy efficiency measures between 2009–2017. (http://www.iea.org/work/2011/bloomsday/Session3_Sathaye.pdf)
3. The official programme of activities (PoA) was launched in February 2009.
4. The market price of a CFL lies in the INR 80–100 range (BEE estimates) while a conventional incandescent bulb costs between INR 10–15.
5. BEE estimates.
6. The TERI Energy Directory 2010 estimates that the residential and commercial sector accounts for about 13.5% of the total energy consumption in the country – need citation to TER ED2010I.
7. Although Indian environmental conditions differ much from these geographies, efficient building design in India has been shown to reduce EPI to 100 to 150 kWh/ sq m/ year.
8. The initial requirement of 500 kW or 600 kVA, was modified in 2010, thereby increasing the number of buildings under purview.
9. Four PSUs viz NTPC (India's largest power producer primarily through coal), Power Finance Corporation (PFC), Rural Electrification Corporation (REC) and POWERGRID (agency responsible for the inter-state transmission of electricity) would form this joint venture, representing an expertise across several relevant sectors.
10. In 2013–14, over 2008-09 values.
11. It is important to realise that the mere presence of a better technology is insufficient for it to be identified as a technology suitable for large-scale deployment. For example, although LED lighting provides a superior efficiency, its prohibitively high cost inhibits any deployment efforts on a meaningful scale.
12. For the ceiling fan case, specification targets of 25–30 W have been proposed, contrasted against the 50W figure for the most efficient fan today.

References

Altenburg, T., and Pegels, A. (2012) Sustainability-oriented innovation systems – managing the green transformation. *Innovation and Development*, forthcoming 2012.

American Energy Innovation Council (2011) Catalyzing American ingenuity: The role of government in energy innovation.

BEE (2009) Bachat Lamp Yojana: CDM based CFL scheme. Bureau of Energy Efficiency, New Delhi.

BEE(I) (2011a) Based on discussions with program/sector experts from BEE.

BEE (2011b) Overview of energy efficiency standards and labeling program. APP Workshop. Bureau of Energy Efficiency, New Delhi.

BEE (2011c) BEE - GEF - WB project: Project overview Ankleshwar cluster (chemical), available at: http://www.emt-india.net/Presentations2011/05-Chemical_21July2011/1BEE.pdf, accessed on: 15 August 2011.

BEE (2011d) About standards and labeling programme, available at: http://urja-nidhi.com/Standards_Labeling/main.htm

Brown, M. (2001) Market failures and barriers as a basis for clean energy policies. *Energy Policy*, 29(14), pp. 1197–1207.

Brundtland Commission (1987) *Our Common Future*. World Commission on Environment and Development (USA: Oxford University Press).

Chaminade, C., Lundvall, B., Vang, J., and Joseph, K. (2009) Designing innovation policies for development: Towards a systemic experimentation-based approach, in: C. Chaminade, B. Lundvall, J. Vang, and K. Joseph (eds) *Handbook of Innovation Systems and Developing Countries: Building domestic capabilities in a global setting*, pp. 360–379 (Cheltenham, UK: Edward Elgar).

Chikkatur, A., Chaudhary, A., and Sagar, A. (2011) Coal power impacts, technology and policy: Connecting the dots. *Annual Reviews of Environment and Resources*, 36, pp. 101–138.

de la Rue du Can, S., Letschert, V., McNeil, M., Zhou, N., and Sathaye, J. (2009). Residential and transportation energy use in India: Past trend and future outlook. Lawrence Berkeley National Laboratory.

EDS (2010) Reducing emissions in the buildings sector in India: A strategy paper. Environmental Design Solutions, New Delhi.

European Commission (2005) Doing more with less: Green paper on energy efficiency. European Commission, Luxembourg.

Fagerberg, J. (2004) Innovation and catching-up, in: J. Fagerberg. *The Oxford Handbook of Innovation* (Oxford University Press)

Flyvbjerg, B. (2011) Case study, in: N. Denzin and Y. Lincoln (eds) *The Sage Handbook of Qualitative Research* (vol. 4, pp. 301–316) (Thousand Oaks, CA: Sage).

Gerring, J. (2004) What is a case study and what is it good for? *American Political Science Review*, 98(2), pp. 341–354.

Greenwood, C. (2007) Global trends in sustainable energy investment 2007: Analysis of trends and issues in financng of renewable energy and energy efficiency in OECD and developing countries. United Nations Environment Programme and New Energy Finance.

Goodland, R., and Daly, H. (1996) Environmental sustainability: Universal and non-negotiable. *Ecological Applications*, 6(4), pp. 1002–1017.

Holdren, J. (2008) Science and technology for sustainable well-being. *Science*, 319(5862), pp. 424–434.

Hekkert, M., Suurs, R., Negro, S., Kuhlmann, S., and Smits, R. (2007) Functions of innovation systems: A new approach for analysing technological change. *Technological Forecasting and Social Change*, 74(4), pp. 413–432.

IEA (2004) Oil crises & climate challenges: 30 years of energy use in IEA countries. IEA/OECD, Paris.

IEA (2006) Energy policies of IEA countries. International Energy Agency, Paris.

IEA (2009a) Lessons learned from the energy policies of IEA countries: Key cross-cutting issues 2007/2008. International Energy Agency, Paris.

IEA (2009b) Energy transition for Indian industry. International Energy Agency, Paris.

IEA (2010a) World energy outlook. International Energy Agency, Paris.

IEA (2010b) Energy technology perspectives 2010. International Energy Agency, Paris.

IEA (2011a) Technology development prospects for the Indian power sector. International Energy Agency, Paris.

IEA (2011b). Energy transition for industry: India and the global context. International Energy Agency, Paris.

IPCC (2007) Summary for policymakers of the synthesis report of the IPCC fourth assessment report. Intergovernmental Panel on Climate Change.

Jacobsson, S., and Bergek, A. (2004) Transforming the energy sector: The evolution of technological systems in renewable energy technology. *Industrial and Corporate Change*, 13(5), pp. 815–849.

JNNSM (2010) Jawaharlal Nehru national solar mission: Towards building SOLAR INDIA, available at: http://india.gov.in/allimpfrms/alldocs/15657.pdf, accessed on: 15 August 2011.

Kates, R., Clark, W.C., and Corell, R. (2001) Sustainability science. *Science*, 292(5517), pp. 641–642.

Kammen, D. (2006, Sept). The rise of renewable energy. *Scientific American* (September), pp. 84–93.

Kumar, S. (2010) National mission for enhanced energy efficiency – PAT mechanism. (World Bank Workshop: Mitigation Actions and Role of Market Instruments, Seoul).

Lundvall, B.-A. (1992) *National Systems of Innovation: Towards a theory of innovation and interactive learning* (London: Pinter).

Levin, S., and Clark, W. (2010) Toward a science of sustainability. Report from Toward a Science of Sustainability Conference, Center for International Development, Cambridge, MA, Harvard University.

Linares, P., and Perez-Arriaga, I. (2009) Promoting investment in low carbon technologies. *European Review of Energy Markets*, 3(2), pp. 1–23.

Margolis, R., and Kammen, D. (1999) Underinvestment: The energy technology and R&D policy challenge. *Science*, 285(5428), pp. 690–692.

Mathur, A. (2007) Energy efficiency in buildings in India: An overview. 2nd Meeting of the Indo-German Energy Forum, New Delhi.

Mathur, A. (2011) Different strokes: (Re)learning diversity in the Design of Energy Efficiency Programmes in 34th IAEE International Conference, Stockholm.

McKinsey (2009a) Version 2 of the global greenhouse gas abatement cost curve, *Pathways to a Low Carbon Economy*. McKinsey & Company, New Delhi.

McKinsey (2009b) *Energy and Environmental Sustainability: An approach for India*. McKinsey and Company, New Delhi.

Modi, V., McDade, S., Lallement, D., and Saghir, J. (2005) Energy services for the millennium development goals. United Nations Development Programme, UN Millennium Project, and World Bank, Energy Sector Management Assistance Programme.

National Research Council (NRC) (1999) *Our Common Journey: A transition towards sustainability* (Washington DC: The National Academies Press).

National Research Council (NRC) (2010) Hidden Costs of Energy. National Research Council (Washington, DC: The National Academies Press).

NCAER (2003) Annual report 2003. National Council for Applied Economic Research, New Delhi.

Nelson, R. (1993) *National Innovation Systems: A comparative analysis.* (vol. 1). USA: Oxford University Press).

Nicholas Lefevre, P., and Waide, P. (2006) Barriers to technology diffusion: The case of compact fluorescent lamps. IEA, Paris.

NMEEE (2008) National mission for enhanced energy efficiency, available at: http://india.gov.in/allimpfrms/alldocs/15659.pdf, accessed on: 15 August 2011.

PCAST (1997) PCAST report on sustainable development. Executive Office of the President, Washington, DC.

Planning Commission (2011) Interim report of the expert group on low carbon strategies for exclusive growth. Planning Commission of India, New Delhi.

Power Ministry (n.d.) Introduction to Energy Conservation Act 2001, available at: http://www.powermin. nic.in/acts_notification/energy_conservation_act/introduction.htm, accessed on: 15 August 2011.

Price, L. (2005) Voluntary agreements for energy efficiency or GHG emissions reduction in industry: An assessment of programs around the world (Berkeley: Lawrence Berkeley National Laboratory).

Rao, N., Sant, G., and Rajan, S. (2009) An overview of Indian energy trends: Low carbon growth and development challenges. Prayas Energy Group, Pune.

REDI (n.d.) Renewable energy development initiative. (IEA), available at: http://www.iea.org/textbase/pm/ ?mode=re&id=70&action=detail, accessed on: 15 August 2011.

Reuters (2009) China offers big solar subsidy, shares up, available at: http://www.reuters.com/article/2009/ 07/21/china-power-solar-idUSPEK12570920090721, accessed on: 15 August 2011.

Sachs, W., and Santarius, T. (2007) *Fair Future: Resource Conflicts, Security and Global Justice* (Black Point: Fernwood Publishing Company).

Sagar, A. (2011) Climate innovation centers: Advancing innovation to meet climate and development challenges. Climate Strategies. Cambridge.

Sagar, A., Bremner, C., and Grubb, M. (2009) Climate innovation centers: A partnership approach to meeting energy and climate challenges. *Natural Resources Forum*, 33(4), pp. 274–284.

Sagar, A., Oliver, H., and Chikkatur, A. (2006) Climate change, energy and developing countries. *Vermont Journal of Environmental Law*, 7(1), pp. 71–94.

Sagar, A.D., and van der Zwaan, B. (2006) Technological innovation in the energy sector: R&D, deployment and learning-by-doing. *Energy Policy*, 34(17), pp. 2601–2608.

Seth, S. (2011) Energy efficiency initiatives in commercial buildings, available at: http://www. globalcoolcities.org/wp-content/uploads/2011/09/Seth-Presentation.pdf, accessed on: 15 August 2011.

Smith, A., Voß, J.-P., and Grin, J. (2010) Innovation studies and sustainability transitions: The allure of multi-level perspectives and its challenges. *Research Policy*, 39(4), pp. 435–448.

Stamm, A., Dantas, E., Fischer, D., Ganguly, S., and Rennkamp, B. (2009) *Sustainability Oriented Innovation Systems: Towards decoupling economic growth from environmental pressures* (Bonn: German Development Institute).

Taylor, R., Chandrasekar, G., Levin, J., Meyer, A.S., and Ward, W.A. (2008) *Financing Energy Efficiency: Lessons from Brazil, China, India and beyond* (Washington, DC: World Bank).

Thaler, R., and Sunstein, C. (2008) *Nudge: Improving decisions about health, wealth and happiness* Penguin).

UNDP (2001) Human development report 2001: Making new technologies work for human development. United Nations Development Programme, New York.

UNDP (2005) Energizing the millennium development goals: A guide to energy's role in reducing poverty. United Nations Development Programme.

UNFCCC (2010) Cancun decision 1/CP.16. United Nations Framework Convention on Climate Change.

United Nations (2000) United Nations millenium declaration. United Nations General Assembly, A/RES/ 55/2, New York.

United Nations (2002) WEHAB framework papers. United Nations World Summit on Sustainable Development, Johannesburg.

USAID (2009) Energy assessment guide for commercial buildings. United States Agency for International Development, USAID ECO-III Project, New Delhi.

van den Bergh, J., Faber, A., Idenberg, A., and Oosterhuls, F. (2006) Survival of the greenest: Evolutionary economics and policies for energy innovation. *Environmental Sciences*, 3(1), pp. 57–71.

Venkataraman, C., Sagar, A., Habib, G., and Smith, K. (2010) The Indian national initiative for advanced biomass cookstoves: The benefits of clean combustion. *Energy for Sustainable Development*, 14, pp. 63–72.

World Bank (2011) *Household Cookstoves, Environment, Health, and Climate Change: A new look at an old problem* (Washington, DC: World Bank).

World Energy Council (2010) *Energy Efficiency: A recipe for success* (London: World Energy Council).

Sustainability-oriented innovation in the automobile industry: advancing electromobility in China, France, Germany and India

Tilman Altenburg, Shikha Bhasin and Doris Fischer

German Development Institute, Bonn, Germany

Many leading economies have recently launched policy initiatives to promote electromobility. E-mobility presupposes innovations that are both radical and systemic, as new charging infrastructure, new mobility concepts and new interfaces with the energy system are needed. The paradigm shift affects an industry that is the backbone of manufacturing in many countries. Policymakers therefore need to strike a difficult balance between competing objectives: to mitigate climate change, reduce urban air pollution, enhance energy security and strengthen the competitiveness of national auto industries. Also, they need to ensure that investments in new vehicles, more efficient batteries and public charging infrastructures are undertaken simultaneously and in a coordinated way. This article shows that China, France, Germany and India deal with these challenges differently. It traces policy differences back to initial industry characteristics, specific political priorities and patterns of economic governance.

Introduction

Automobile production is a strategic industry, forming the backbone of the manufacturing sector in many countries. Including parts- and component-manufacturers, it accounts for over 5% of the world's total manufacturing employment (OICA, 2012) and is a major contributor to global production, trade, and R&D investments. Its economic importance also stems from extensive linkages with related industries, be it the consumption of steel, iron, aluminium, glass, plastics, glass and rubber; or production of parts and components; and its range of related services such as distribution, maintenance and mobility services. Each direct job in the auto industry is estimated to support 'at least another five indirect jobs [...], resulting in more than 50 million jobs owed to the auto industry' (OICA, 2012). Latecomer economies, especially those with a substantial internal market, have therefore traditionally tried to develop the automobile industry as a catalyst of industrial development – including China, South Korea, Brazil, Mexico, India and Thailand (UNIDO, 2003).

With the emergence of a global consuming middle class, demand for cars is increasing at a very rapid pace. Middle classes worldwide are willing to spend a considerable part of their income on individual mobility and automobile ownership constitutes an important element of social status. Car and commercial vehicle production in China alone jumped from 2 million in 2001 to 18 million in 2010 and the global rise was from 59 to 78 million cars between 2001 and 2010 (OICA, 2010). This trend is expected to continue as consuming middle classes in population-rich BRIC countries expand (Óneill et al., 2004).

At the same time, climate change presents the automobile sector with the largest challenge it has had to face yet. According to the IPCC, by 2050 there needs to be a reduction in global greenhouse gas emissions to 50% of 1990 levels (IPCC, 2007). Road transport, which contributes 16% of man-made CO_2 emissions (OICA, 2010), is a priority target for climate change mitigation efforts.

However, carbon emission and energy consumption reductions per car have so far been modest. In the EU, CO_2 emissions were reduced from 175 g CO_2/km in 2000 to 145 in 2009 (European Environment Agency, 2010). Some progress was achieved through lightweight construction, the development of hybrid engines and other innovations, but these have not been sufficient to bring emissions down to the desired level. To substantially lower the emissions from the road transport sector, it is necessary to substitute a large part of vehicle fleets running on internal combustion engines (ICE). Electric vehicles provide an alternative that allows combining convenient individual mobility with low emissions.

A transition to large scale deployment of electric vehicles, or e-mobility, requires both *radical* and *systemic* changes (Smith, 2009). *Radical* in the sense of going beyond incremental improvements of existing designs and introducing completely different core technologies; and *systemic* in that it involves a substantial change of the underlying technological regime, with new combinations of industrial sub-systems, and the emergence of new institutions and power relations between industry actors. The challenge remains to achieve major and simultaneous technological breakthroughs in several fields including battery technology, electric power trains, light materials, new charging technology and infrastructure, new 'smart' interfaces between the transport and the energy system, and innovative mobility concepts. Taking all these interrelated technical and organisational innovations into consideration, we may classify the transition from a fossil fuel-based transport system to e-mobility as a *techno-economic paradigm* shift that gradually devalues and replaces established subsystems and 'takes root in collective consciousness, replacing the old ideas and becoming the new "common sense" of engineers, managers and investors for the most efficient and "modern" productive practice across the board' (Pérez, 2004, p.12).

To avoid disastrous environmental damage at a global scale, particularly with regard to the atmosphere's rapidly decreasing sink capacity for greenhouse gases,[1] this paradigm shift has to be achieved under considerable time pressure. Organising such a techno-economic paradigm shift under conditions of considerable uncertainty about future technologies and markets puts high demands on governance. Therefore, large and well-coordinated government efforts are needed to accelerate this transition to e-mobility, suggesting that technological pathways depend to a considerable extent on policymakers' assumptions about the future and on political settlements between conflicting stakeholder interests. This policy-driven character of technological development eventually implies a strong divergence of national technological trajectories (see Altenburg and Pegels in this Special Issue).

This article explores how four countries (France, Germany, China and India), all amongst the top 10 motor vehicle producing countries, are managing the transition from traditional, fossil-fuel based transport systems towards e-mobility. All four nations embarked on ambitious national e-mobility development programmes and set up coordinating institutions between 2008 and 2011. At the same time, they have very different initial conditions regarding the structure and competitiveness of their incumbent motor vehicles industries; the power relations between industrialists and environmentalists also differ, as do patterns of economic governance. Such variation presents an interesting case for comparing how initial economic conditions, constellation of interest groups and political settlements lead to diverging technological trajectories.

As innovations related to e-mobility are so manifold, it is necessary to delimit the scope of our subsequent comparative policy analysis. E-mobility concepts may imply different kinds of vehicles – from bicycles, scooters and three-wheelers to passenger cars, vans, buses and trains.[2] This paper focuses on policies that seek to promote the development and deployment of vehicles that provide a minimum of 50 km of purely electric range. It includes battery and fuel cell-driven vehicles, range-extended electric vehicles and plug-in hybrids. Other activities related to e-mobility, such as new mobility services, are considered insofar as they increase the complexity of the systemic transition, but exploring their competitive performance is beyond the scope of this paper.

We develop our argument in four steps. First, we describe the transition to e-mobility as a techno-economic paradigm shift, resulting from radical and systemic changes within and between technological subsystems. Second, we address the governance implications of the paradigm shift, and we highlight the need for a coordinated 'big push' to overcome multiple market failures as well as the politically negotiated character of the transition. Third, we present the main characteristics of the approach taken by each of the four countries in managing the transition towards e-mobility. Here the focus is on initial conditions of industry structure, power relations between interest groups and existing patterns of economic governance. Finally, in the fourth section we draw some lessons from the comparison of country strategies.

1. The transition to e-mobility – a multidimensional challenge

The transition to e-mobility can be regarded as a techno-economic paradigm shift. It implies a substantial reorganisation and recombination of technological subsystems, different underlying institutions and a new 'common sense' (Pérez, 2004) for what is generally regarded to be a 'good practice'. The need to create completely new technological subsystems and recombine them in innovative ways can be exemplified both within the field of electric vehicle production and in its integration in wider e-mobility concepts.

With regard to *electric vehicle manufacturing*, two major technological subsystems are already undergoing a fundamental change and need to be further optimised in order to increase the competitiveness of electric vis-à-vis ICE vehicles. First, the performance of batteries needs to be improved in several ways (Bundesregierung, 2009, p. 10). Even the best available batteries generate fairly little energy per kg of battery; hence vehicles need to carry large and heavy batteries (around 200 kg) in order to reach an acceptable driving range. Also, recharging times need to be reduced. Recharging a typical 16 kWh battery at home with the normal single-phase current takes around four to five hours. Quick charging with poly-phase current is possible, but requires a special charging system and reduces the economic life-time of the battery (Kaiser et al., 2011, 23f). Also, the cost of batteries needs to be reduced substantially. In 2010, the cost of a 16 kWh lithium-ion battery was about €5,700 (Sankey et al., 2010). Although considerable research is being undertaken to improve battery performance and reduce costs, it is impossible to predict how long it will take until electric vehicles are able to compete without subsidies.

Second, different electric and hybrid drive technologies need to be developed. In the case of automobiles, electric drives look very different from those based on ICE. Different technological options are available. For example, electric motors can be housed in the wheels. In this case, the vehicle does not need any other engine, gearbox, transmissions and ancillary systems. Free space at the front and rear of the car can be used for storage, but additional impact absorbing collapse zones have to be built in as there is no engine block to absorb shocks. Wheel hub motors are only one option, but the example shows that new drive technologies lead to fundamental redesigns of the whole vehicle. Also, development of light construction materials becomes more important to compensate for the weight of the battery.

Looking at *e-mobility more broadly*, the complexity of the paradigm change becomes even more evident. Electric vehicles require infrastructure for battery charging. While charging can partly be done at home or at the work place, there is a need for public charging stations as well. As charging takes time, it needs to be offered at public parking sites, which in densely populated areas creates challenges for urban planning. Another technological option is electromagnetic induction, whereby induction loops in the pavement generate a magnetic field which is used for wireless energy transfer. This again has far-reaching implications for road construction and requires huge infrastructure investments. Smart software systems can integrate vehicles in power grids to encourage charging outside peak load periods. Intelligent billing systems will have to be developed to charge respective energy consumption. While in the first stage of e-mobility development, the main challenge is to recharge batteries, gradually vehicle batteries should also be used for storage with the ability to feed energy back to the grid and buffer energy input fluctuations. 'Larger fleets of vehicles could be linked into combined renewable power plants [. . .] and thus contribute to the continuity, cost reduction and improved marketability of electricity from renewable energy' (Bundesregierung, 2009, p. 11). The two-way interaction between vehicles and the energy system requires the development of new information and communication technologies to ensure continuity of load supply and reduce reserve capacities.

Furthermore, e-mobility calls for a new interface between the production of innovative electric vehicles and urban and mobility planning. As electric vehicles have a limited range, they are best suited for urban transport. New multimodal mobility concepts are being tested to combine the specific advantages of different means of transport, mainly rail and road.

All of the above goes much beyond usual incremental innovations, whereby individual artefacts are improved or substituted in the process of competition. Rather, they amount to radical and systemic changes. For such changes to occur, many new system interfaces need to be explored, giving rise to new business models, such as battery changing services or ICT solutions for innovative smart-charging and billing. Moreover, the technology shift will affect attitudes towards mobility and consumer behaviour.

2. The policy challenge

The advantages of e-mobility compared to carbon-emitting transport systems benefit the general public more than the individual who (currently) has to pay a higher price for a vehicle that pollutes less and conserves energy, but has considerable disadvantages in terms of range, velocity and disposability (acatech, 2010, p. 19). This public goods nature justifies political support.

Moreover, the systemic change from combustion-engine to electricity-based transport requires coordinated policy interventions to overcome coordination failures at different levels. Coordination failure occurs when desirable activities fail to take place because they presuppose simultaneous investments in interrelated activities. Entrepreneurs may not be willing to invest in activity A unless investments in B (which are crucial for A's success) are guaranteed and vice versa. Moving ahead with one component of an interdependent system is particularly risky when the other components are not yet technologically mature and commercially viable. This is exactly the case with e-mobility.

The most obvious risk of coordination failure in the case of e-mobility development relates to the interdependencies between investing in vehicle production and setting up a charging infrastructure. Electric vehicles are expensive. In Europe, they cost between €6,000 and €10,000 more than a comparable ICE vehicle (Buttner, 2012). This is a strong disincentive for customers, especially when other disadvantages of electric vehicles are taken into account. Hence it is important to reach the stage of mass manufacturing that would bring unit production costs down and reduce the price gap between conventional and electric vehicles. Mass production, however, is unlikely to take off as long as a network of charging stations is not developed. Conversely, investment in charging infrastructure is held back as long as the number of electric vehicles on the road is low. A large, coordinated public policy push is therefore needed to develop mass production of vehicles and infrastructure concurrently.

This is not the only possible coordination failure. As the previous section has shown, simultaneous improvements are needed in a number of interrelated technologies, including battery and vehicle technology, smart grids, multimodal mobility concepts and international standard-setting.

Part of the necessary coordination can be provided by alliances among large corporations with a strategic long-term orientation. In fact, auto manufacturers and energy providers have already engaged in manifold strategic alliances, for example, between Volkswagen and E.ON, Daimler and RWE, and Ford and Southern California Edison. New alliances have also emerged between car manufacturers and local governments to organise local fleet tests (Nissan Motor and City of Houston). A.T. Kearney (2009) predicts the emergence of many new e-mobility alliances, for example, between energy utilities and mineral oil companies to build upon the latter's network of petrol stations; between fleet operators and car park operators; between railways and car-sharing companies and so forth. But no private alliance can be big enough to organise the 'big push' that would be needed to ensure the simultaneous development of all the necessary subsystems. This is one explanation why market penetration of electric vehicles has so far been very slow. Worldwide, less than 16,000 battery electric vehicles and 2000 plug-in hybrids were produced in 2010 (Buckley, 2011). As a consequence, many governments have recently adopted ambitious coordinated 'missions' or 'platforms' to advance e-mobility (see section 3).

It should be noted that such concerted efforts involve difficult choices on the part of policymakers. Given the urgency of climate change mitigation, policymakers need to accelerate the transition towards low carbon transport systems. At the same time, early stages of technological development are typically characterised by high levels of uncertainty, that is policymakers have to take funding and regulatory decisions at times when no one can predict which technological solutions (for example, batteries or fuel cells?) will finally make it to the commercial stage.

In addition to the uncertainty problem, the choice of policies occurs in a highly contested political arena with many conflicting interests involved. Conflicts of interests tend to increase when (a) public goods are involved and (b) a paradigm change can potentially shake up the market and threaten incumbents. Both arguments apply to e-mobility. Roadmaps towards e-mobility therefore require complex stakeholder negotiations and political settlements:

Balancing public and private goods. The transition to e-mobility will have a positive effect on urban pollution and public health. Assuming that electricity comes from low carbon sources, it will furthermore contribute to climate change mitigation and energy security. Some interest groups will therefore lobby for higher budgets for e-mobility research and deployment, stricter emission standards, and regulations ensuring that additional electricity supply comes from renewable energy sources. At the same time, the transition will affect the competitiveness of different industrial activities. Some companies stand to gain from the new techno-economic paradigm, whereas others are likely to lose market shares and profits. Implications also depend on firm strategies. The OECD (2011a, p. 193) characterises private sector responses to the transition as

> a complex strategic game, with newcomers exploring radical alternatives, on the one hand, and, on the other, incumbent firms, with their large accumulated assets, divided between taking a leading exploratory role to rapidly leverage their market power in this emerging sector, and an imitative behaviour to avoid the costs of search-and-try errors and protect their historical brand.

Effects on competitiveness will thus vary greatly between sectors and firms, which in turn will affect labour markets and economic growth. Furthermore, consumers will be affected through changes in mobility services and in prices for energy and transport. Governments will need to strike a fine balance between these various private interests and the creation of public goods.

Market shake-up. As the transition is radical and systemic, new technologies and business models are sometimes developed by completely new industry players. For example, tyre manufacturer Michelin has developed an electric vehicle on the basis of two wheel hub motors, one for traction and braking and the other for electric active suspension control (Evans, 2008). If this concept became the dominant design, it would devalue many assets held by incumbent producers of combustion engines, gearboxes, cardan shafts and the like, and it would establish a tyre manufacturer as a competitor of traditional car makers. Likewise, the Chinese company BYD started expanding as a battery producer around 1996 and entered automobile production in 2003. Such examples indicate a major potential for market shake-ups and newcomers leapfrogging into the new technologies. Governments need to be aware of the effects of their policies on national competitiveness. When they establish new industry standards for batteries or plugs, for example, some big industry players who have developed other standards may have to write off multi-million investments. Encouraging innovation and avoiding technological lock-in without sacrificing existing competitive advantages is a challenging task.

In sum, governments need to play a very pro-active role in managing the transition. They need to facilitate stakeholder dialogue and pursue political settlements between competing interest groups, incentivise the search for new technologies and organise demonstration projects, develop technological roadmaps and bundle resources for their implementation, discourage old polluting technologies and coordinate simultaneous investments in emerging technological subsystems in order to avoid being locked into path-dependent technological trajectories.

3. Managing the transition: governance responses in four countries

France, Germany, China and India are all important motor vehicle manufacturers, and all four have, between 2008 and 2011, set up comprehensive e-mobility innovation policies. All four, however, are managing the transition differently, reflecting customary patterns of economic governance, industry conditions, and interest groups.

France: big public-private push

France is the tenth largest global motor vehicle manufacturer, but the country would rank higher if outsourced production were taken into account. The automotive sector accounts for almost 10% of France's manufacturing and energy employment, 12% of exports and 17% of R&D expenditure (Colling et al., 2010). However, sales of French cars stagnated around 2003, as did car registration in France. Moreover, French carmakers have gradually been crowded out of the high-end market segment and instead concentrated on compact cars and the lower middle-sized class (Jullien 2010, 6f). Although the competition is fierce and margins are small in the latter, this competitive edge may provide France with a big advantage in meeting emissions reduction targets and shifting to electric vehicles.

Moreover, French carmakers have pioneered a number of environmental innovations, such as the diesel particulate filter, for which the country is still the market leader. France is also the technological leader in Europe for electric vehicles, having launched the first models for mass production in 2010 (Peugeot iOn) and 2011 (Renault Kangoo Z.E. and Fluence Z.E.).

However, a coherent national policy to promote e-mobility was only adopted in 2009. Still in 2007, when a prominent national environmental summit, the 'Grenelle Environnement', was convoked by President Sarkozy, e-mobility did not figure prominently.[3] But in 2009, as a reaction to the economic crisis, the *Pacte automobile* was agreed, a multi-billion rescue package for the French car industry which aimed at fostering structural adjustments and making the automobile industry fit for the post-crisis period. While the *Pacte automobile* was not specifically geared towards e-mobility, it served to bundle earlier agreed support measures for electric vehicles, encourage collective industry initiatives and scaled up financial support for R&D and demonstrations projects (Présidence de la République, 2009).

The French policy is driven by a dual policy objective: mitigating climate change and increasing the competitiveness of French car manufacturers, who have recently seen their market shares decline. The EU has decreed specific emissions reduction targets for European car manufacturers, and non-compliance fines have been set at a standard €95 for every gCO_2/km in excess of the target multiplied by the number of cars from 2019.[4] As such, there is a clear economic rationale to gear national mobility policies towards emissions reduction. At the same time, stricter emission standards may favour the French industry. First, the French energy mix is strongly based on nuclear energy and is therefore 'low carbon'. The average CO_2 emissions for electricity generated in France (85 g/kWh) are only a fraction of the European average of 400 g/kWh (ADEME, 2009, p. 6). Electric vehicles in France thus have a smaller carbon footprint than electric vehicles in other European countries, where most electricity comes from coal-fired power plants. Stricter emission standards would therefore only affect the European rivals. Second, French carmakers Renault and PSA Peugeot Citroën have an early mover advantage in electric vehicles and a product portfolio dominated by small cars.

The French government has therefore set ambitious e-mobility targets. It aims to have two million electric cars in France in 2020 (Guillou et al., 2009). This is the most ambitious target in Europe, clearly exceeding those of its main sectoral rival in Europe; despite a larger domestic market, Germany targets 'only' one million electric cars on German roads in the same year (discussed below).

To overcome the coordination failure of electric vehicle markets (*technological innovations* in various fields, *mass production of electric vehicles* and a *national charging infrastructure* need to be promoted simultaneously) the government adopted a coordinated big push approach (Ministère de l'Ècologie, 2009):

- To step up technological innovations, a €400 million-fund was established to provide soft loans for 'green' demonstration projects in 2009–2012. An additional € 50 million were allocated to the French Environment and Energy Management Agency specifically for e-mobility pilots projects. In addition to French funds, industries can also access a €5 billion fund from the European Green Car Initiative. Besides funding, the government encourages partnerships between public agencies, the auto industry and research centres to work on improvement of the power train and batteries.
- To create an incentive for mass production of electric vehicles that would bring unit prices down, the government offers a subsidy of €5,000 for the purchase of electric vehicles with less than 60 g/km CO_2. In addition, the coordinated procurement of 100,000 electric cars by public and private companies until 2015 was agreed and leading car manufacturers committed to produce 60,000 electric vehicles in 2011–2012. To accelerate the production of batteries, the French government is also directly involved as a shareholder in the construction of a battery factory near Paris, together with Renault.
- To ensure the development of a national charging infrastructure, a working group including central and local authorities, automobile manufacturers and private service providers was established to develop solutions for the charging and battery exchange infrastructure. One of its priorities is to develop common standards for battery charging. Also, a road map for the development of charging stations was defined, targeting 4 million private

and 400,000 public charging points. Local authorities made commitments to install standardised charging stations; from 2012 construction companies are obliged to install charging points in new car parks, and all companies are expected to equip company car parks with charging points by 2015 (Colling et al., 2010). In addition, funds were set aside to develop a million charging points in private homes, car parks and roadside sites (OECD, 2011a, p. 208).

In sum, France has the most ambitious electric vehicle policy in Europe, providing a coordinated big push for R&D, rollout of electric cars and infrastructure development. As an OECD study denotes, 'the distinctive feature of the French strategy for electric vehicles is the key role of the state and national programmes. The orientations and selected players are defined by the administration' (OECD, 2011a, p. 208). Purchase subsidies, coordinated public-private procurement that takes advantage of close relationships between the state and large corporations, R&D grants, legal requirements to install charging points in company parking lots and state-business agreements to harmonise public investments in charging infrastructure with private car production add up to a strong state-led strategy.

Germany: from high-emission luxury cars to competitive advantages in electric vehicles?

Germany is the fourth largest car manufacturer worldwide and by far the largest in Europe (OICA, 2010). The automotive industry is Germany's most important, with sales reaching €315 billion in 2010 (BMWI, 2010), contributing 20% of total German industry revenue in 2009 and providing employment for 723,000 persons (GTAI, 2010, p. 11). The German car industry, with brands including Daimler-Chrysler, BMW, Audi and Porsche, has a strong competitive edge in upper middle-sized and luxury class vehicles. Average emissions per vehicle are therefore high, which is why Germany – otherwise a frontrunner in environmental policies – successfully lobbied against more ambitious CO_2 emission reduction targets at EU level.[5] Given its current pattern of specialisation within the global motor vehicle industry, escaping a carbon lock-in (Cowan and Hultén, 1996) could prove even more difficult for Germany.

However, the German car industry has taken up the challenge of e-mobility. The EU's graduated scheme for emissions reduction does not leave any alternative. German carmakers need to reduce emissions per vehicle across all size categories of cars and at the same time develop a substantial number of low emission cars to compensate for the traditional luxury cars in their portfolio that are unlikely to reach the prescribed limits. BMW and Opel will launch mass-manufactured battery-electric vehicles in 2013, two years behind France and about four years behind Japan. Despite this time lag, the industry is optimistic that it can catch up with the frontrunners, as Germany's sectoral innovation system for the automotive industry is particularly strong. Germany was not only the European leader in the *number* of electric and hybrid vehicle patents filed in 2003–2008, but it also had the second-highest *share* of this sector in national patents overall, topped only by Japan (OECD, 2011b, p. 28). With €20 billion in 2010, the automobile industry is by far the largest contributor to Germany's private R&D expenditure (VDA, 2011). Germany hosts 42% of all European Original Equipment Manufacturer and tier 0.5 supplier automotive R&D centres (Invest in Germany, 2008). Furthermore, large energy utilities including E.ON and RWE show strong commitment to developing e-mobility and have entered a number of strategic alliances with carmakers to experiment with electric vehicle fleets and local charging networks.

Germany has competitive advantages in most industries that feed into the automotive value chain. However, a SWOT analysis conducted in preparation for the National Electromobility Development Plan identified battery technology as the Achilles heel of the German innovation system for electric vehicles (Bundesregierung, 2009, p. 15). Lithium-ion battery technologies have mainly been developed in Japan and Korea in conjunction with the electronics and optical industries. When these industries gradually relocated to Asia in the 1980s and 1990s, Germany's interest in battery technology diminished,[6] and relatively more research was dedicated to hydrogen and fuel cell technology development.

A coordinated policy approach for electric vehicles started in 2008 when an inter-ministerial committee was formed and the decision was taken to establish the National Platform Electromobility with the mandate to coordinate a systemic, market-oriented and technology-neutral approach to make Germany a leading provider and lead market for 'electromobility made in Germany' (NPE, 2011, p. 5). By the end of 2011, the platform had 147 members, including enterprises from different industries, state agencies and civil society organisation, ranging from the national automobile club to environmental NGOs. To ensure day-to-day coordination, a Federal Government Joint Unit for Electric Mobility was created, with personnel seconded from four ministries. Seven thematic working groups were established within the unit to deal with issues such as 'drive technology and systems integration', 'charging infrastructure and grid integration', 'battery technology' and 'norms and standards'. While these working groups involve a broad range of stakeholders, their agenda is in most cases very much industry-led. At the same time, the broad range of stakeholders helps to avoid political capture, because members pursue different interests, and it would be difficult for one particular industry to impose its interests.[7]

The programmes for R&D and deployment in the different fields of technology under the umbrella of the National Platform Electromobility amount to €4 billion (NPE, 2011, p. 6). As in France, research funding benefited from the German governments' second stimulus package to overcome the deep recession in late 2008, early 2009. The national strategy has set the objective of having 1 million electric vehicles circulating on German roads by 2020 and a minimum of 6 million by 2030 (Bundesregierung, 2011, p. 10).

German strategy also supports regional experiments, typically executed by alliances between energy utilities, carmakers and municipalities. Starting with a tender in late 2011, three to five of these regional pilots will be up-scaled to so-called 'Schaufenster' (showcases) for large-scale experimentation. €180 million have been earmarked for such showcases.

As in France, the main motives behind Germany's national e-mobility strategy are emissions reduction and competitive repositioning of the national automotive industry. A major difference, however, relates to the interface between electric vehicles and the energy system. While France's energy policy regards nuclear energy as an appropriate source of low carbon energy, Germany is phasing its nuclear energy programme out. In Germany, fossil fuels account for the lion's share of electricity generation. Promoting e-mobility on the basis of this energy mix would hardly have any positive effect on greenhouse gas emissions.[8] Therefore, the 'Government Programme Electromobility' states that 'additional demand for electric energy for this sector is to be covered by renewable energies' (Bundesregierung, 2011, p. 8). The Ministry of Environment even claims that renewable energy used for the purpose of electric vehicles should be on top of the already committed national renewable energy targets. Hence, electromobility development in Germany is contingent upon energy system reforms. This is reflected in a strong research focus on ways of integrating electric vehicles into intelligent power supply systems that provide for using the vehicle fleet for intermediate energy storage and feeding energy back into the grid when supply is low, thereby mitigating the typical fluctuations of solar and wind energy supply.

The German approach relies more on market-based experimentation, private sector-led initiatives, allocating the bulk of its subsidies to research and demonstration projects. There are neither direct subsidies for purchasing electric vehicles in Germany nor concerted public-private procurement initiatives, in contrast to France. The National Platform Electromobility explicitly states that it is preferable to support R&D than to subsidise the cost of vehicles. This reflects a generally less interventionist position of German governments and of the current Christian-liberal coalition in particular, but it may also be due to more pragmatic reasons: as long as German carmakers have no electric vehicles on offer, a purchase subsidy would use German taxpayers' money to buy almost exclusively French and Japanese cars.

The German government is also avoiding getting deeply involved in infrastructure development. While France uses an integrated package of state funding, mandatory requirements for companies and nudging of municipalities to build up a dense country-wide charging infrastructure, the German government trusts in demonstration effects from the regional showcases and a mainly voluntary and market-driven process of infrastructure expansion. Also, Germany's federal political system favours competing regional experiments, whereas France's highly centralised political system allows the government to implement one nation-wide infrastructure initiative.

China: industry change as a leapfrogging opportunity?

In 2009 China surpassed Japan as the world's largest motor vehicle producer and in 2010 production exceeded 18 million vehicles (OICA, 2010). China today is also the largest auto market. The history of China's rapid automobile industry growth goes back to the 1990s when the government defined the industry as a pillar of China's economic development and, for the first time since 1949, allowed private car ownership. The industry developed on the basis of Joint Ventures between Chinese state-owned companies and major foreign companies, as a means to accelerate technology transfer. In recent years, some larger Chinese-owned companies emerged, mostly regional government-backed state-owned enterprises, with the notable exception of the private company Geely. The innovation approach of Chinese-owned companies was characterised by making production processes simpler and production cheaper, thereby challenging the Joint Ventures and foreign car brands in the Chinese market. While the long-term government strategy is to develop indigenous brands for export, so far exports remain at a low level. Chinese car manufacturers have yet to achieve the aspired competitiveness in global markets. They still struggle to meet the safety and quality standards of industrialised countries and continue relying on foreign (for example, powertrain) technologies (Gao et al., 2008; Zhang, 2011).

Against this background, Chinese politicians and industry experts have identified the shift to e-mobility as an opportunity for technological leapfrogging (Wang and Kimble, 2011). The starting conditions for this shift appear to be good: China is already the global lead market for battery technology, especially lithium-ion batteries used in the electronics industry, and is expected to contribute considerably to lowering battery costs as the industry scales up for mass production of large batteries for electric vehicle application (World Bank, PRTM Management Consultants, 2011). In addition, China has the largest market for e-bikes in the world. This market is supplied by Chinese firms based on mainly indigenous technology. It has also accustomed Chinese consumers to the idea of e-mobility.

Policy support for electric vehicles originates from three sources (Wu, 2010). First, technological development and innovation has received support from government research funds since the 10th Five-Year Plan (2001–2006). The 12th FYP (2011–2015) has included electric vehicles in the list of priority emerging industries, encouraging R&D accordingly. Also, specific development goals have been defined in the science and technology policies of the Ministry of Science and Technology (MOST, 2011). Second, the government selected 13 cities to experiment with 'energy efficient and new energy automobiles' in 2009. The number of cities has since been increased to 25. While these cities are supposed to experiment with public vehicle fleets, five more cities were selected in 2010 to experiment with purchase subsidies for private electric vehicles. Third, in July 2010 the Ministry of Industry and Information Technology (MIIT) circulated a

'Draft development plan for the energy efficient and new energy car industry (2011–2020)' for comment from other ministries and dissemination by the State Council. Even as draft, this document currently serves as major guideline for the industry.

Both central and local governments define ambitious projections for e-vehicle production and diffusion. The MIIT draft development plan describes a preparatory period until 2012 for the development of relevant standards, construction of recharging infrastructure and local experiments. A modest degree of mass production and commercialisation is expected to develop until 2015. Until then, 'indigenous' know-how in the technology of core parts (such as battery, electric motor and electric control systems) shall be available in China. The envisaged market volume for 2012 is a minimum of 500,000 battery-electric and plug-in hybrid electric vehicles. Mass production at the highest international technology level shall be achieved by 2020, allowing for production and sales capacities for five million vehicles. The draft plan includes objectives for industry structure; by 2020 there should be a small number of large enterprise groups dominating the different steps of the electric vehicle value chain, namely vehicle, battery, raw materials as well as motor and automatic gearing production (Wu, 2010).

To overcome coordination failure, central government support includes supply and demand side incentives, including subsidies for private purchases of new energy vehicles, tax holidays, reduction of VAT, demonstration projects and incentives for corporate R&D (Liu, 2010). In addition, appropriate energy efficient and new energy cars will be integrated in government procurement priority lists for environment-friendly and indigenous innovation products. Some of the policies suggested in the draft document have since been implemented or specified at the local level. For example, at least six cities (Shanghai, Changchun, Shenzhen, Hangzhou, Hefei and Beijing) already apply the subsidy scheme for private electric vehicle purchases. In these cases, the central government provides up to €6600[9] purchasing subsidy for battery-electric and €5500 for plug-in hybrid electric vehicles. Local governments are allowed to add a purchasing subsidy of up to €6600. In addition, some local governments have announced highly ambitious policies that envisage production capacities for new energy vehicles in 2015 that go far beyond the national targets formulated in the draft industrial policy.[10]

Apart from local governments, enterprises also reacted to the policies of 2010. Three major alliances were formed. First, the 'China Electric Vehicle Alliance' links 16 large state-owned enterprises under the guidance of the State-owned Asset Supervision and Administration Commission (SASAC) with the intention of establishing a national platform for electric vehicle technology. Second, the 'Top 10 Electric Vehicle Alliance' unites 10 carmakers based on an initiative of the China's Automobile Industry Association. In addition, some Chinese and US firms created the Sustainable New Energies International Alliance. These alliances were allegedly created to foster cooperation along the electric vehicle value chain. However, the enterprises also hope to get better access to financial support through the alliances, as the government policies promise overall financial support in the range of €11 billion. SASAC additionally promised to invest €140 million in the China Electric Vehicle Alliance. Given the size and status of the state-owned enterprises joining this alliance, one additional hope was to define future electric vehicle standards.

Electric vehicle sector development has thus received substantial government support in recent years. The government hopes that electric vehicles will help push the Chinese automobile industry from being a production hub to becoming a centre of cutting-edge innovation. The thriving e-bike industry is not an integral part of the e-mobility strategies described above. This has been criticised in China by researchers who see a stronger potential for China to develop indigenous e-mobility technology from upgrading e-bike know-how. However, the e-bike industry is driven by private small and medium enterprises and, as such, is far less important for the economy than the large state-owned automobile producers.

Other considerations support the electric vehicle strategy. First, e-mobility is expected to reduce China's dependence on oil imports, while the country's endowment with some rare earths which are strategic for electric vehicles adds a geopolitical advantage. Second, e-mobility is seen as a way to reduce urban air pollution. Climate change considerations so far play a minor role in e-mobility policies, as electricity comes mainly from coal-fired power plants and e-mobility thus does not reduce overall emissions.

In sum, the recent national electric vehicle initiatives show typical traits of Chinese industrial policies in that they favour large and state-owned enterprises, formulate technological and structural goals, and emphasise the importance of indigenous innovation in order to lessen the dependence on imported technologies. The policies are initiated top-down but intentionally pick specific regions as testing grounds and encourage them to come up with more specific or additional initiatives. This approach of 'competition under hierarchy' (Fischer, 2010; Heilmann, 2011) has shown strengths and weaknesses in the past. Often production targets are reached much earlier than expected due to a 'run' into the industry triggered by the policies and local initiatives. Fierce competition then leads to rapidly decreasing prices. While Chinese enterprises often have thrived in this competition due to cost advantages arising from economies of scale, process management, etc., the approach has so far hardly ever produced technological leadership. It therefore must be doubted that China's current policies will support big gains in innovation capacities of China's automobile industry. However, China will probably make major contributions in cost reduction of the battery system and other components.

India: hesitant national mission and niche market development

After independence in 1947, India followed a protectionist policy to build up a national automotive industry and indigenise the production of components. While this helped to build up basic manufacturing infrastructure and capabilities, the captive market also reduced competitive pressure and resulted in low levels of productivity and competitiveness. This changed with the deregulation and liberalisation policies that were introduced for the automobile sector in the mid-1980s (Narayanan, 1997, p. 4). Today, the Indian car industry is booming. The country manufactures the largest number of tractors, fifth largest number of commercial vehicles, and ninth largest number of cars in the world. Automobile production doubled in India between 2004 and 2010, with the total number of produced units going beyond 17.9 million, and the number of automobiles exported increased from 629 thousand in 2004 to 2.3 million in 2010 (SIAM, 2012a). In addition, the auto component industry exported goods worth US$5.2 billion in 2010–11 (ACMA, 2012, p. 9). In total, the automobile industry has an annual turnover of US$38 billion per year (2008–2009) (SIAM, 2012b).

India's motor vehicle industry benefits from a rapidly evolving domestic market. At present, only about 1.6% of the population owns a vehicle (Pasvantis, 2011a), but car ownership is expected to multiply rapidly as the number of households that can afford motor vehicles grows. India's real average household disposable income has doubled between 1985 and 2005 and will almost triple over the next two decades if India continues on its current growth path. If this were the case, its consuming 'middle class' would grow tenfold, from 50 to 583 million people (McKinsey Global Institute, 2007, pp. 9–10).

However, with low average household incomes, the automotive market is very price-sensitive, and demand is concentrated on simple low-cost cars. This severely restricts the market for e-vehicles, whose cost of acquisition is high compared to conventional vehicles. Also, the supply of public charging stations is insufficient. The high frequency of power cuts in India further reduces the attractiveness of electromobility. Due to these constraints, the domestic market for e-vehicles is almost entirely limited to two-wheelers. The Society of Manufacturers of Electric Vehicles estimates that in fiscal year 2010–2011, 100,000 two-wheelers and 600 e-cars have been sold (Pasvantis, 2011b).

Only one company manufactures e-cars in India. Mahindra-REVA, then a medium-sized family business, started producing electric cars as early as 2004. Since then, it has sold about 3500 units. While Mahindra-REVA has an installed capacity of 6000 cars per year, annual production is only about 800. Fewer than 2000 e-cars have been sold domestically; the remainder has been exported to 24 countries, mainly to the United Kingdom (Visier and Pasvantis, 2010). All REVA models are simple low-cost cars for specific niche markets, for example, use within city limits, as they do not meet the safety requirements for circulating on European highways. In India, the main target market is families interested in REVA as a second car for inner-urban use.[11] Still, REVA claims that it has the second largest fleet of electric cars running in the world (Mahindra REVA, 2012). Carmakers Tata, Hero Honda, Maruti Suzuki and GM (all significant players in India's auto industry) have announced India-specific electric vehicle launches, but none have embarked on any production plans for these. As it appears, most carmakers are still awaiting supporting policies to step in. Two-wheelers are produced by three industrial companies, Hero Electric, Electrotherm und Lohia Auto, as well as many small informal workshops. The latter mainly assemble imported parts and account for 50% of electric two-wheeler production.

Without substantial policy support, the domestic e-mobility market will remain insignificant. Until 2010, the Government of India hesitated to set up major support schemes; subsidising a fairly wealthy segment of urban consumers in poverty-stricken India could not be justified easily. Some research activities were supported, for example, to develop a small electric trolley bus for public urban transport at the Central Mechanical Engineering Research Institute. However, research on electric and hybrid vehicle technology is not a research priority in India. This is manifested in the patent applications filed in 2003–2008 by India, where the share of patents related to these technologies in overall Indian patents was low, compared, for example, to the OECD average or to China (OECD, 2011b, p. 28).

In 2010, the government's attitude partly changed. In May 2010, REVA sold almost 55% of its stake to Mahindra & Mahindra, a large Indian automobile conglomerate, whose leadership was also leading the Society for Indian Automobile Manufacturers until the end of 2011 (SIAM, 2012c). Since then, e-mobility became more commonplace in government announcements. In November, the Ministry for New and Renewable Energy launched a subsidy for the purchase of electric cars, two- and three-wheelers: Manufacturers get up to 20% on the ex-factory price of every e-vehicle sold up to a maximum of INR100,000 (approximately €1500) per car and INR4000–5000 (€60–75) per two-wheeler until the end of fiscal year 2011–2012. Although the programme's total budget was only €14 million, it triggered an immediate increase in sales. Mahindra REVA tripled its vehicle sales and expects to sell 2500 e-cars in 2011–2012 (Pasvantis, 2011b).

In February 2011, the Finance Minister announced in his budget speech a National Mission for Hybrid and Electric Vehicles. The mission set a target of 800,000 electric vehicles – including two-wheelers – in the Indian market. Under the mission, a National Council for Electric Mobility has been set up headed by the Heavy Industries & Public Enterprises Minister. Also, a National Board for Electric Mobility has been set up at the secretary level. These bodies have representation from several Ministries (Environment and Forest, New and Renewable Energy, Heavy Industries & Public Enterprises) as well as the automobile sector. In addition to purchase subsidies, certain imported components for hybrid and battery-electric vehicles were exempted of custom duties, and support for e-mobility experiments in certain model cities is envisaged. Additional incentives, including reduction of the value-added tax and reimbursement of registration fees and road tax are under scrutiny (Pasvanti, 2011b). Recent media reports state that the Ministry of Heavy Industry will ask the central government to create a €860 million financial package for the development and deployment of electric vehicles (Shukla, 2012).

The National Mission claims that its main objective is to build a sustainable and environment-friendly transport system. However, electrical energy generation in India is strongly reliant on coal-fired power plants, and there are so far no explicit targets to decouple e-mobility from the overall energy mix. Under these conditions, electric vehicles are unlikely to reduce greenhouse gas emissions or improve energy efficiency. The fact that the mission was launched precisely at a moment when global carmakers started to launch electric cars and Mahinda & Mahindra had acquired REVA suggests that competitiveness issues played a major role in starting to support the national industry. The automotive industry has become the backbone of India's manufacturing sector, and the industry does not want to miss a technological trend that may become relevant for the competitiveness of the motor vehicle industry worldwide. Also, the facts that (a) the subsidy is tied to a local content requirement of 30% and (b) the coordinating role of the National Mission was given to the Ministry of Heavy Industries & Public Enterprises – rather than the Ministries of New and Renewable Energy or Environment and Forests – points to industrial policy interests.

Overall, it seems unlikely that India will become a major electric vehicle market in the near future, with the exception of two-wheelers. The car market is price-sensitive and the government's financial scope for subsidising market entry is not comparable to the other three countries studied in this paper. While Mahindra REVA has been able to export to international niche markets, it is unlikely that it will be able to challenge large-scale electric vehicle deployment by global car manufacturers such as Mitsubishi.

4. Insights from comparison

Many commonalities exist between the e-mobility strategies of France, Germany, China and India. While small-scale experimentation with electric vehicles has been going on for several decades, all four countries recently tapped on e-mobility and the manufacturing of electric vehicles in particular as a strategic industry in the global race for green growth. This is mainly due to one political and one technological driver. On the political front, all four governments have committed to reducing greenhouse gas emissions and motor vehicles are one of the main contributors to those emissions. On the technological front, recent progress in the performance of lithium-ion batteries has created optimism that the disadvantages of the new technology vis-à-vis ICE in terms of cost and range can be reduced substantially.

All four governments have recently set up institutions for inter-ministerial coordination and stakeholder engagement in order to develop roadmaps and overcome the market failures that currently hold the industry back. France, Germany and China have allocated substantial incentives for R&D and technology deployment and encourage experimentation in pilot regions and with specific fleets. India is lagging behind in this regard, but has currently announced a National Mission for Hybrid and Electric Vehicles which creates similar incentives, albeit at a more modest scale.

At the same time, the comparison reveals big differences in terms of

- initial industry structure and technological capabilities;
- the political priorities for policymaking; and
- policy packages reflecting specific national patterns of economic governance.

With regard to *industry structure and technological capabilities*, the motor vehicle industries of the four countries have started developing e-mobility from different bases. France traditionally had a strong car industry which has recently seen its competitiveness decline, particularly in the upmarket range. Producing small eco-efficient cars is therefore seen as a strategy for regaining competitive advantages and French car makers have indeed gained an early mover advantage in electric vehicles. Stricter EU emissions standards would therefore benefit French industry vis-à-vis most international competitors, which may explain the determined and ambitious electric vehicle policy pursued. Germany's car industry, in contrast, is currently very competitive, particularly in upper middle and luxury class cars. In electric vehicle manufacturing, Germany is a latecomer, but EU emission standards are forcing the industry to develop low emission cars. China has the largest and fastest growing home market and is the world leader in motor vehicle production, but still has limited innovative capabilities. Competitive advantages exist in two-wheeler production and in lithium-ion battery technology, partly as a spillover from the electronics and optical industries. India's conventional motor vehicle market is also booming. Automobile and auto parts manufacturers are rapidly catching up and gaining export shares, but technological innovation is still very modest. Low purchasing power of private households and huge deficits in electricity supply are severely constraining electric vehicle development, with the exception of two-wheelers.

How governments try to manage the paradigm change and how they design policy packages depends on their *political priorities*. In Europe, climate change mitigation is the main driver of change. The EU has made binding commitments for emission reduction, which have been broken down into targets for the transport sector. German and French car manufacturers are obliged to reduce the emissions of their fleets to levels that cannot be achieved by incremental improvements of the incumbent ICE technology. Hybrid vehicle technologies alone are insufficient to reach the targets. With climate change mitigation being the main driving force behind the European e-mobility efforts, both the French and German governments want to ensure that the electricity used for e-mobility comes from low carbon sources. Here, differences between French and German energy systems come into play. As electricity in France mainly comes from nuclear power plants, French policymakers consider electric vehicles as having a very small carbon footprint. Germany, in contrast, is phasing nuclear energy out and its energy system is heavily reliant on fossil fuels. The German government therefore promotes e-mobility only if the additional electricity comes from renewable energy sources. As a result, considerable research efforts are being made to use batteries of the electric vehicle fleet for intermediate energy storage and to promote smart grids. At the same time, both European governments are trying to strike a difficult balance between climate change mitigation and protecting their national auto industries. In this regard, the French government sees strict EU emission standards as an opportunity, whereas such standards are a threat for Germany's upmarket producers and therefore opposed by the German government.

China's interest in e-mobility is different; emphasis is on reducing urban air pollution and creating indigenous innovation capabilities. In order to reduce urban air pollution, it is important to replace ICE with electric drives. Whether the electricity is generated from polluting coal-fired power plants (as long as they are not in the midst of the polluted cities) or from renewable energies is only a secondary concern. Furthermore, China's automobile industry has been trying for decades to catch up with technological leaders in Japan and the West without success. Electric vehicles are now seen as a paradigm change that might help China to leapfrog into the group of technological leaders, taking advantage of its technological capabilities in battery manufacturing and its ability to push the new industry through coordinated large-scale research and deployment policies. In India, there is less pressure to reduce GHG emissions; and, given the high upfront investments required to create a national market (subsidies, energy and charging infrastructure), it is unlikely that a major internal market will arise in the next 10–20 years, aside from two-wheelers. While climate change mitigation is cited as the driving force for the new electric vehicle mission, the main reason appears to be the desire of auto industries to avoid being left behind in an emerging field of technology; moreover, producing low-cost electric vehicles for export may be a niche market for Indian manufacturers.

The comparison also reveals how *differences in national patterns of economic governance* influence policy design. First, the policies adopted reflect different attitudes towards industrial policy. In China and France, the governments adopt strongly state-led strategies aimed at giving a coordinated big push to the industry, in Germany, policy coordination is sought through voluntary cooperation and regional experiments, whereas in India, electric vehicle sector coordination is still weak. This is reflected in different attitudes to setting up charging infrastructure. In China and France, central and local governments are strongly involved as an investor and by making investments mandatory for certain market actors. In Germany and India, setting up a charging infrastructure is largely left to private investors. Stronger state intervention is furthermore manifested in the willingness to subsidise the purchase of e-vehicles in China and France, and recently, with modest subsides, also in India, whereas Germany prefers to invest strongly in R&D. Second, the degree to which governments can influence company decisions varies. If the Chinese government sets targets, state-owned automobile manufacturers or energy utilities align their strategies accordingly. China's central government even tries to influence the size and structure of the emerging electric vehicle industry in the way it thinks is most appropriate. The French state has reached an agreement with leading carmakers, offering public engagement in setting up a charging infrastructure in exchange for private sector commitments to produce a minimum number of cars. Also, a state-business deal has been made to jointly procure 100,000 vehicles among state-owned, parastatal and private corporations. Such political deals are not customary in Germany's and India's market economies, where industry collaboration is strictly voluntary. Also, in Germany, many regional experiments are led by industry alliances with only minor participation of local governments. Third, decision-making is more centralised in France and China compared to Germany and India, were many relevant policies are state matters. Setting up a homogeneous country-wide charging infrastructure is probably easier in centralised France than in federal Germany. On the other hand, regional experimentation and competition of policy approaches may also be a driver of innovation. German and Indian governments are already testing different policy packages to promote e-mobility. This also applies to China, where policy guidelines come from the top, but local experimentation and 'competition under hierarchy' are encouraged.

In sum, we have found big differences between the four countries in terms of initial market conditions, political priorities, policy packages and the way policies are implemented. As the paradigm change is still at its nascent stage with only very few electric vehicles actually running (with the exception of two-wheelers), it is too early to predict which countries will be more successful than others and which policies will work best. It seems likely that the French governments' big push to accelerate market introduction will extend its early mover advantages; but it is not clear how long this will last, as Germany's car industry has performed better in recent years and may catch up quite rapidly in electric vehicles. China benefits from its strong competences in battery technology, its head start in two-wheeler production, its ability to align leading Chinese manufacturers, especially state-owned enterprises, with a national strategy and, last but not least, its unprecedented boom of automobile demand and production. Whether this will suffice to manage the breakthrough 'from production to innovation' (Altenburg et al., 2008) is not yet foreseeable. In the past, the Chinese auto industry successfully boosted production, but failed to create cutting edge innovations. Likewise, it is not clear whether the successful export strategy of two Indian electric vehicles manufacturers can be maintained as the leading global car manufacturers are just starting to bring mass-manufactured e-cars to the market place.

We expect the existing differences to result in country-specific technological trajectories. France, for example, may exploit technological early mover advantages related to its pioneering investments in building up charging infrastructure; Germany may build expertise in smart solutions for integration electric vehicles into power grids, because this is one of its specific key challenges ahead; China may exploit its economies of scale to gain an advantage in mass manufacturing for e-cars or in battery production; and India may exploit international niche markets for low-cost e-vehicles. Only future research will show whether these assumptions prove to be right. This research will also help to assess the effectiveness of different national policy approaches.

Notes

1. McKinsey has calculated that 'a 10-year-delay in taking abatement action would make it virtually impossible to keep global warming below 2 degrees Celsius' (McKinsey, 2009, p. 8).
2. Furthermore, electrification of transport describes a continuum spanning from energy-saving devices that can be added to traditional internal combustion engines (ICE), for example, an electric start-stop system; hybrid engines which combine an ICE with an electric propulsion system, mainly by regenerating energy as the car brakes to charge the battery; plug-in hybrids which have an electric motor as well as an ICE which can be connected to external power sources to recharge their batteries; range-extended electric vehicles which use an additional ICE powering a generator when the batteries are low; to entirely electric vehicles driven by a battery or fuel cell.
3. See agreements under http://www.legrenelle-environnement.fr/-Workgroups-.html
4. See Regulation 443/2009/EC, Article 9.
5. The 130g CO2/km target was initially set for 2012, but was postponed to 2015 due to German resistance. Stricter norms were advocated by UK and the Netherlands who do not have substantial car industry.
6. Interview with Dr. Randolf Schließr, VDI/VDE, Berlin, 9 November, 2011.
7. Interview with Ingrid Ott, Federal Government Joint Unit for Electric Mobility, Berlin, 9th November, 2011.
8. According to ADEME (2009, p. 6), indirect CO2 emissions of electric vehicles are above 250 g CO2/km if electricity is generated in conventional coal-fired power plants, compared to average emissions of ICE vehicles in the range of 150 g CO2/km and a 2020 target of 95 g CO2/km.
9. Calculated with a currency exchange rate 1RMB = 0,11 Euro.
10. 2015 electric vehicle production projections of Wuhan, Shenzhen and Shanghai alone add up to 600,000 cars, which is far more than the national production envisaged for that year (The Climate Group, 2011). These objectives seem particularly ambitious considering that only about 10,000 electric vehicles were sold in 2011. Of these, only about 1,000 vehicles were private purchases (Lan, 2011, p. 30).
11. Interview with Kartik Gopal, General Manager – Business Development, Mobility Solutions, Mahindra Reva Electric Vehicles Pvt. Ltd.; 31 August 2011.

References

acatech (2010) Wie Deutschland zum Leitanbieter für Elektromobilität werden kann. Acatech bezieht Position, no. 6. Fraunhofer IRB Verlag, Stuttgart.

ACMA (2012) Automotive Component Manufacturers Association of India, growing capabilities of Indian auto component industry & its sustainability, available at: http://acmainfo.com/pdf/Status_Indian_Auto_Industry.pdf

ADEME (2009) Les transports électriques en France: Un développement nécessaire sous contraintes. ADEME&vous, 21, 21 juillet.

Altenburg, T., Schmitz, H., and Stamm, A. (2008) Breakthrough? China's and India's transition from production to innovation. *World Development*, 36(2), pp. 325–344.

Kearney, A.T. (2009) Energiewirtschaft macht mobil. Düsseldorf.

BMWI (Bundesministerium für Wirtschaft und Technologie) (2010) Automobilindustrie. Branchenkonjunktur, available at: http://www.bmwi.de/BMWi/Navigation/Wirtschaft/branchenfokus, did=195926.html

Buckley, P. (2011) Global electric car production forecast to top 16 million in 2021, EE Times Europe, 24 June, available at: http://www.automotive-eetimes.com/en/global-electric-car-production-forecast-to-top-16-million-in-2021.html?cmp_id=7&news_id=222901645

Bundesregierung (2009) German federal government's national electromobility development plan. Berlin.

Bundesregierung (2011) Regierungsprogramm Elektromobilität. Berlin.

Buttner Von, R. (2012) Elektroautos: Fürchtet euch nicht!. *Spiegel Online*, 4 January, available at: http://www.spiegel.de/auto/aktuell/0,1518,806020,00.html

Colling, S., Tuononen, S., and Salo, R. (2010) Electric mobility in France, available at: http://www.finpro.fi/documents/10304/799ceeb6-77e8-483f-8c65-4d388cefbccf, accessed on 20 January 2012.

Cowan, R., and Hultén, S. (1996) Escaping lock-in: The case of the electric vehicle. *Technology Forecasting and Social Change*, 53(1), pp. 61–80.

European Commission (2011) White paper. Roadmap to a single European transport area – Towards a competitive and resource efficient transport system. COM/2011/0144 final, Brussels, available at: http://eur-lex.europa.eu/LexUriServ/LexUriServ.do?uri=CELEX:52011DC0144:EN:NOT

European Environment Agency (2010) Monitoring the CO2 emissions from new passenger cars in the EU: Summary of data for 2010, available at: http://www.eea.europa.eu/data-and-maps/data/co2-cars-emission/monitoring-of-co2-emissions-from-1/monitoring_co2_emissions_from_new_passenger_cars_in_eu27.pdf

Evans (2008) Michelin active wheel system to hit Roads in 2010. *Gizmag*, 2 December, available at: http://www.gizmag.com/michelin-active-wheel-production-electric-car-by-2010/10489/

Fischer, D. (2010) Comparing transitions: Insights from the economic transition processes in former socialist countries for sustainability transitions. *Osteuropa-Wirtschaft*, 55(4), pp. 289–310.

Gao, P., Wang, A., and Wu, A. (2008) China charges up: The electric vehicle opportunity. McKinsey Company, October.

GTAI (Germany Trade and Invest) (2010/11) *The Automotive Industry in Germany*. Issue 2010/2011, available at: http://www.gtai.de/GTAI/Content/EN/Invest/_SharedDocs/Downloads/GTAI/Industry-overviews/industry-overview-automotive-industry.pdf

Guillou, C., Massy-Beresford, H., and Hardcaste, E. (2009) France to launch electric car plant on Thursday, Reuters, 30 September, available at: http://www.reuters.com/article/2009/09/30/electriccars-france-idUSLU28944520090930.

Heilmann, S. (2011) Policy-making through experimentation: The formation of a distinctive policy process, in: S. Heilmann and E.J. Perry (Hrsg.) (eds) *Mao's Invisible Hand – The political foundations of adaptive governance in China* (Cambridge and London: Harvard University Asia Center), pp. 62–101.

Invest in Germany (2008) The automotive industry in Germany: Driving performance through technology. Berlin.

IPCC (2007) Climate change 2007: Synthesis report. 4th Assessment report of the intergovernmental panel on climate change. IPCC, Geneva.

Jullien, B. (2010) Wie krisenanfällig ist die Automobilindustrie Eine Analyse am Beispiel des französischen Automobilmarkts. DGAPanalyse, April 2010, N° 2.

Kaiser, O.S., Meyer, S., and Schippl, J. (2011) Elektromobilität. ITA-Kurzstudie. VDI Technologie-zentrum, Düsseldorf.

Lan, X. (2011) Gaining green ground. *Beijing Review*, November 10, 2011, 28–31.

Liu, W. (2010) Exposing the new energy plan: More than half of central financial support goes to private cars (Xin nengyuan guihua baoguang, guoban zhongyang zhuanxiang zijin butie sijia che), available at: http://auto.163.com

Mahindra REVA (2012) Official Website of Mahindra Reva, available at: http://www.petrolfreeworld.com/

McKinsey (2009) Pathways to a low-carbon economy. Version 2 of the global greenhouse gas abatement cost curve. McKinsey and Company.

McKinsey Global Institute (2007) The 'bird of gold': The rise of India's consumer market. McKinsey and Company.

Ministère de l'Ècologie (2009) Dossier de presse: Lancement du plan national pour le développement des véhicules électriques et hybrids rechargeables. Ministère de l'Ècologie, de l'Énergie, du Développement Durable et de la Mer.

MOST (2011) 12th national five year plan for science and technology development. Ministry of Science &Technology plan announcement (2011) #270, Beijing 4.7.2011, available at: http://www.most.gov.cn

Narayanan, K. (1997) Technology acquisition, deregulation and competitiveness: A study of Indian automobile industry. *Discussion Paper Series # 9703*, United Nations University, INTECH Institute for New Technologies.

NPE (2011) Zweiter Bericht der Nationalen Plattform Elektromobilität. Nationale Plattform Elektromobilität, Bonn.

OECD (2011a) Better policies to support eco-innovation. OECD Studies on Environmental Innovation, OECD Publishing.

OECD (2011b) Fostering innovation for green growth. OECD Green Growth Studies, OECD Publishing.

OICA (2010) Production statistics, available at: http://oica.net/category/production-statistics/

OICA (2012) Economic contributions, available at:http://oica.net/category/economic-contributions/

ÓNeill, J., Lawson, S., and Purushothaman, R. (2004) The BRICs and global markets: Crude, cars and capital. Goldman Sachs (2004). *Global Economics Paper*, No. 118, 14 October 2004.

Pasvantis (2011a) Indiens Automobilbranche bietet großes Potential, Germany Trade & Invest, available at: http://www.gtai.de/GTAI/Navigation/DE/Trade/maerkte,did=251182.html

Pasvantis (2011b) Indiens Markt für Elektrofahrzeuge gewinnt an Tempo, Germany Trade & Invest, available at: http://www.gtai.de/GTAI/Navigation/DE/Trade/maerkte,did=77766.html

Pérez, C. (2004) Technological revolutions, paradigm shifts and socio-institutional change, in: E. Reinert (ed.) *Globalization, Economic Development and Inequality: An alternative perspective* (Cheltenham and Northampton), pp. 217–242.

Présidence de la République (2009) Pacte automobile. Dossier de presse, Palais de l'Elysée, Paris, Lundi 9 février 2009.

Sankey, P., Clark, D., and Micheloto, S. (2010) The end of the oil age 2011 and beyond: A reality check. Deutsche Bank Global Markets Research, available at: http://bioage.typepad.com/files/1223fm-05.pdf

SIAM (2012a) Society of Indian automobile manufacturers, industry statistics: Production trends, available at: http://www.siamindia.com/scripts/production-trend.aspx

SIAM (2012b) Society of Indian automobile manufacturers, industry statistics: Gross turnover, available at: http://www.siamindia.com/scripts/gross-turnover.aspx

SIAM (2012c) Society of Indian automobile manufacturers, profile: President, available at: http://www.siamindia.com/scripts/president.aspx

Shukla (2012) Budget 2012–2013: Electric, hybrid cars to get boost. *India Today*, 12 January, available at: http://indiatoday.intoday.in/story/budget-2012-2013-electric-hybrid-cars-to-get-boost/1/168393.html

Smith, K. (2009) Climate change and radical energy innovation: The policy issues, *TIK Working Papers on Innovation Studies, No. 20090101*, Oslo.

The Climate Group (2011) China's clean revolution IV – Financing China's low carbon growth. Beijing.

UNIDO (2003) The global automotive industry value chain: What prospects for upgrading by developing countries. *Sectoral Studies Series*, United Nations Industrial Development Organization, available at: http://www.unido.org/fileadmin/media/documents/pdf/Services_Modules/Automotive_Industry.pdf

VDA (Verband der Automobilindustrie) (2011) Annual report, available at: http://www.vda.de/en/publikationen/jahresberichte/

Visier, A., and Pasvantis, V. (2010) Indiens Markt für Elektrofahrzeuge soll Fahrt aufnehmen, Germany Trade & Invest, available at: http://www.gtai.de/GTAI/Navigation/DE/Trade/maerkte,did=68432.html?view=renderPrint

Wang, H., and Kimble, C. (2011) Leapfrogging to electric vehicles: Patterns and scenarios for China's automobile industry. *International Journal Automotive Technology and Management*, 11(4), pp. 312–325.

World Bank, PRTM Management Consultants (2011) The China new energy vehicles program – Challenges and opportunities, Beijing 2011, available at: http://www.prtm.com/uploadedFiles/Thought_Leadership/Articles/External_Articles/The_China_New_Energy_Vehicles_Program_.pdf

Wu, Q. (2010) Comments on draft for comment of the 'Development plan for the energy efficient and new energy car industry (2011–2020)'. Dongfeng Qichewang, 30.08.2010, available at: http://mag.oauto.com/news/html/5959.html

Zhang, L. (2011) 2013 could bring the opportunity for commercialization of EVs in China (2013 nian, diandong qiche huo ken zai woguo yinglai shichanghua de jiyu). TX Investment Consulting Co.Ltd, Beijing.

Different routes to technology acquisition and innovation system building? China's and India's wind turbine industries

Rainer Walz[a] and Jonathan Nowak Delgado[b]

[a]Competence Center Sustainability and Infrastructure Systems, Fraunhofer Institute for Systems and Innovation Research, Karlsruhe, Germany; [b]Virtual Consulting International, New York, Hongkong, Perth, Johannesburg

Shaping economic development to be environmentally compatible is becoming increasingly urgent. The wind turbine industry has been successfully developed as a domestic industry in both China and India. Important success factors here are policies to facilitate learning and integrated environmental, technological and industrial policy schemes. There are clear differences between the countries, e.g. with regard to the importance of electric utilities, the international focus of the main players and the level of industrial policies to support domestic suppliers. There is not just 'one successful way' of developing a domestic wind turbine industry: India has taken a more market driven approach compared to China, where the development is more government induced and is taking place even more rapidly.

Introduction

In newly industrialising countries (NICs) sustainability innovations are becoming increasingly urgent from a global perspective. NICs have made significant economic progress in the last years, but they are still facing the challenge of having to upgrade their energy infrastructure. An important question is whether they are ready to integrate sustainability technologies into their economic development. Recently there has been a strong increase in the diffusion of clean energy technologies in countries such as China and India (Pew Environment Group 2011). Some NICs have also started to develop a domestic supply industry. This opens up the question of how the respective innovation system is working, and what strategies, e.g. with regard to technology acquisition and policy support, are best suited to such a development.

This paper takes up these questions in a case study of the wind energy industry development in China and India. It describes the results of an innovation system analysis of this technology in each country. In addition to analysing how the respective innovation system is operating in each country, the aim is to find out what role those factors play, which are known to be important for the innovation systems for renewable energy technologies in OECD countries. Furthermore, aspects which relate to the development of an innovation system are important, such as the strategy used to acquire knowledge. Finally, it will be interesting to see how diverse the experience has been between the countries, and whether we can identify more than one possible route to the successful build-up of a domestic wind turbine industry in a newly industrialising country.

The paper starts with conceptual issues: The prerequisites for sustainability innovation are presented, and the methodology of the bottom-up case studies and general development of the wind turbine industry are addressed. This is followed by chapters on the wind innovation systems in China and India, respectively. Finally, the results are discussed and conclusions are drawn.

Conceptual and empirical state-of-the-art and methodology

Prerequisites for sustainability innovations in newly industrialising countries

In the past, green technologies have been developed and supplied mainly by OECD countries. NICs have to develop their competences in order to be able to absorb green technologies. They are more likely to move towards green technologies if this is not only supported by environmental concerns, but also opens up the economic perspective of contributing to industrial development (Walz and Marscheider-Weidemann, 2011).

The first aspect addresses the long-standing debate on absorptive capacities and competence building. Competence building has to take into account the changing conditions for learning and knowledge acquisition. One aspect to consider is the growing tendency for technological and production capabilities to be developed separately (Bell and Pavitt, 1993). Another aspect relates to the effect of globalisation on the mechanisms for knowledge dissemination. Archibugi and Pietrobelli (2003) stressed the point that importing technology per se has little impact on learning and called for policies to upgrade cooperation strategies in the direction of technological partnering. Nelson (2007) highlighted the changing legal environment and the fact that the scientific and technical communities have moved much closer together. All these factors lead to the conclusion that indigenous competences in science and technology fields related to green technologies are increasingly a prerequisite for the successful absorption of green technologies in NICs.

The debate on the economic interest of NICs in the environment often refers to the pollution haven hypothesis and the resulting disincentive for strong environmental policies in NICs in order to attract pollution-intensive industries (Copeland and Taylor, 2004). However, there are also economic incentives for NICs to push environmental technologies. Many green technologies are related to infrastructure so they have the potential to contribute to modernisation e.g. in the energy, water or transport sectors. Furthermore, the movement towards environmental sustainability will create huge international markets for these green technologies. Thus, another incentive for NICs to engage in the development and production of these technologies is that they can then compete for a leading role in supplying the world market with sustainability technologies. Various factors have to be taken into account when assessing a country's potential to realise such an export potential, such as demand side factors, regulation and the level of technological capabilities (Walz, 2006 and 2010).

In summary, it is argued that green technologies are important for NICs for environmental reasons and infrastructure build-up on the one hand and, on the other, because they offer an industrial development opportunity. It is increasingly acknowledged that the absorption of developed technologies and developing the abilities to further advance them and to bring them to international markets are closely interwoven (Nelson, 2007). Thus, for both strategies – absorption of technology and establishing domestic suppliers able to compete on international markets – it is necessary to have an innovation system which can provide the necessary competences.

Innovation system research

The heuristics of systems of innovation has been developed for national, sectoral and technological systems (see e.g. Lundvall et al., 2002; Edquist, 2005; Malerba, 2005; Carlsson et al., 2002).

The innovation system concept also has great potential to analyse sustainability-oriented innovation systems. Innovations in such systems are typically more influenced by public needs and public discourse than 'traditional' sectoral or technological innovation systems, and are subject to various specificities (Markard, 2011). Regulation must address environmental externalities, and long time horizons of sunk costs into infrastructure, supported by traditional economic sector regulation, leads to a triple regulatory challenge (Walz, 2007). From a methodological point of view, this results in the need to adapt the systems of innovation approach towards sustainability oriented innovation systems (Altenburg and Pegels, 2012).

The majority of applications of technological systems of innovation on green innovations so far have been in the renewable energy field (e.g. Bergek and Jacobsson, 2003; Agterbosch et al., 2004; Foxon et al., 2005; Walz, 2007; Bergek et al., 2008a; Suurs and Hekkert, 2009; Dantas, 2011; Mohamad, 2011). The empirical evidence suggests a strong impact of policy on innovations in renewable energy technologies for power generation. Both public R&D spending as well as policies which induce domestic demand increase the innovation activities. Likewise, policy factors such as introducing targets for renewable energy and providing stable policy support lead to higher innovation output. There is also empirical evidence that success on international markets seems to foster further innovations.

It has been suggested that a technological innovation system can be analysed by looking at how the different functions it is supposed to carry out are fulfilled (Bergek and Jacobsson, 2003; Hekkert et al., 2007; Bergek et al., 2008 a, b; Hekkert and Negro, 2009; Suurs and Hekkert, 2009). Abstracting from differences in wording, the following categories of an innovation system's functions can be distinguished:

- *creation and development of knowledge*;
- *knowledge diffusion* through exchanging information in networks, but also along the value chain (including supplier-user interaction);
- *guidance of search*, that is directing R&D and searching for new solutions with respect to technology and market;
- *legitimacy* of a new technology, which is closely connected with recognising a growth potential for the technology and the ability to counteract political resistance;
- facilitation of *market formation*;
- *mobilisation of resources*, which is especially important for new technologies associated with a higher risk of failure; and
- *entrepreneurial experimentation*, leading to diversity and a variety of solutions in order to allow for a sufficiently large stock of technologies enabling the selection process to result in a dominant design.

These functions are not disjunctive. Bergek et al. (2008c) point out that the mechanisms and interactions of the actors of an innovation system, and the feedback loops between the different functions, need to be taken into account to properly understand the innovation process (Bergek et al., 2008c). These feedback mechanisms can induce an increase in innovations but also block further development (Bergek et al., 2008b; Hekkert and Negro, 2009). It is within these dynamic relationships that the development of an innovation system takes place.

Research concept

The research concept follows a technological innovation system approach (Figure 1). The empirical development of the wind turbine industry provides the background for the development which has been taking place in the analysed countries. Analysing the wind turbine innovation systems in

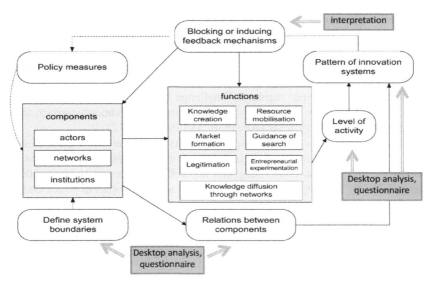

Figure 1.   Scheme of technological innovation system analysis performed for China and India.
Source: adapted from Bergek et al. 2008c

China and India started with a desktop analysis. Statistics and publications on the energy system and the wind turbine industry were used to delineate the innovation system. This research was complemented by a patent analysis for the wind turbine industry. The patent analysis followed the transnational patent approach described in Frietsch and Schmoch (2010). Various indicators were calculated such as patent shares, but also specialisation profiles. Grupp's definition was used (1998) for the Relative Patent Advantage (RPA). For every country i and every technology field j the Relative Patent Activity (RPA) is calculated according to:

$$RPA_{ij} = 100 * \tanh \ \text{In} \left[(p_{ij} / \sum_i p_{ij}) / (\sum_{ij} p_{ij}) \right]$$

Very often the Revealed Comparative Advantage (RCA) is used for measuring specialisation in trade. However, it can be misleading for indicating related technological capabilities, if the imports are restricted by protectionist policies. Therefore we use the relative export activity (RXA). It is calculated in a similar way as the RPA, by substituting patents (p) by exports (x). All specialisation indicators are normalised between +100 and −100 (see Grupp, 1998). Positive values indicate an above average specialisation in wind turbines; a negative value shows that the country is more specialised in other technologies.

The use of such indicators must be accompanied by careful interpretation and additional analysis of the links between the actors in the innovation system, their interactions with the numerous institutions, and the nature of the learning processes taking place. Therefore, the heuristics of a technological innovation system was used to develop a detailed questionnaire, which was conducted among experts in wind energy development and industry in China and India. This questionnaire contained about 100 questions, which were grouped under the headings of competences and level of experimentation in wind energy and turbine manufacturing, governmental policies and regulations for supporting both the diffusion and manufacturing of wind turbines, channels of access to (foreign) knowledge, assessment of competences in various subfields of wind turbines, linkages with and knowledge spillovers from complementary sectors, and framework conditions with regard to legitimacy and financing and interaction in networks. Based on the results from the questionnaire, the components and the performance of the innovation system, but also the communication patterns and the performance of the various innovation functions were analysed. The questionnaire was conducted with support from local partners from the Chinese Academy of Sciences Institute of Policy and Management (CAS-IPM, China) and The Energy and Resources Institute (TERI, India). The questionnaire formed the basis for 10 interviews with experts in each country, which took place between October 2009 and January 2010. The experts were assured strict confidentiality. They were identified by the local partners as representing the relevant policy arena, the wind power industry, manufacturing and research. The results of the interviews and the desktop analysis were then interpreted. The interpretation results were discussed with renewable energy experts in India and China, and were also presented and discussed at conferences such as the 9th Annual GLOBELICS Conference 2010 and the 11th Biennial Conference of International Society for Ecological Economics (ISEE) 2010.

Empirical background of the development of the wind turbine industry

Most renewable energy technologies are closely related to the electrical and non-electrical machinery industry, which has been classified by the OECD as medium-high tech (Hatzichronoglou, 1997; Grupp, 1998). Wind turbine manufacturing is not a mass industrial process to the same extent as PV production and application of tacit knowledge makes technology transfer more difficult (McInerney, 2011). Comparing wind turbine patent development with all patents indicates rather high innovation dynamics. Renewable energy technologies show very strong dynamics, much stronger than the average patent dynamics (Figure 2). Of the various renewable energy technologies, wind energy has experienced even stronger dynamics in recent years, even above photovoltaics. This supports the analysis made by sector consultants which sees new generations of turbines in the pipeline (Roland Berger, 2011). Thus, new market entrants from NICs cannot count on the future market for wind turbines being driven solely by the cost competition of the existing technologies. This all underlines the necessity to develop a strong innovation system in order to become internationally successful.

Figure 3 demonstrates the enormous growth in the wind turbine industry over the last 15 years. Currently, there are about 200 GW of wind turbines installed globally. This growth has been driven by the German market in the early 2000s, followed by expansion in Spain and other European countries. Since the mid-2000s, the US, China and India have become important markets, too.

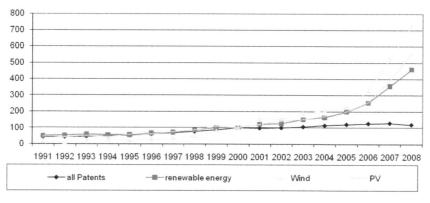

Figure 2. Patent dynamics for green technologies (2000 = 100).
Source: calculations of Fraunhofer ISI.

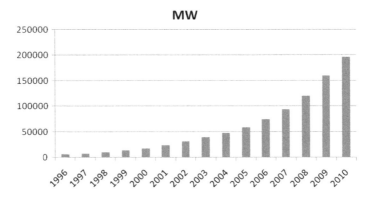

Figure 3.   Development of accumulated installed wind energy capacity.
Source: data from Global Wind Energy Council and World Wind Energy Association.

The wind turbine industry developed around many newcomers in the field, which started as small companies. The industry has become more mature since then Some of the early pioneers have grown into medium sized companies. There have been mergers between these pioneers and some of them have been taken over by more established players, such as General Electric and Siemens. Today, many of the leading companies operate international subsidiaries or are involved in joint ventures, and newcomers from China and India have been joining the playing field. The industry has become more international in its focus. According to UN-COMTRADE data, world exports of wind turbines grew from less than USD 400 million in 1996 to USD 1 billion in 2000 and around USD 5 billion in 2008.

Thus, the wind turbine industry has left its niche to become a very dynamic industry. Globalisation is a major factor within the industry, as is the emergence of China and India as major markets and important suppliers. This raises the question of how new players China and India have managed to become a successful part of this dynamic industry.

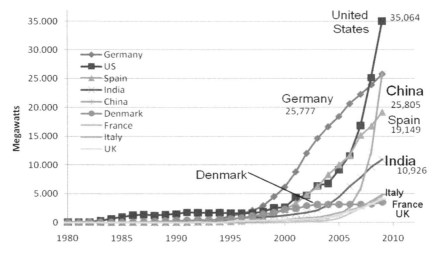

Figure 4.   Accumulated installed wind power capacity in the top nine countries between 1980 and 2009.
Source: data from Global Wind Energy Council and World Wind Energy Association.

Innovation system for wind energy in China

Performance of wind turbine industry

Wind energy technologies have been successfully integrated into the economic catching-up processes taking place in China, in particular since 2006. China has taken the development path of a fast follower within a period as short as five years. Wind technology has been diffusing through China at a rapid pace and has expanded with a cumulated average growth rate of more than 100% over the last four years. In terms of cumulative wind energy installations, China has taken the global lead by 2011, surpassing the USA.

This diffusion has been accompanied by a steady increase in the average size of installed turbine (Figure 5). The number of international patents in China has risen rapidly (Figure 6). Between 2004 und 2008, China accounted for about 4% of transnational patents. The revealed patent advantage (RPA) amounts to 47. Thus, compared to other sectors, China has been specialising very significantly in building up knowledge in the wind turbine sector. However, the overall number of wind turbine related patents is still much lower than the leading countries such as Germany, the US and Denmark. This gap is underlined by a look at the trade data, which show that China is not yet a significant exporter of wind turbines. The RXA shows a value of -71 for 2008.

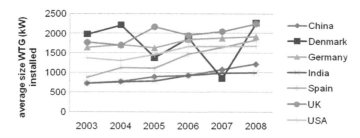

Figure 5.   Average size of newly installed wind turbines in various countries.
Source: Data from BTM Consult ApS, 2009.

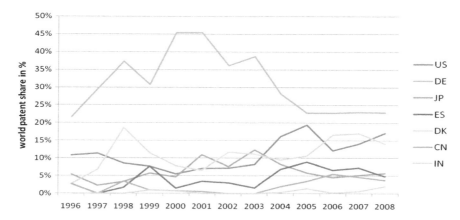

Figure 6.   Annual world patent shares in wind turbine technology between 1996 and 2008.
Source: calculation by Fraunhofer ISI.

Driving forces of development

Wind resources in China are abundant and the estimated exploitable onshore potential lies between 600 and 1400 GW. The driving forces for China's involvement in wind power are threefold:

- Driver 1: Energy security through technology leapfrogging
  Electricity consumption has increased rapidly (on average by 10% yearly), forcing China to make sure that its emerging economy has a guaranteed power supply. Power generation capacity is expected to double by 2020 (IANS, 2006). At the same time energy independence has political priority as well. The Chinese government aims to diversify its energy supply and minimise the oil-price risk. Renewable energy sources and wind in particular have been identified as a way of doing so.
- Driver 2: Environmental benefits
  Environmental pressure on China is growing as it is the world's biggest CO_2 polluter, emitting 6.1 billion metric tons of energy-related CO_2 in 2007, 55% of which are attributed to power generation (IEA/OECD, 2009). The costs associated with accelerated climate change are staggering. Furthermore, there are other effects: Sixteen of the world's twenty most polluted cities are located in China and at least 400,000 deaths occur each year in China due to pollution-related diseases (World Bank, 2008). The power sector has been identified as a key sector for emission reductions. After hydro, which generates about 16% of China's electricity needs, wind is the most promising source of clean energy.
- Driver 3: Economic and social potentials
  Chinese governmental agencies have identified the wind energy sector as a strategic economic growth sector (Wen et al., 2008). The Chinese wind market alone will see investments of USD 91.1 billion over the next 10 years (WPM, 2009). This anticipated market demand provides great potential for domestic supply chain developments and job creation. As most Chinese wind resources are situated in the country's northwest, it is hoped that wind energy development will contribute to this region catching up economically.

Structure of the innovation system

Actors and networks

China's wind energy innovation system has been developing very strongly along the value chain (Figure 7). A comprehensive supply chain has developed. The five state-owned electric utilities, also called the 'Big Five', dominate the wind farm market and are the major buyers of wind turbines made in China. They obtained the concessions for large scale wind farm developments planned by the government throughout the country. These Wind Power Base projects make up the majority of the new installations.

While both domestic and foreign owned wind energy equipment suppliers have production facilities in China, it has become increasingly difficult for foreign players to be successful on the Chinese market. This is attributed to the government's protectionist stance towards domestic suppliers (Zhang et al., 2009). In 2009 some 77% of the market was served by Chinese suppliers. Today, the first tier of domestic suppliers is led by Sinovel, Goldwind and Dongfang Electric, followed by the two foreign owned companies Gamesa and Vestas. The rest is comprised of a second and third tier of domestic suppliers and the residual subsidiaries of foreign-owned companies.

A closer look at the first tier reveals the following strategies and development path of the leading Chinese manufacturers of wind turbines. All of them started to develop their manufacturing through technology transfer (Zhang et al., 2009):

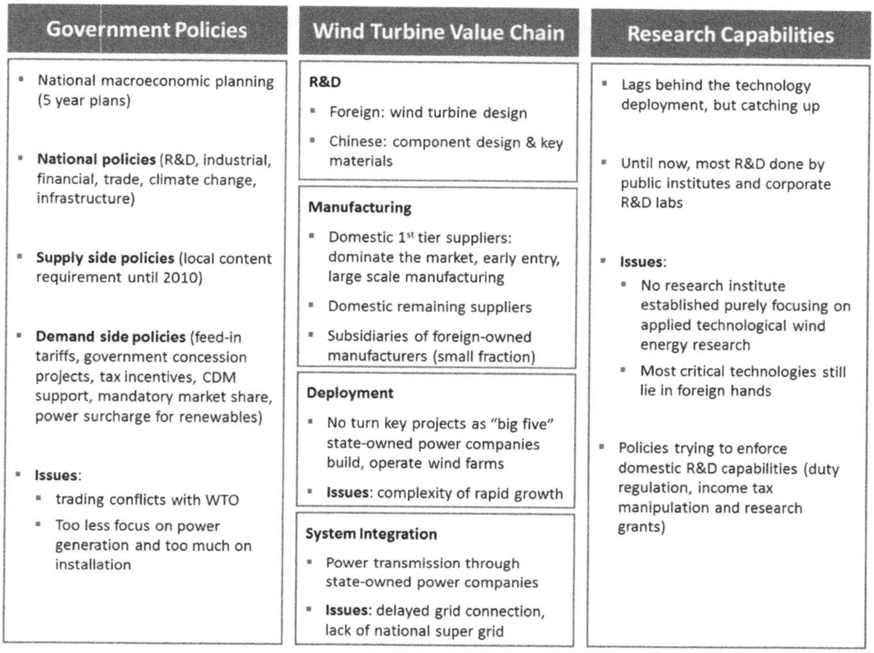

Government Policies	Wind Turbine Value Chain	Research Capabilities
• National macroeconomic planning (5 year plans)	**R&D** • Foreign: wind turbine design • Chinese: component design & key materials	• Lags behind the technology deployment, but catching up
• **National policies** (R&D, industrial, financial, trade, climate change, infrastructure)	**Manufacturing** • Domestic 1st tier suppliers: dominate the market, early entry, large scale manufacturing	• Until now, most R&D done by public institutes and corporate R&D labs
• **Supply side policies** (local content requirement until 2010)	• Domestic remaining suppliers	• **Issues:** • No research institute established purely focusing on applied technological wind energy research
• **Demand side policies** (feed-in tariffs, government concession projects, tax incentives, CDM support, mandatory market share, power surcharge for renewables)	• Subsidiaries of foreign-owned manufacturers (small fraction) **Deployment** • No turn key projects as "big five" state-owned power companies build, operate wind farms	• Most critical technologies still lie in foreign hands
• **Issues:** • trading conflicts with WTO • Too less focus on power generation and too much on installation	• **Issues:** complexity of rapid growth **System Integration** • Power transmission through state-owned power companies • **Issues:** delayed grid connection, lack of national super grid	• Policies trying to enforce domestic R&D capabilities (duty regulation, income tax manipulation and research grants)

Figure 7. Scheme of wind energy innovation system in China.
Source: Authors, based on literature review and expert interviews.

- Xinjiang Goldwind Science and Technology Company Limited (Goldwind) is a subsidiary of the Xinjiang Wind Energy Company (XWEC) and was established in 1998. Its parent organisation, Xinjiang Wind Energy Research Institute (XWERI), a research-oriented industrial group, was founded 10 years before in 1988. Substantial support was provided by foreign government programmes for the first wind-related research and piloting activities of the group (XWERI, 2010). The state holds the majority ownership (55%), the rest is under Chinese ownership (Lewis, 2007). Goldwind has secured high control over its supply chain. Technological capabilities have been acquired through licence agreements with various German companies (Jacobs, Repower, Vensys Energiesysteme GmbH). Following the emergence of a Chinese supplier network for wind turbine components over the last decade, Goldwind has been able to continuously increase the local content in its turbines (Lewis, 2007). In early 2008, Goldwind acquired 70% of Vensys, intensifying its already close collaboration on large-scale direct drive turbines.
- The market share of Sinovel in China amounted to 22.1%. Sinovel was founded in 2004 as a spin-off of the giant Dalian Heavy Industry. It took the chance to enter the market by securing a production licence for 1.5 MW turbines from the German company Fuhrlaender. In line with the market's trend towards larger turbines and the prospects of China's offshore potentials, Sinovel has added a 3 MW turbine to its portfolio, which has been developed together with the US company AMSC Windtec. Moreover, a 5 MW turbine is also underway (WPM, 2008). Sinovel wanted to tackle quality and reliability issues from the outset and contracted the German company Germanischer Lloyd for certification of its turbines.
- Dongfang has succeeded in winning large-scale government orders. Dongfang was established as a strategic diversification of one of the world's largest power generation

equipment manufacturers, Dongfang Electric Corporation, and is based in the southwest Sichuan province of China (Wen et al., 2008). Dongfang's product portfolio includes a 1.5 MW turbine (production licence from REpower) and a 2.5 MW turbine (joint development with German Aerodyn). Dongfang will own the intellectual property rights for the latter.

In China, most wind energy projects are not set up on a turnkey basis. The wind turbine manufacturers themselves only focus on manufacturing the wind turbines to the customer's requirements. Project developers then build and run the wind power plants. The experts in our questionnaire pointed to the fact that wind operators in China are mostly big corporations owned by the state. The 10 most active project developers in China are all state-owned and represent more than 75% of installed capacity (Recknagel, 2008; Meyer, 2009). The residual capacity is covered by more than 180 companies, only a few of them being privately held (domestic or foreign).

Regulation as the most important part of institutions

The main governmental agencies in charge of renewable energy policies are the National Development and Reform Commission (NDRC) and its Energy Bureau, the National Energy Commission. Early key actions include the power sector reform in 2002, which aimed to facilitate access to the grid for renewable energy generation (Cherni and Kentish, 2007). China has clear targets for and a political commitment to renewable energy sources and wind, and major progress was made in 2006 when the Renewable Energy Law took effect (Figure 8). This law created a more stable and long-term perspective for renewable energy (see Zhang et al., 2009; Wang et al., 2010; Yu and Zeng, 2011). The features of Chinese regulation and policies can be grouped into policies affecting the supply and demand side.

On the supply side, wind energy research has been an important focus of China's three key programmes: the national basic research programme (973 Program), the national high-tech R&D programme (863 Program) as well as the national key technology R&D programme (Zhang et al., 2009). However, so far, no research institute has been established which focuses purely on applied technological wind energy research.

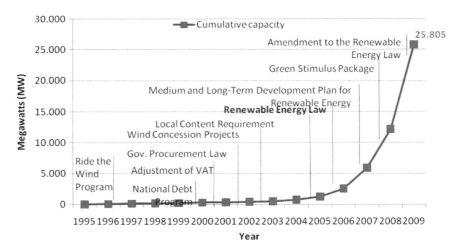

Figure 8. Development of wind energy policies in China.
Source: Authors, based on literature review and data from Global Wind Energy Council.

The Ride the Wind Program required for the first time locally made components (40% of the total value) and effectively introduced the wind turbine manufacturing technology into China (Changliang and Zhangfeng, 2009). During the Wind Concession period from 2003 to 2007 it was then mandated to source at least 70% of the total value from domestic manufacturers (Zhang et al., 2009). The local content requirement has been a very direct way to support the formation of a domestic wind energy industry (Lewis and Wiser, 2007). The local content requirement was officially abolished in December 2009. However, whether this will facilitate access to the mega base projects for foreign players remains unclear. In any case, the local content requirement seems to have accomplished what it was designed for: the creation of a strong domestic wind energy supply chain large enough to cope with China's rising demand for wind turbines.

There are also more indirect forms of supporting the build-up of a domestic wind turbine industry. One of them is procurement. In 2006, three Chinese ministries jointly released the Provisional Measures for the Accreditation of National Indigenous Innovation Products (NIIP). These establish a procedure under which products made with 'indigenous' (e.g. Chinese) intellectual property can qualify for 'priority' in government procurement. Because it is proving very difficult for foreign enterprises to qualify for 'indigenous' status under this programme, the measure effectively leads to procurement preferences favouring domestic renewables equipment manufacturers. Furthermore, the Ministry of Finance issued a regulation on import tax and customs duty exemption for wind turbine components. Only wind turbines with a capacity larger than 2.5 MW as well as some stand-alone key components (converters, bearings, controls) are eligible. The goal is to ease the supply bottleneck for components which are not yet produced in China.

The use of technical standards is also an important instrument which can be used to foster home industries. There are a number of internationally recognised standards in the field of renewable energy (e.g. issued by the International Organization for Standardization (ISO) or the International Electrotechnical Commission (IEC)). As many countries such as Germany and the United States have done, China released also its own technical standards. Such standards are typically scrutinised whether or not they hinder international trade, and are often subject to WTO disputes. Another WTO related dispute involving wind energy has been resolved after the United States challenged the Special Fund for Wind Power Equipment Manufacturing (Special Fund) as WTO prohibited subsidies.

The main policies on the demand side are associated with the Renewable Energy Law, which was enacted in 2006, and the Medium and Long-Term Development Plan for Renewable Energy, which was released by NDRC in 2007. The Renewable Energy Act established a framework under which utilities should be required to pay the full price for electricity generated by renewable energy sources, while offering consumers of renewables-generated electricity discounted rates (Cherni and Kentish, 2007). It was amended in 2009 to require utilities to purchase all the renewable power generated in China. This measure has encouraged entry into the renewable energy generation business and increased the demand for renewable power equipment.

The Medium and Long-Term Development Plan for Renewable Energy in China from 2007 called for a medium target of 100 GW installed capacity in 2020 (Yu and Zheng, 2011). It required power companies which owned installed capacity of more than 5 GW to have non-hydro renewable energy installed power capacity accounting for 3% of total capacity by 2010 and 8% by 2020. This measure has triggered a surge of investment in wind energy, reflecting the fact that wind power equipment is less costly to install and operate than solar and biomass alternatives. In March 2011, the Chinese government updated the targets and called for a medium target for 2020 of 180 GW installed capacity (Yu and Zheng, 2011).

International climate change collaboration also contributed to the success of wind turbine development. By September 2009, the clean development mechanism (CDM) pipeline encompassed around 387 wind projects representing 21.6 GW of capacity (WPM, 2009). Over 90% of the smaller wind projects in China have applied or are applying to become CDM registered projects. The income provided by the certified emission reductions amounts to 10% to 15% of a wind project's total income. Thus, especially in this segment of the market, CDM has been of high importance in contributing to the surge in wind power diffusion (Zhang et al., 2009; Bodas Freita et al., 2011).

Functioning of the innovation system

Based on the results from our questionnaire, the performance of the innovation functions can be summarised as follows:

- Knowledge development is being driven by incentives such as the R&D subsidies and corporate R&D efforts, and innovation pressure such as fierce price competition and the need to improve turbine performance.
- Knowledge diffusion has been best served by a twentyfold increase in wind power over the last four years. Clearly, the Wind Mega Bases were driving this growth and the supply side policies were channelling a lot of this demand towards domestic suppliers.
- Legitimacy has gained momentum due to the framework regulation of the Renewable Energy Law in 2006 and the targets for renewable energy. The success in building a domestic turbine industry, and the increase in the targets, have reinforced the legitimacy of the technology furthermore.
- Guidance of search was not as well served as it could be. The legitimacy enforced by policies often lacked sufficient implementation. The need to improve the grid was not sufficiently communicated in the actions, supported by the early focus of the demand regulation on installed capacity instead of electricity fed into the grid. Moreover, the sheer success and speed in market growth, which was achieved by the big state owned electric utilities, also had its downside. The Chinese manufacturers were not forced to look into new business models, such as turnkey projects, and the tremendous demand pushed quality concerns somewhat in the background.
- Market formation is extremely strong, as the onshore market is moving towards a mass market in the face of a 100+ GW project pipeline. However, high potential niche markets (offshore, decentralised solutions) still have to be explored.
- Entrepreneurial activity is high, with a value chain clearly dominated by domestic players. China's wind power equipment supply chain is growing and expected to become the largest in terms of output in the near future.
- The resource supply situation has improved for some resource categories (financial resources, site resources, industrial resources), while for others there are still obstacles on the path to professional industrialisation (human resources and infrastructural resources).

To sum up the experience, the main force has been the strong political commitment to renewable energy. The large projects implemented to follow the targets led to increasing demand, which fostered entrepreneurial activity. Positive feedback loops have been established with knowledge development, entrepreneurial experimentation and market formation reinforcing each other. The regulatory mechanisms have successfully contributed to the emerging of a massive wind turbine and component supply chain. Target setting and massive market formation increased the legitimacy of this technology. The large electric utilities were picking up the targets and were installing capacity very quickly. However, to maintain this in the future, action needs to be taken today, by both policy and (state-owned) corporations. Based on the results of the expert questionnaire, the following challenges and barriers have been identified in China:

- integration of large-scale wind power supply into the grid without reducing quality and functionality of the electricity system; which requires investments on the one hand, but also improved grid management with regard to fluctuating wind power supply on the other;
- lagging behind in developing technology innovations and adapting wind turbines to national conditions through indigenous R&D;
- lack of technical standards, testing activities and certifications;
- lack of operational and managerial experience with wind farm management, including maintenance; and
- overcapacities in the Chinese wind energy equipment market. This refers to the numerous companies starting to enter the equipment market with sometimes very little experience and low quality products aiming to win on their low cost production.

Some of the challenges relate to quality problems, which lower the full load hours per year. Furthermore, various reports are complaining about problems in connecting all the new capacity to the grid (Zhang, et al., 2009; Yu and Zheng, 2011). These problems seem to be connected to a policy which was focusing on wind capacity installation instead of wind power generation, and to an institutional structure, in which large state-owned utilities, which are less subject to direct market pressure than small IPPs, are the main investors. Furthermore, this incentive system also seems to be consistent with manufactures putting less emphasis on testing and quality checks relative to a quick increase in output of wind turbines. With Chinese manufactures still focusing on the domestic market, there was also no need to fulfil the quality standards of international customers. Finally, even if foreign licenses are taken, it takes more time to build tacit knowledge, which is necessary to come up with a high level of quality. Thus, some of the quality problems also seem to be related to the rapid speed with which the development of the wind turbine industry was taking place.

However, the Chinese innovation system is in a process of further development: With the Amendment to the Renewable Energy Law in December 2009, a major step towards a generation-based performance metric was undertaken. It remains to be seen what the effect of this change on the challenges ahead will be. Furthermore, Sinovel and Goldwind are putting forward plans to develop larger turbines (Roland Berger, 2011). This would bring them closer towards developing cutting edge innovations and could also make Chinese companies more competitive on international markets and on the markets for offshore wind farms.

Wind turbine industry development in India

Performance of wind turbine industry

India took the development path of a fast follower. Wind technology is diffusing rapidly and has grown by 28% each year over the last decade. This catch-up is expected to continue at a rapid pace in the future. As illustrated in Figure 4, India's installed wind capacity ranks fifth globally, after the US, Germany, China and Spain. However, capacity is still very unevenly distributed within the country: some 44% of Indian wind installations are located in the southern state of Tamil Nadu. Nevertheless, other states are starting to catch up, setting ambitious goals as well as policy support mechanisms. Clearly, future wind energy will be installed in high potential, low penetration states, such as Gujarat, Karnataka, Rajasthan, or Andhra Pradesh.

The average size of installed turbines has been increasing steadily. However, there is still a considerable gap between India and the leading countries (Figure 5). The number of patents is still very limited. Furthermore, patent numbers and also the specialisation profile fluctuate strongly, which indicates a rather volatile basis for patenting new knowledge. India reached a 1% share of world wind turbine patents between 2006 and 2008. On the other hand, India has already experienced significant success in exporting wind turbines. Based on UN-COMTRADE data, India held more than 8% of world exports in wind turbines in the late 2000s. Clearly, India shows extreme positive specialisation in exporting wind turbines: the Relative Export Advantage (RXA) was 97 in 2007, which makes this technology a very remarkable example of India's export success.

Driving forces of development

Wind resources in India are abundant and the estimated exploitable onshore potential lies between 48 and 100 GW. The driving forces for India's involvement in wind power are threefold: energy security, environmental pressure, and socio-economic potentials:

- Driver 1: Energy security
  India needs a secure power supply: The power generation capacity of 147 GW installed in 2006 is expected to grow sixfold by 2030 (IANS, 2006). At the same time energy independence and diversification of supply has political priority as well. Renewable energy sources and wind in particular have been identified as one way of doing so.
- Driver 2: Environmental benefits
  India is emitting 1.3 billion metric tons of CO_2 in 2007, 56% of which can be allocated to power generation (IEA/OECD, 2009). Local air pollution is a major issue. It is estimated that a low-carbon development path could save India some USD 1 billion until 2020 and USD 3 billion until 2030 in local air pollution costs (IEA/OECD, 2009). The power sector has been identified as a key sector for emission reductions. After hydro, which generates about 25% of India's electricity needs, wind is the most promising source of clean energy.
- Driver 3: Economic and social potentials
  The Indian economy has a strong interest in the power generation industry. Some additional USD 550 billion investments in low-carbon power generation will be required between 2010 and 2030 (IEA/OECD, 2009). Investments in the Indian wind power market reached INR 96.3 billion or USD 3.28 billion in 2008 alone and are expected to increase to USD 91.1 billion during the period 2010 to 2020 (WPM 2008). This anticipated market demand holds great potential for domestic supply chain developments and job creation.

Structure of the innovation system

Actors and networks

The wind energy innovation system of India (Figure 9) has developed based on one strong domestic player. At the same time, international players are closely involved in turbine production and, increasingly, in financing. In 99% of all cases, turnkey projects are realised. These turnkey projects have turned wind turbine manufacturers into wind farm operators. The incentive structures have led to many concomitant testing and quality control services being developed.

Both domestic and foreign owned suppliers of wind turbines are present in India. The liberal investment and incentive structure is attracting increasing numbers of foreign players to open production facilities in India. In total, over a dozen companies are manufacturing wind turbines in India and domestic manufacturing capabilities are well established. Besides Suzlon

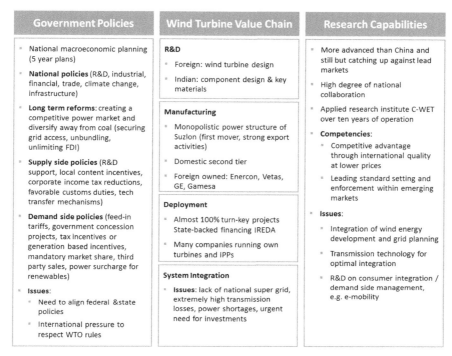

Figure 9.   Scheme of the wind energy innovation system in India.

(69% market share in 2008), which dominates the Indian market, India is served by the domestic RRB Energy Limited (9.6% market share in 2008) as well as a number of smaller players (8.5% market share). Global foreign suppliers that have set up production facilities in India (still) supply only a fraction of India's market. The Danish company Vestas has managed to hold and even slightly increase its market share (2003: 8%, 2008: 13%). The Indian subsidiary of the German firm Enercon has lost a significant market share over the last few years (2003: 24%, 2008: less than 8.5%). Numerous new entrants from overseas have set up new production facilities in India. These include GE, Gamesa, Siemens, ReGen Power Tech, LM Glasfiber, WinWinD, Kenersys and Global Wind Power (GWEC, 2009).

The Indian-owned wind turbine producer Suzlon has played a pioneering role and has managed to establish itself as one of the top five suppliers globally. Ownership structure changed in 2005 when Suzlon went public after 10 years under family ownership. Investors include two major American investment funds, City Group and Chrystal Capital, each providing USD 25 million (WPM, 2004). Suzlon also controls other up- and downstream activities in the value chain. Upstream activities include research and development and component manufacturing. Downstream activities include project development and wind farm management. Suzlon's broad range of activities as well as its global orientation are mirrored in its subsidiary structure which includes technological development centres in Germany and The Netherlands, a rotor blade manufacturing company (Suzlon Energy B.V) in The Netherlands, a US market subsidiary (SWECO), an Australian market subsidiary (Suzlon Energy Australia Pty Limited) and its international headquarters in Aarhus, Denmark. The production locations in India help to keep manufacturing and labour costs low, the R&D centres overseas enable it to have access cutting edge technology innovation, and its regional management and representation offices offer close proximity to its customers. The main instrument used by Suzlon to access wind technology expertise was to license production technologies, e.g. from the German 'Suedwind GmbH Windkraftanlagen' in 1996, and with Enron Wind Rotor Production B.V. in 2001 for rotor blade manufacturing. Suzlon is currently capable of assembling wind turbines with ratings from 350 kW to 2.1 MW and of manufacturing components such as rotor blades, tubular towers, control panels, generators and gearboxes. Through a joint-venture with the Austrian Elin EBG Motoren GmbH, Suzlon started to manufacture generators in 2005. In what can be seen as a second step of technological knowledge acquisition, Suzlon acquired the German manufacturer, Repower in 2007.

Wind energy development is influenced by the structure, development and future of electric utility industry in India. India has taken a market-based approach to restructuring the power sector. Key actions taken include the Electricity Act of 2003, aiming to liberalise and unbundle power generation and distribution, facilitating privately owned independent power producers' (IPPs) access to the grid. Utility structure in India has undergone a clear shift from state-ownership to liberalisation.

Indian R&D activities are shaped by the government institute C-WET and corporate R&D labs. The Indian R&D subsystem is highly developed compared to those of other NICs. However, the number of patents and results from the questionnaire point towards the fact that India still lags behind compared to the leading countries.

Regulation as the most important part of institutions

The government agencies in charge of renewable energy policies are the Ministry of New and Renewable Energy and the State Electricity Boards, which set the feed-in tariffs at state level. Those factors which have been identified as crucial for a manufacturing base to take off globally, namely stable demand and sufficiently high reimbursement resulting in a sizable domestic market, have been achieved in the case of wind energy in some Indian states. Most remarkable has been the success in Tamil Nadu, where demand policies, human and infrastructural resources, and entrepreneurial activities led to the formation of a wind turbine manufacturing cluster around the city of Chennai. Fixed feed-in tariffs and tax incentives create a strong base for market confidence. However, regulation is still very scattered among the different states and so far there is no well developed harmonised national policy.

Demand-side regulation in India currently comprises very different instruments:

- Access to the monopolistic bottleneck of energy transmission has been guaranteed to wind operators in India. According to our expert questionnaire, access to the grid is evaluated as 'effectively realised at the state level'.
- Fixed feed-in tariffs are granted at state level. The feed-in tariffs vary across states from INR 3.14 per kWh or EUR 0.048/kWh (Kerala) to INR 4.5 per kWh or EUR0.069/kWh (Rajasthan) with the average around INR 3.50/kWh or EUR 0.054/kWh. In an international context, this price range is low compared to countries like Germany, but comparable to other NICs such as China.
- Tax incentives are granted at federal level, including a 10-year income tax break for wind power generation projects, an 80% accelerated depreciation over one or two years and a sales tax exemption (P. Purohit, 2009). Moreover, there is an excise duty relief on certain components. Evaluating our expert questionnaire indicates that, besides the feed-in tariffs, tax incentives are the most powerful demand-side incentives for investments in wind power in India.
- On top of the state feed-in tariffs, a federal generation-based incentive scheme for grid connected wind power projects under 49 MW provides INR 0.5/KWh or EUR 0.0076/kWh.

Investors who may not benefit from the tax incentives described above due to their small size or lack of tax liability can choose this alternative incentive instead. This price instrument is limited in its scope and therefore its impact on wind economics remains to be evaluated. Nevertheless, selected Indian wind energy experts in our survey mentioned the generation-based incentives as vital for promoting operational efficiency over simply adding MW capacity.

- Mandatory market share: The Electricity Act of 2003 requires the State Regulatory Commissions to set state-wide renewable portfolio standards. Ten of the 29 Indian states have introduced varying quotas for renewable energy (from 2% up to 10%). The wind-generated electricity is then sold to the electric utilities via a power purchase agreement or a so-called energy buy-back (MNRE, 2009).

- The Indian electricity market – with its insufficient and unreliable grid – makes distributed power supply an attractive option. Decentralised power supply from wind has been identified by some large industrial cooperations as one way to overcome grid problems (Prime Minister's Council on Climate Change, 2008). Selling wind power to third parties has been facilitated in order to support off-grid wind applications (Kristinsson and Rao, 2007).

- The Clean Development Mechanism has played a key role as a profitability factor in about half of India's wind projects. As of August 2009, 301 Indian wind projects had been registered with the CDM Executive Board, accounting for 5659 MW (GWEC, 2009).

- The Indian Renewable Energy Development Agency (IREDA) is the premier financing agency of the Government of India used to provide soft loans for renewable energy projects, particularly for demonstration and private sector projects. Other national and international organisations like the International Finance Corporation or the Asian Development Bank are also active on the Indian wind market promoting private sector investments (Kristinsson and Rao, 2007).

It is characteristic of the Indian way of fostering demand that different instruments are used in parallel. The findings of our expert interviews point to the structural challenge of India having separate federal and state level legislation, which makes the country-wide synchronisation of policies and stabilisation of wind power markets difficult to manage.

The Indian government has also assisted the development of a local manufacturing industry through supply-side policies, however on a limited scale. India has treated foreign and domestic wind turbines more or less the same (Lewis, 2007). Public R&D spending levels in India have been comparatively low. Our expert survey reveals that R&D subsidies for developing indigenous technology exist at national level, but are not effectively realised. Incentives for certification and testing programmes have contributed to India's capabilities in the field of wind turbine testing. Their wind energy certification and standards are among the highest in the world. This is clearly an inducing factor resulting in more competitive turbines for the Asian and world market. However, this factor does not specifically target Indian manufactures, as it is also available to foreign wind turbine manufacturers producing in India.

Functioning of the innovation system

India's wind turbine industry is in the midst of a rapid growth phase during which the industry has followed the path of capacity expansion, internationalisation and liberalisation. The main inducing forces include the financial attractiveness of wind investments, a growing demand-supply gap and increasing internationalisation. Learning effects, strong private sector participation and notions of industrialisation are observable in the Indian wind component industry. Results from our questionnaire indicate the following functional pattern:

- Knowledge development is driven by competition and collaboration co-existing in close proximity, enabling learning networks to be established and bringing wind turbine technology made in India closer to the global technological frontier.
- Knowledge diffusion is well served because wind generation capacity is continuously being added.
- Legitimisation is mostly induced through profitable wind investments and energy security, but increasingly also through national and international environmental pressure to reduce GHG emissions.
- Guidance of search has improved. The early export successes helped to highlight the need for internationally competitive designs. As operators of wind farms, the suppliers had access to first-hand experience of the strengths and weaknesses of their turbines.
- There has been a tenfold capacity increase in market formation, but niche markets are still lagging behind despite their large potentials. Positively influencing factors were stable feed-in tariffs, high export activities and a very early industry formation; on the other hand, the lack of national harmonisation represents an obstacle to greater market confidence.
- Entrepreneurial activity is high, but the rise of other strong domestic manufacturers could be hindered by Suzlon dominating the supply market in India.
- The resource supply situation has improved for some resource categories (financial resources, site resources, industrial resources), while others are still blocking the path to the further development of the industry.

To sum up, the successful national and international market expansion of Indian suppliers has improved knowledge development, which is reinforcing entrepreneurial experimentation. Currently, this is also driving improvements to directing research. Entrepreneurial experimentation has pushed legitimacy, which reinforces resource mobilisation and knowledge development. The success of the Indian wind turbine industry is closely related to one company. It has become possible through a combination of individual entrepreneurial decisions within that company, acquisition of technology from abroad and an electricity market, which was opened to newcomers plus demand policies, which supported diffusion in some provinces. These conditions led to a high number of turnkey projects and forced the players to increase reliability and accompanying services, which enabled them to compete rather early on international markets. Nevertheless, there are still obstructions remaining. These include lack of national harmonisation of incentives, which prevent an even stronger diffusion and additional scale effects. Another issue is lack of adoptability of national R&D and high reliance on further technology acquisition from abroad. The development of cutting edge innovations, for example, is still performed by Suzlon's subsidiary Repower, and not by Suzlon itself (Roland Berger, 2011). It has to be seen whether the positively reinforcing cycles characterised above will also help to reduce these shortcomings in the future.

Discussion and interpretation of results

The analysis of both countries revealed some similarities: Both countries have successfully built up a domestic wind turbine industry. Wind markets in both countries are now undergoing a rapid growth phase. Similar drivers were involved: mainly energy security, environmental pressure, socio-economic potentials, political commitment and regulatory support. However, the analysis also highlighted some differences in the innovation system of each country:

- In China, five state-owned electric utilities dominate wind farm operations and are the major customers for Chinese wind turbines. In India, turnkey projects have turned wind turbine manufacturers into wind farm operators and electric utilities are not as important a factor as in China.

- Market development in China closely follows the development plans of the Chinese government. In India, the incentive structures resulted in a wind market driven more by private sector participation.

- In China, major support policies are managed on the federal level, but policy coordination of wind and grid planning is still a major issue. In India, support policies are still managed on an individual state level and lack national harmonisation and coordination.

- A comprehensive supply chain has developed in China with domestic firms dominating the market, supported by strong industrial policies aimed at building up a domestic industry. In India, there is a higher involvement of international players in turbine production and, increasingly, in financing.

- The leading Indian wind turbine player Suzlon enjoyed early success on the world markets and so was exposed early on to the requirements of international markets with regard to reliability and quality. The development in China, in contrast, has focused more on the home market so far. Global success still has to be achieved by the leading Chinese players.

- Project performance and technical standards and certification are still underdeveloped in China compared to India.

To sum up the differences, China followed a path which is characterised by concise governmental policies. Strong industrial policy support for manufactures was combined with demand policies which let state owned power companies to invest heavily in wind energy. Chinese manufacturers started to acquire international know-how and moved on to develop a domestic value chain. Rapid diffusion of capacity and rapid development of a domestic value chain for wind turbines developed in parallel. However, the combination of fast increase of scale in a huge domestic market plus incentives for installed capacity instead of electricity supplied to the grid also pushed quality aspects more in the background. It remains to be seen whether the latest policy changes and the move of Chinese manufactures to develop larger turbines will lead to improved quality and cutting edge innovations.

Compared to China, there was a more fragmented, market driven approach in India, in which the lack of involvement of electric utilities opened up opportunities for wind turbine manufacturers. One domestic key player emerged, also acquiring technology from abroad. Higher international openness with regard to the role of foreign manufacturers in India increases competition. More emphasis had to be put on quality issues and organisational innovations. This made the Indian wind turbine industry also able to succeed on international markets early on. However, the lower level of domestic R&D capabilities makes the Indian wind turbine industry more dependent on its strategy to source additional new technological knowledge from the European producers it has acquired over the years.

Apart from these differences, there are also similarities between the two countries with regard to the knowledge acquisition strategies of the domestic first tier turbine suppliers. All of them started by acquiring production licences from second tier European suppliers, followed by joint ventures. The selection of these second tier European suppliers also seems to follow a similar pattern: None of them were strong enough to break into the market in India or China on their own so they opted for cooperation with emerging Chinese and Indian suppliers as the only way of profiting from the growing market in these countries.

The results for China also fit in with the conclusions Altenburg et al. (2007) have drawn with regard to China's and India's economic development. China's development of wind turbine industry shows the unique combination of dynamic growth, market size, emphasis on development of domestic skills, all of it supported by strong governmental policies. Thus, the wind turbine success story seems to fit into an overall pattern and it remains to be seen if China will repeat success on international markets in this technology, too. India's case of wind turbine also fits some of the general patterns of development seen by Altenburg at al. (2007) in India, such as market institutions being better developed than in China and lagging behind in terms of domestic R&D. However, wind turbine development in India also shows an above average international openness and early success on international markets, which makes it a much more particular success story.

Conclusions

The case study on the wind turbine industry development in India and China yields various methodological and policy conclusions. In both countries, the successful development of a domestic wind turbine industry can be explained by looking at the dynamics of system of innovation development. Using the heuristics of systems of innovation to analyse infrastructure in NICs looks like a promising way to also analyse sustainability innovations in newly industrialising countries. The same methodological scheme was successfully used for NICs as for OECD countries. Clearly a technology innovation system approach which looks at the functions of an innovation system and feedback loops is also suitable for analysing the catching-up processes in infrastructure-related areas in NICs.

However, the Chinese and Indian cases also demonstrate that there is not just 'one successful way' of building a domestic wind turbine industry. India has used policies in line with its economic model and with its typical, more fragmented policy approach. There is a higher level of international openness, which concerns both a greater involvement of international companies in India and the early focus on exports by the leading Indian player. China has used policies which are compatible with its current economic model and achieved a more top-down development of the private sector. The policy goals of building a domestic wind turbine industry are much more influential. There is a greater focus on developing domestic knowledge and capabilities, which is supported by industrial policies. This translates into the emergence of big players in a short period of time and a focus on expanding the domestic knowledge base. Compared to this, India relies more on international knowledge and on acquiring this by exchanging experiences and learning by exporting. Thus, it is not surprising to see a higher number of patents from China and domestic initiatives towards developing cutting edge turbine sizes, but a stronger presence of India at international R&D locations.

There are also similarities between the two cases. The importance of policy regulation can be seen in both countries, e.g. with regard to stimulating demand. Furthermore, the first tier domestic companies used a similar strategy to acquire foreign knowledge, starting with production licences, moving on to joint ventures and finally taking over these companies.

There are also important policy making conclusions for both countries. Strengthening environmental regulation in NICs should not be seen as a trade-off between environmental protection and economic development, but rather as one instrument of a demand-side driven innovation policy in one of the most dynamically growing economic sectors. Indeed, if NICs can master the various policy challenges, they are likely to improve their competitiveness even further, which would reinforce the view that achieving sustainability does not lead to diminished economic growth, but can yield additional economic benefits.

Acknowledgements

Research for this paper has been performed within the Research Project 'Integration of Sustainability Innovations in the Catching-Up Process (ISI-CUP)'. The financial support of the German BMBF is acknowledged. Two anonymous reviewers provided us with many helpful suggestions. We are grateful to Prof.

Wang Yi from CAS-IPM and Alok Kumar from TERI for their help in conducting the questionnaire in China and India.

References

Agterbosch, S, *et al.* (2004) Implementation of wind energy in the Netherlands: The importance of the social and institutional setting. *Energy Policy*, 32(18), pp. 2049–2066.

Altenburg, T., and Pegels, A. (2012) Sustainability-oriented innovation systems – Managing the green transformation. *Innovation and Development*, forthcoming 2012.

Altenburg, T., Schmitz, H., and Stamm, A. (2007) Breakthrough? China's and India's transition from production to innovation. *World Development*, 36(2), pp. 325–344.

Archibugi, D., and Pietrobelli, C. (2003) The globalization of technology and its implications for developing countries – Windows of opportunity or further burden. *Technological Forecasting and Social Change*, 70(9), pp. 861–883.

Bell, M., and Pavitt, K. (1993) Technological accumulation and industrial growth contrasts between developed and developing countries. *Industrial and Corporate Change*, 2(1), pp. 157–210.

Bergek, A., and Jacobsson, S. (2003) The emergence of a growth industry: A comparative analysis of the German, Dutch and Swedish wind turbine industries, in: S. Metcalf and U. U. Cantner (eds) *Change, Transformation and Development*, pp. 197–227 (Heidelberg: Physica-Verlag).

Bergek, A., Hekkert, M., and Jacobsson, S. (2008a) Functions in innovation systems: A framework for analysing energy system dynamics and identifying system building activities by entrepreneurs and policy makers, in: T. Foxon, J. Köhler and C. Oughton (eds) *Innovations in Low-Carbon Economy,* (Cheltenham: Edward Elgar), pp. 79–111.

Bergek, A., Jacobsson, S., and Sandén, B. (2008b) Legitimation' and 'development of positive externalities': Two key processes in the formation phase of technological innovation systems. *Technology Analysis and Strategic Management*, 20(5), pp. 575–592.

Bergek, A., Jacobsson, S., Carlsson, B., Lindmark, S., and Rickne, A. (2008c) Analyzing the functional dynamics of technological innovation systems: A scheme of analysis. *Research Policy*, 37(3), pp. 407–429.

Bodas Freitas, I.M., Dantas, E., and Iizuka, M. (2011) The Kyoto mechanisms and the diffusion of renewable energy technologies in the BRICS. *Energy Policy*. doi:10.1016/j.enpol.2011.11.055.

BTM Consult ApS (2009) International wind energy development. BTM Consult ApS, Ringkobing, Denmark.

Carlsson, B., Jacobsson, S., Holmén, M., and Rickne, A. (2002) Innovation systems: Analytical and methodological issues. *Research Policy*, 31(2), pp. 233–245.

Changliang, X., and Zhanfeng, S. (2009) Wind energy in China: Current scenario and future perspectives. *Renewable and Sustainable Energy Reviews*, 13(8), pp. 1966–1974.

Cherni, J.A., and Kentish, J. (2007) Renewable energy policy and electricity market reforms in China. *Energy Policy*, 35(7), pp. 3616–3629.

Copeland, B.R., and Taylor, M.S. (2004) Trade, growth and the environment. *Journal of Economic Literature*, 42(1), pp. 7–71.

Dantas, E. (2011) The evolution of the knowledge accumulation function in the formation of the Brazilian biofuel innovation system. *IJTG*, 5(3&4), pp. 327–340.

Edquist, C. (2005) Systems of innovation: Perspectives and challenges, in: J. Fagerberg, Mowery D. and Nelson R.R. (eds) *The Oxford Handbook of Innovation*, pp. 181–208 (Oxford: Oxford University Press).

Foxon, T.J., Gross, R., Chase, A., Howes, J., Arnall, A., and Anderson, D. (2005) UK innovation systems for new and renewable energy systems: Drivers, barriers and system failures. *Energy Policy*, 33(16), pp. 2123–2137.

Frietsch, R., and Schmoch, U. (2010) Transnational patents and international markets. *Scientometrics*, 82(1), pp. 185–200.

Grupp, H. (1998) *Foundations of the Economics of Innovation: Theory, measurement and practice* (Cheltenham: Edward Elgar).

GWEC (2009) Indian wind energy outlook 2009. Global Wind Energy Council, Brussels.

Hatzichronoglou, T. (1997) Revision of the high-technology sector and product classification. *STI working papers 1997/2, OECD/GD 97/216*, Paris.

Hekkert, M.P., and Negro, S.O (2009) Functions of innovation systems as a framework to understand sustainable technological change: Empirical evidence for earlier claims. *Technological Forecasting and Social Change*, 76(4), pp. 584–594.

Hekkert, M.P., Suurs, R.A.A., Negro, S.O., Kuhlmann, S., and Smits, R.E.H.M. (2007) Functions of an innovation system: A new approach for analysing technological change. *Technological Forecasting and Social Change*, 74(4), pp. 413–432.

IANS (2006) India envisages about 950,000 MW power requirement by 2030. Indo-Asian News Service, New Delhi.

IEA/OECD (2009) How the energy sector can deliver on a climate agreement in Copenhagen. International Energy Agency / Organization for economic Co-Operation and Development, Paris.

Kristinsson, K., and Rao, R. (2007) *Learning to Grow: A comparative nalysis of the wind energy sector in Denmark and India* (Aalborg: Danish Research Unit for Industrial Dynamics).

Lewis, J. (2007) Technology acquisition and innovation in the developing world: Wind turbine development in China and India. *Studies on Comparative International Development*, 42(3–4), pp. 208–232.

Lewis, J., and Wiser, R.H. (2007) Fostering a renewable technology industry: An international comparison of wind industry policy support mechanisms. *Energy Policy*, 35(3), pp. 1844–1857.

Lundvall, B-A., Johnson, B., Andersen, E.S., and Dalum, B. (2002) National systems of production, innovation and competence building. *Research Policy*, 31(2), pp. 213–231.

Malerba, F. (2005) Sectoral systems – How and why innovation differs across sectors, in: J. Fagerberg, J.D. Mowery and R.R. Nelson (eds) *The Oxford Handbook of Innovation*, pp. 380–406 (Oxford: Oxford University Press).

Markard, J. (2011) Transformation of infrastructures: Sector characteristics and implications for fundamental change. *Journal of Infrastructure*, 17(3), pp. 107–117.

McInerney, M. (2011) Tacit knowledge transfer with patent law: Exploring clean technology transfers. *Fordham Intellectual Property, Media & Entertainment Law Journal*, 21(2), pp. 449–493.

Meyer, S. (2009) China wind market growth prospects. Azure International, Beijing.

MNRE (2009) Annual report 2008–09. Ministry of New and Renewable Energy, New Delhi.

Mohamad, Z.F. (2011) The emergence of fuel cell technology and challenges for catching up by latecomers: Insights from Malaysia and Singapore. *IJTG*, 5(3&4), pp. 306–326.

Nelson, R.R. (2007) The changing institutional requirements for technological and institutional catch up. *International Journal of Technological Learning, Innovation and Development*, 1(1), pp. 4–12.

P. Purohit, I.P. (2009) Wind energy in India: Status and future prospects. *Journal of Renewable and Sustainable Energy*, 1(4), pp. 1–17.

Pew Environment Group (2011) Who is winning the clean energy race? The Pew Charitable Trust, Washington.

Prime Minister's Council on Climate Change (2008) National action plan on climate change. Government of India, New Delhi.

Recknagel, P. (2008) Wind power in China 2008. China Wind Power Center, Beijing.

Roland Berger Strategy Consultants (2011) Wind turbine manufacturing – A case for consolidation. Industry overview and key trends. Hamburg, November 2011.

Suurs, R.A.A., and Hekkert, M. (2009) Cumulative causation in the formation of a technological innovation system: The case of biofuels in the Netherlands. *TFSC*, 76(8), pp. 1003–1020.

Walz, R. (2006) Impacts of strategies to increase renewable energy in Europe on competitiveness and employment. *Energy & Environment*, 17(6), pp. 951–975.

Walz, R. (2007) The role of regulation for sustainable infrastructure innovations: The case of wind energy. *International Journal of Public Policy*, 2(1–2), pp. 57–88.

Walz, R. (2010) Competences for green development and leapfrogging in newly industrializing countries. *International Economics and Economic Policy*, 7(2&3), pp. 245–265.

Walz, R., and Marscheider-Weidemann, F. (2011) Technology-specific absorptive capacities for green technologies in newly industrializing countries. *International Journal of Technology and Globalisation*, 5(3–4), pp. 212–229.

Wang, F., Yin, H., and Li, S. (2010) China's renewable energy policy: Commitments and challenges. *Energy Policy*, 38(4), pp. 1872–1878.

Wen, F., Hua, D., and Wang, Q. (2008) Wind power generation in China: Present status and future prospects. *Int. J. Energy Technology and Policy*, 6(3), pp. 254–276.

World Bank (2008) Midterm evaluation of China's 11th five year plan (Washington, DC: The World Bank).

World Bank & SEPA (2007) Cost of pollution in China. The World Bank and the State Environmental Protection Administration of China (SEPA), Washington, DC.

WPM (2004) Suzlon ownership structure. *Wind Power Monthly*, March 2004.

WPM (2008) Special report China 2008. *Wind Power Monthly*, November 2008.

WPM (2009) Special report China 2009. *Wind Power Monthly*, October 2009.

XWERI (2010, 04 29) Introduction of Xinjiang wind energy company, available at: http://www.xjwind.com/companyE.html, accessed on 29 April 2010, from Xinjiang Wind Energy Research Institute.

Yu, J., and Zheng, J. (2011) Offshore wind development in China and its future with existing renewable policy. *Energy Policy*, 39(12), pp. 7917–7921.

Zhang, Z., Chang, S., Huo, M., and Wang, R. (2009) China's wind industry: Policy lessons for domestic government interventions and international support. *Climate Policy*, 9(5), pp. 553–564.

Key actors and their motives for wind energy innovation in China

Frauke Urban[a], Johan Nordensvärd[b] and Yuan Zhou[c]

[a]*School of Oriental and African Studies SOAS, University of London;* [b]*London School of Economics and Political Science LSE;* [c]*School of Public Policy and Management SPPM, Tsinghua University*

Today China is the world's largest wind energy manufacturer and has the world's largest installed wind capacity. To create an improved understanding of the Chinese wind energy sector, this paper assesses the role of the key actors including key government authorities, energy firms, research institutions and non-governmental organisations (NGOs). The paper also assesses the motives of these key actors for driving wind energy innovation at industrial level. The paper finds that the primary motives driving wind energy innovation in China seem to be concerns related to energy security and economic growth rather than only concerns about climate change. The paper also finds that the key actors and their motives tend to influence the direction, speed, development and implementation of wind energy policies and technological trajectories for wind energy innovation. Hence analysing the key actors' motives can provide new insights into how the Chinese wind sector will develop in the future – both in terms of policy and in terms of technological trajectories.

1. Introduction: climate change and wind energy in China

China is currently the world's largest emitter of greenhouse gas emissions in absolute terms, at the same time it is the world leader in renewable energy, most notably in wind energy, solar energy and hydropower. China is leading the renewable energy field in terms of investments, production and installed capacity (IEA, 2011). It is often indicated that one of the primary causes for increasing global and Chinese investments in renewable energy is concerns about climate change.

Global climate change is considered one of the greatest threats to humanity and could seriously undermine the recent development efforts of countries such as China. The Intergovernmental Panel on Climate Change's (IPCC) Fourth Assessment Report indicates that global greenhouse gas emissions leading to climate change must be reduced by 80% in 2030 compared to 2000 levels to avoid 'dangerous climate change', defined as a global temperature rise above 2 degrees Celsius (IPCC, 2007).

Low carbon energy, including wind energy, plays a key role in mitigating climate change. Sustainability-oriented innovation systems, particularly wind and solar, have seen a rapid and radical increase in investments, production and installed capacity in recent years in China (Altenburg and Pegels, 2012). The wind energy resources in China are reported to be large. China has a total exploitable wind energy potential of 3000 GW according to the World Energy Council (WEC), of which 750 GW are reported to be situated offshore (Lewis and Wiser, 2007)[1].

Earlier studies in this field have assessed wind power potential, wind energy development to date, wind energy policies and prospects (Liu and Kokko, 2010; Liao et al., 2010; Wang, 2010; Xu et al., 2010; Liu et al., 2002; Li, 2010; Hong and Moller, 2011). Other studies have assessed institutional dynamics and the performance of the wind power industry (Zhao and Zuo, 2009; Liu et al, 2002). Lewis and Wiser (2007) have compared wind industry policy support mechanisms for various leading countries including China, Denmark, Germany, India, Japan, Spain and the US. Zhou et al. (2011) have elaborated how the policy dimension can be strengthened for technology road-mapping for the wind energy industry. Lema et al. (2011) have discussed opportunities and risks associated with competition and cooperation between China and Europe in the wind energy sector. There is a growing body of literature about China's innovation capabilities in low carbon technologies, such as Altenburg (2008) and Lewis (2007).

While these earlier studies shed some light on achievements in the wind energy sector today, the role of innovation and key policies, there is a knowledge gap regarding the role of key actors and the motives that drive innovation in wind energy and how this can influence policy and technological trajectories. This paper therefore aims to assess the role of the key actors in the Chinese wind energy sector and their motives for driving wind energy innovation, and elaborate the implications this has for wind energy policy and technological trajectories. The key actors and their motives influence the direction, speed, development and implementation of wind energy policies and technological trajectories for wind energy innovation. Hence, understanding the key actors and their motives is important for understanding the wind energy sector and its development.

The study of motives and actors are based on three empirical approaches:

1. Qualitative interviews with 33 key actors from government, wind energy industry, research organisations and NGOs to assess the motives that drive innovation in wind energy technology in China and to assess the position of various actors.
2. The interviewees were asked to give quantitative scores for the motives that drive innovation in wind energy in China. A 5-point Likert-type scale was used.
3. The third empirical step was to conduct an actor analysis to assess who plays a key role in the wind energy sector in China and in driving wind energy innovation.

The paper finds that key motives behind the development of wind energy innovation are mainly related to energy security and economic growth, despite the prevailing climate change discourse in policy documents. Poverty reduction is another motive which is mentioned by interviewees in relation to decentralised wind energy provision, but seems to have marginal importance as the key emphasis is on creating competitive domestic wind firms which can rival international wind firms, create economic growth and ensure domestic energy security. Despite the interviewees' emphasis on energy security and economic growth, the academic debate often seems to be about climate change mitigation as a key driver of innovation in renewable energy, while the economic and political aspects behind the growth of the renewable energy industry tend to be downplayed to some extent.

Section 2 briefly discusses the development and current status of the Chinese wind energy sector, section 3 elaborates the conceptual framework and the methodology of this study, section 4 elaborates on the empirical findings of the study, section 5 discusses the findings and their implications and section 6 concludes the paper.

2. The Chinese wind energy sector

Lewis and Wiser (2007) stress how the development of the wind energy sector sets itself apart from other sectors. This is mainly due to two factors: (1) The importance of the home market, meaning that in the early years of the development of a wind sector, firms tend to trade domestically and then expand abroad (Lewis and Wiser, 2007) and; (2) The importance of sizable, stable demand, meaning that annual market demand for wind turbines has to be large to develop a domestic market (Lewis and Wiser, 2007). Both factors can be observed in China. Lema and Ruby (2007) further suggest that the Chinese wind energy sector is different from the wind energy sector in other countries by having undergone three transformations from fragmented authoritarianism in the 1980s and 1990s to coordinated market regulations and an incentivised system from 2000 onwards.

The development of the Chinese wind energy sector can be differentiated by four phases:

Phase 1: The early beginning of the Chinese wind energy sector dates back to the years between 1975 and 1985 when China invested in off-grid micro-wind systems to provide household energy supply in remote areas. This was followed by modest up-scaling between 1985 and 1995 when turbines with capacities of 100 to 300kW were developed and the first demonstration wind farms were built (Xu et al., 2010).

During this time, the Chinese government promoted *technology transfer* through foreign donations and Foreign Direct Investment (FDI)-funded wind pilot projects from Denmark, Germany and Spain as domestic wind innovation capacity was still in its infancy (Dai, 2011).

Phase 2: In the late 1990s and the early 2000s, the Chinese government promoted the development of *indigenous wind energy innovation for turbines of up to 1MW*, accelerated the construction of large-scale wind farms and created a Chinese wind power market (Xu et al., 2010). Despite these efforts, until the early 2000s the Chinese wind power market was mainly dominated by foreign firms that were global leaders in wind technology innovation.

Phase 3: A further step by the Chinese government to promote indigenous innovation was to introduce a *local content requirement*, which was 50% from 2004 to early 2005 and was then augmented to 70% from mid 2005 to 2009. The local content requirement meant that 70% of the wind turbine and its components had to be sourced locally (Wang, 2010). The local content requirement meant that foreign firms still had access to the Chinese market, but their production capacity had to be in China.

Many *domestic firms and joint ventures* emerged in the period between 2004 and 2008. Market access was consequently traded for part-Chinese ownership. Within only five years, the market share of domestic turbines rose from 25% to more than 60%, while the market share of foreign turbines plummeted from 75% to 40% in 2008 (Zhao et al., 2009). In 2003, none of the world's top 10 turbine manufacturers were Chinese. In 2010, the Chinese firms Sinovel, Goldwind, Dongfang Electric and Guodian United Power lead the global top 10 in wind turbine manufacturing (Lema et al., 2011; BTM, 2010).

After 2005, the Kyoto Protocol and the UN regime for climate change was an external driver for expanding the Chinese wind market due to government policies (Dai, 2011).

Phase 4: Since the abolishment of the local content requirement in 2009, the Chinese domestic market booms – in terms of installed capacity, manufacturing and investments. Chinese State-Owned Enterprises (SOEs) make up the majority of leading wind firms in China (Liu and Kokko, 2010).

China's wind capacity has recently overtaken the US, Germany and Spain, and China now has the world's largest installed wind capacity. China achieved an approximate doubling of its installed wind energy capacity in five consecutive years (IEA, 2011; GWEC, 2011; Jingfeng et al., 2006). Figure 1 shows the rapid increase in installed wind turbine capacity in China

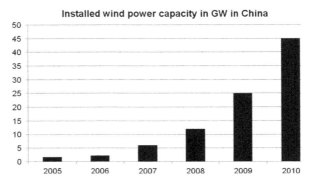

Figure 1.   Installed wind power capacity in China in GW between 2005 and 2010. Data source: Amended from IEA, 2010; Liu and Kokko, 2010.

between 2005 and 2010. Since 2010, the government aims to scale up its wind farms, markets and technologies and to export Chinese wind energy technology globally (Dai, 2011).

Nevertheless, the impressing figures and policies supporting China's wind energy development have to be considered with caution. China's rapidly growing economy, its large population and its surging energy demand mean that only 1.2% of China's electricity came from wind power in 2010 (WWEA, 2011). Wind energy policies issued by the central government in Beijing are sometimes only reluctantly implemented by provincial and local governments and authorities. Recent research by Wang et al. (2010) shows there are major barriers to China's wind energy development. First, the share of renewable energy in total energy consumption is decreasing, instead of increasing, due to rapid growth of fossil fuel capacity (Wang et al, 2010). Second, the efficiency of wind energy technology tends to be low as often the quality of the technologies is not to the latest standard in China and efficiencies for wind energy technology are generally rather low. Third, many wind farms are not connected to the grid as this requires high costs and logistic resources. There is a lack of adequate transmission lines and supporting infrastructure and a part of the installed wind energy capacity is therefore often wasted (Liao et al., 2010; Wang et al., 2010). The WWEA (2010) reports that in 2010 only 31GW out of the total capacity of 45GW was connected to the grid; this means that 31% of the installed capacity was standing idle.[2]

3.   Conceptual framework and methodology

3.1   *Innovation*

This paper addresses the actors relevant to wind energy *innovation* at the industrial level in China and their motives. This section discusses the key concepts related to innovation in general and innovation in wind energy technology in specific.

Innovation is here defined as something that is new to a firm or a market (Van de Ven et al., 1989). According to Rogers, innovation is usually perceived as uncertain and risky. It requires a group of individuals with the same interests to first adopt a technology and then disseminate it. This process usually takes months or years before the diffusion of innovation takes place (Rogers, 2003). Innovation policies in China are defined broadly as including industrial policy, science and technology policy, financial, tax and fiscal policy (Liu et al., 2011). Altenburg et al. (2008) make a distinction between production and innovation capabilities. While China has significantly invested in production capabilities or innovation input, such as spending on R&D and investment in human resources, the innovation capabilities or innovation output still seem to lag behind as China produces significantly fewer patents, trademarks, journal publications and citations than OECD countries (Altenburg et al., 2008; Altenburg, 2008). Similar findings are presented by Sun and Du (2010) who mention the increasing investments China makes in industrial innovation, but who also stress the importance of technology transfer as a source of innovation and the fact that China does 'not compete on the basis of original innovation in the international market' (Sun and Du, p.548). Very little research exists so far to assess whether this lack in innovation capabilities can also be observed for low carbon innovation and wind energy innovation.[3]

Low carbon innovation is an umbrella term for innovation related to low carbon technologies, such as wind turbines, solar panels and carbon capture and storage (CCS) technology.

Low carbon innovation has the specific characteristic of being a 'global public good' by reducing greenhouse gas emissions that lead to climate change. Low carbon innovation also often contributes to energy security as most of its technology is based on renewable energy, low carbon energy or energy efficiency, which can offer an alternative to finite fossil fuels or save energy resources. Decentralised low carbon innovation is further considered for its contribution to poverty reduction, particularly in relation to reducing energy poverty in developing countries through decentralised renewable energy technology (IEA, 2010). Finally, low carbon innovation has been used by governments and firms as a way to stimulate economic growth, by creating employment, tax revenues, profits and by attempting to become first-movers in a new sector of technology innovation (e.g. European Energy Programme for Recovery, EC, 2011).

Low carbon innovation involves a complex process, which includes research, development, demonstration and deployment of low carbon technologies (Watson, 2008). Low carbon innovation comprises three elements: (1) capital goods and equipment for low carbon technologies; (2) skills and know-how for operation and maintenance; (3) knowledge and expertise for low carbon innovation (Ockwell et al., 2007). Innovation is thus not only limited to the 'hardware', but also to the 'software' such as skills and knowledge. This can be related to horizontal flows of hardware and software for innovation between firms and vertical flows from R&D to commercialisation.

The role of low carbon technology transfer for China has been vividly discussed (see Ockwell et al., 2007; Watson, 2002; Lewis, 2007; Barton, 2007), although more recently the focus has been on China's capacity for indigenous innovation or *Zizhu Chuangxin* (Dobson and Safarian, 2008; Sun and Du, 2010; Liu et al., 2011). This means a move from absorptive capacity – a recipient firm's ability to absorb new technology – to developing innovative capacity to enable the recipient firm to move from technology transfer to innovation.

More specifically, wind energy innovation relates mainly to capital, skills and experience for technology innovation, such as the design of the tower, rotor blades and gear box/turbine generator. Technology innovation in the beginning of the wind energy sector in the 1970s to early 1990s was characterised by finding the most adequate design for small-sized turbines (Gipe, 1995; Johnson and Jacobsson, 2000). Experimentations with horizontal and vertical axis innovations in the end led to a commercially dominant vertical axis design. This resulted in out-competing a number of firms which had invested primarily in horizontal axis innovation, such as some Dutch firms which have since then vanished from the scene of the world's top wind turbine firms (Kamp et al., 2002; Gipe, 1995). In the late 1990s and 2000s, innovation in wind energy technology was mainly related to designing bigger, more efficient turbines, particularly moving from kW to MW-turbines. In very recent years, the main emphasis has been on scaling up and developing even larger, more robust offshore turbines, which can withstand higher wind speeds offshore and have very high yields (Zhang et al., 2011, Wang et al., 2009; Chen, 2011; Yu and Zheng, 2011).

3.2 *Climate change as a motive for driving wind energy innovation?*

The deployment of wind energy and other low carbon energy technology is a key strategy for reducing greenhouse gas emissions to mitigate *climate change* and for increasing energy security. Climate change mitigation is defined as 'an anthropogenic intervention to reduce the anthropogenic forcing of the climate system; it includes strategies to reduce greenhouse gas sources and emissions and enhancing greenhouse gas sinks (IPCC, 2001, p. 379).

In recent energy and climate policy documents, Chinese government authorities stress the importance of climate change mitigation, the transition to a low carbon economy and low carbon energy including wind energy. Two examples are China's National Climate Change Programme from 2007 and China's Pathway Towards a Low Carbon Economy Plan from 2009. The National Climate Change Programme mentions that 'To address climate change and promote sustainable development, China has carried out various policies and measures, such as [. . .] development and utilization of hydropower and other renewable energy [. . .] which has contributed significantly to the mitigation of climate change' (NDRC, 2007a, p. 4). 'China will stick to its sustainable development strategy and take such measures as energy efficiency improvement, energy conservation, development of renewable energy [. . .] to control its greenhouse gas emissions and make further contribution to the protection of the global climate system' (NDRC, 2007a, p. 58). The Low Carbon Economy Plan first reports the need for global climate change mitigation: 'To avoid dangerous levels of climate change, global temperature rises need to be restricted to no more than 2°C above pre-industrial level. [. . .] In order to achieve this, energy systems that are close to zero emissions will need to be developed' (CCICED, 2009, p. 2). The report then outlines China's role and the importance of low carbon energy technology, including wind energy: 'China's move towards a low carbon economy is inevitable, necessary and urgent. There are considerable benefits to China of taking early action. [. . .] Investments made now and over the next decade will determine China's exposure to energy security and climate change risks for decades to come. [. . .] The country is already a world leader on critical low carbon technologies such as solar power, heat and wind turbines and is rapidly developing key technologies for electric vehicles' (CCICED, 2009, pp. 7–8). Both documents mention wind energy 11 times each.

While a few years ago the debate about climate change and renewable energy was mainly dominated by a focus on energy and industrial policy (see e.g. Richerzhagen and Scholz, 2008), the debate has gradually shifted towards a focus on climate and low carbon policy. This is due to several factors: (1) China becoming the world's largest carbon dioxide emitter in absolute terms in 2007 (IEA, 2010); (2) China's ambitious climate change and low carbon policies and initiatives since 2007 (e.g. NDRC, 2006; NDRC, 2007a; NDRC, 2007b; State Council, 2008; CCICED, 2009; Climate Policy Initiative Tsinghua, 2010; UNFCCC, 2010; State Council, 2011); (3) its recent emergence as a globally leading market in wind, solar and hydropower; (4) its growing capacity in climate and low carbon research. Hence one key question of the motives part of the paper (see section 4.2) is whether climate change is a key motive for innovation in the Chinese wind energy sector – as recent trends, debates and policy rhetoric seem to suggest – or whether other motives such as energy security, economic growth and poverty reduction are the prime motives.

The motives energy security, economic growth and poverty reduction are being analysed due to two key reasons: (1) these motives are closely related to the specific characteristics of low carbon innovation (see section 3.1); (2) these motives have been selected based on scoping interviews with Chinese energy experts. This led to four predominant motives: climate change mitigation, energy security, economic growth and poverty reduction.

Energy security is defined as the availability of energy supply at cost-effective prices at adequate times and in adequate quantities to such an extent that the economic and social development of a country can be ensured (Kowalski and Vilogorac, 2008). Economic growth is defined as an increase in GDP (GDAE, 2011). Poverty reduction is defined as any process that reduces poverty levels (ICT4D, 2011.)

3.3 Methodology

The following part of this section addresses the *methodology* adopted for this study:

1. Qualitative interviews with 33 key actors from government, energy industry, research organisations and NGOs to assess the motives that drive innovation in wind energy technology in China and to assess the position of various actors. The interviewees were selected based on their leading positions in their organisations and their expertise in relation to the Chinese wind energy sector.

Interviewees from the *government* were officials involved in the energy, climate change and environment programmes at government bodies like the National Development and Reform Commission (NDRC), Environmental Protection Agency (EPA), Ministry of Finance (MOF), and the Ministry of Science and Technology (MOST).

Interviewees from *research institutions* were researchers on energy and climate change from various departments such as from Tsinghua University, the Energy Research Institute and the Chinese Academy of Sciences. Interviewees from *firms and business associations* were managers from various energy firms such as Goldwind, Vestas, Huaneng Corporation, as well as senior managers from the Chinese and Global Wind Energy Associations and the Chinese Renewable Energy Association.

Interviewees from *NGOs* were managers involved in the energy, climate change and environment programmes at NGOs such as WWF, Greenpeace, and the Natural Resources Defence Council.

Thirty-three interviews were conducted in 2011. In total six government representatives were interviewed, 11 representatives from research institutions, 10 representatives from the private sector and six representatives from NGOs. The authors attempted to interview an equal number of interviewees from government, energy industry, research organisations and NGOs, nevertheless this was not possible due to lack of availability and time constraints of potential interviewees. The authors recognise that representatives from research institutions and firms were slightly overrepresented.

The interview questions were semi-structured, qualitative questions. Interviewees were first asked the same general questions in the beginning of the interview, secondly followed by more specific questions depending on whether the actors were from government, industry, research organisations or NGOs. These specific questions were systematically developed to identify the role of the different organisations, their specific influence and linkages in relation to other types of organisations. Here we provide two examples of specific questions to elaborate how this system of developing specific questions worked. For example, government organisations were asked about their specific role in wind energy innovation and policy-making, their powers to draft and implement policies and regulations, and their influence on firms and other relevant organisations. As another example, firms were asked about their role in wind energy innovation, their influence on the wind sector and their links to the government.[4]

This methodological approach is particularly relevant for assessing the interactions between the actors and motives that drive wind energy innovation.

2. The second empirical approach was to ask interviewees for quantitative scores for the motives that drive innovation in wind energy in China. A 5-point Likert-type scale was used. The scores ranked from 1 to 5 with 1 meaning 'unimportant', 2 meaning 'not very important', 3 meaning 'neither important nor unimportant', 4 meaning 'important', 5 meaning 'very important'. The

5-point Likert-type scale is often used in social science research and is globally acknowledged as a valid scale for questionnaires and multiple choice enquiries. Four motives were selected based on scoping interviews with Chinese energy experts: climate change mitigation, energy security, economic growth and poverty reduction. The interviewees were asked to give scores for each motive. The motives were then ranked in a spider diagram to compare the motivations that drive wind energy innovation and their perceived importance by the interviewees.

This methodological approach was developed by Pegels et al. (2011) at the German Development Institute for the project 'Low carbon innovation policies in China, India and South Africa'.

3. The third empirical approach was to conduct an actor analysis to assess which institutions and organisations play a key role in the wind energy sector in China and in driving wind energy innovation. For this particular task the interviewees were asked to draw a stakeholder map of the relevant key government authorities at national and provincial level, firms, research institutions and NGOs and to explain the links and relationships between different actors. The motives and the actor mapping approach can provide insights into how various actors and their motives influence policy-making for wind energy innovation and how they influence technological trajectories.

The next section discusses the empirical findings of the study.

4. Empirical findings

4.1 *Interviews*

For this study, 33 interviews were conducted with respondents from governments, energy industry, research institutes and NGOs (see section 3.3 for methodological details).

The interviewees stressed the importance of understanding the actors and motives engaged in the wind energy sector as they influence the direction, speed, development and impact of *policy for wind energy* and *technological trajectories for wind energy innovation* (Interviews with government officials, energy firms, energy experts and NGOs, 2011).

In terms of *wind energy policy*, the interviewees mentioned the importance of industrial, energy and climate policy for driving wind energy policy. This related particularly to the following policies and legislations mentioned by the interviewees:

- The Five-Year Plans, for example the 11th and 12th Five Year Plans that set targets for renewable energy development, including wind power development. The 12th Five Year Plan for 2011–2015 aims for 70 GW installed wind energy capacity by 2015. These national targets are translated into provincial and firm-level targets.
- Mid and Long Term Plan on Renewable Energy by the NDRC in 2007 which aims for 15% of total primary energy consumption to be from renewable energy by 2020 (NDRC, 2007b) and includes targets for wind energy.
- Renewable Energy Law which came in effect in 2006 and sets a legislative framework for promoting wind energy, introduces obligatory grid connections for renewable energy systems, pricing agreements like feed-in tariffs and concessions to guarantee the market.
- Local content requirement: As mentioned in section 2, the Chinese government introduced a local content requirement between 2004 and 2009 which led to a rapid increase of joint ventures and domestic Chinese wind firms and sharply reduced foreign competition (Interviews with government officials, energy firms, energy experts and NGOs, 2011).

The key actors involved are the NDRC and the national government, as well as the provincial government. Key motives seem to be related to energy security and economic growth. Several representatives from research organisations also mentioned the importance of the 2007

Climate Change Programme, and the 2008 and 2011 White Papers on Climate Change for driving wind policy and innovation. These policies set targets for emission reductions as well as targets for renewable energy and wind energy more specific, hence the motive is climate change mitigation rather than energy security or economic growth (Interviews with firms and energy experts, 2011).

Different actors at the national, provincial and firm level influence wind energy policy and incentives, hence understanding their motives is important for understanding the direction and development of policies for the wind energy sector.

In terms of *technological trajectories for wind energy innovation*, the interviewees mentioned the following trends:

- While foreign firms tend to aim at building larger turbines, particularly for offshore use, Chinese firms seem to predominantly aim at developing wind energy innovation which is suited to the local Chinese conditions. This relates particularly to improving integration between wind farm and grid, reducing voltage fluctuations and enabling long-distance transport of electricity as the load centres are often located far away from the demand centres (Interviews with government officials, energy firms, energy experts and NGOs, 2011). Key actors are foreign and domestic firms and key motives seem to be economic growth and energy security.
- Larger turbines for the offshore market tend to be mainly produced in the country of origin such as Denmark, Spain, the US and Germany to limit conflicts regarding Intellectual Property Rights (IPRs) in China. This enables foreign firms to do the cutting-edge R&D at home rather than in China, while turbines larger than 1.5MW are mainly imported to China (Interviews with business associations, firms, wind energy experts, 2011; Liu and Kokko, 2010). Key actors are foreign firms and key motives seem to be economic growth, economic competitiveness and protecting IPRs.
- In the manufacturing industry, China currently has 80 turbine manufacturers, approximately 50 rotor blade manufacturers and approximately 100 tower manufacturers. More than 80% of the Chinese wind equipment manufacturers are state-owned (Liu and Kokko, 2010). Many of these SOEs operate in the smaller and medium turbine segment of the Chinese wind manufacturing market with turbines below 1.5MW. There is concern that the smaller turbine segment of the Chinese wind manufacturing market might soon be saturated. The strong engagement of SOEs like Sinovel and Goldwind creates risks that the market might be distorted by state-funded and state-owned firms that are large, have access to abundant funding, can lower prices excessively, are strategically nurtured and protected by the state and have limited responsibility to shareholders. This might have implications for foreign firms in the long run, but also for domestic SOEs and provincial firms. SOEs are competing against SOEs which might in the long run have an effect on the number of firms surviving and the power play between national and provincial actors (Interviews with NGO and business associations; Liu and Kokko, 2010). Key actors are domestic firms, mainly SOEs promoted by the national and provincial government, and key motives seem to be economic growth and energy security.
- The smaller turbine segment of 300–800kW is partly made up by Chinese SOEs, which are new to the wind energy business. They are established energy and electronics companies, small and medium-sized enterprises and provincial government companies. As these companies are new to the wind power sector and have limited technological skills in this field, their strategy is to buy licences from foreign companies that are not based in China, hence technology transfer and cooperation is a key strategy. Many licences come with restrictive clauses, such as restricting export of these turbines (Interviews with energy experts, 2011).

Key actors are domestic firms, promoted by the national and provincial government, and key motives seem to be economic growth and energy security.

- There were different opinions about the role of indigenous innovation. Most respondents mentioned the importance of indigenous innovation and the increasing innovation capabilities in China's wind energy sector (Interviews with government officials, energy firms, energy experts and NGOs, 2011), whereas a small minority of interviewees –mainly from non-Chinese firms – questioned whether indigenous innovation is happening and rather referred to licensing and technology acquisition (Interviews with wind energy firm, 2011). Key actors are domestic and foreign firms, and key motives seem to be economic growth, economic competitiveness and protecting IPRs.

Different actors at the national, provincial and firm level influence technological trajectories for wind energy innovation, and understanding their motives is important for understanding how the wind energy sector and wind energy innovation is likely to develop in the future.

The next section discusses therefore the motives for wind energy innovation in China, while section 4.3 discusses the role of various actors relevant to wind energy innovation.

4.2   *Motives for wind energy innovation in China*

This section discusses the motives various stakeholders have for contributing to wind energy innovation at the industrial level. This section draws on the interviews conducted with government, industry, research organisations and NGOs.

While a few years ago the debate about climate change and renewable energy was mainly dominated by a focus on energy and industrial policy (see e.g. Richerzhagen and Scholz, 2008), the debate has gradually shifted towards a focus on climate and low carbon policy. Hence one key question of section 4.2 is whether climate change is a key motive for innovation in the Chinese wind energy sector – as recent trends, debates and policy rhetoric seem to suggest – or whether other motives such as energy security, economic growth and poverty reduction are the prime motives.

The authors intend to address the overall policy targets of China's wind energy sector. There may be different motives, but they do not have to be conflicting, as some targets can be beneficial or complementary to other targets. For example, the policy target of energy security can be beneficial to climate change mitigation when there is more reliance on indigenous renewable energy resources such as wind and hydropower. Likewise poverty reduction and economic competitiveness can go hand in hand. Hence, there are co-benefits between climate change mitigation and energy security, as well as economic growth and poverty reduction. On the other hand there can be trade-offs, for example, when high carbon economic growth increases emissions leading to climate change. However, low carbon growth can be in line with climate change mitigation.

To identify what drives wind energy innovation in China at the government and firm level, the interviewees were asked to give quantitative scores for four motives: climate change mitigation, energy security, economic growth and poverty reduction. The scores ranked from 1 to 5 with 1 being the lowest and 5 being the highest score. Motives were then ranked in a spider diagram to compare the motivations that drive wind energy innovation and their perceived importance by the interviewees (see section 3.3 for methodological details). One actor can have many motives and all can be equally valid or equally plausible.

With 33 respondents this study is representative, but works with a selected sample. The study does by no means attempt to make a claim about the Chinese wind energy sector as a whole, but only draws on the motives of a selected sample. Whether the same patterns can be observed in a larger sample remains to be seen in future research.

The interviews showed that most respondents indicated energy security and economic growth as the key motivation for wind energy innovation. The next highly ranked motivation was climate change mitigation. Overall the respondents indicated that poverty reduction tends not to be a key motivation for expanding the wind energy sector and for driving low carbon development. It was mentioned that although decentralised energy provision and access to electricity in rural areas play a role for wind energy development, there are only limited linkages between wind power developments, profits from the wind energy industry and benefits to the poor (Interviews with energy firms, energy experts and NGOs, 2011).

The respondents showed an interesting divide between government authorities, research organisations, firms/business associations and NGOs.

The government authorities ranked energy security as the overriding motivation for wind energy developments at the industrial level with an average score of 4.4 out of 5, followed by climate change concerns with an average score of 4 out of 5 (Interviews with government officials, 2011). This could be explained by the fact that the national and local government has the responsibility to ensure energy security, in terms of quantity of supply, quality of supply and affordability. The high government concern with climate change is reflected in recent national policies on climate change, particularly since 2007. Economic growth scored an average score of 3.75 out of 5 and poverty reduction scored an average score of 2.4 by the interviewed representatives of government authorities.

There was strikingly little variation between the motives mentioned by government representatives, even though different ministries and organisations were involved such as NDRC, EPA, MOST, MOF, etc. This might be explained by the fact that some institutions follow several goals at the same time (e.g. energy security, economic growth and climate change mitigation for NDRC and MOST). These goals do not have to be competing, but can be complementary. In addition, the study only interviewed central government representatives, not representatives from provincial or local governments. Central government is generally more concerned with energy security and environmental issues, while local governments are generally more concerned with economic growth, firm competitiveness, employment and tax income.

Research institutions ranked climate change mitigation and energy security both as the most important motivation for driving wind energy innovation at the industrial level with average scores of 4.3 each out of 5, followed by economic growth which received an average score of 4.2 out of 5 (Interviews with energy experts, 2011). This might be explained by the fact that some of China's energy experts also operate as climate policy experts, for example, in the position of negotiators for the Chinese government in the UN climate change negotiations and for drafting the energy and climate government policies. There was marginal variation among the individual representatives regarding the motives energy security, economic growth and climate change mitigation; however this seemed to be based more on personal preferences than on institutional affiliations. Nevertheless, there were some interesting differences between the role of poverty reduction. While the average score was 2.8 out of 5, the ranking ranged from 0.8 to 3.3, depending on institutions and personal preferences. Those research institutions which are closer to the government scored poverty reduction higher than more independent research institutions.

Firms and business associations ranked energy security, with an average score 4.5 out of 5, and economic growth, with an average score of 4.3 out of 5, as the most important motivations for driving wind energy innovation at the industrial level. Climate change mitigation scored an average 3.5 out of 5. On average, firm representatives gave the lowest scores of all respondents to poverty reduction, namely only 2 out of 5, classifying it between 'unimportant' and 'not very important' in relation to wind energy (Interviews with managers from energy firms and wind business associations, 2011). This could be explained by the fact that firms need to be profitable, hence the wind energy sector is regarded – like any other sector – as a way of creating profits and generating income and economic growth. The authors expected to find trends or major differences between SOEs and private firms, foreign firms and Chinese firms, business associations and firms; however surprisingly it seemed difficult to find coherent trends or patterns of differences regarding the motives between different types of businesses. In total, the scores were rather homogenic between different respondents and different institutions.

NGOs ranked economic growth as the most important motivation for driving wind energy innovation at industrial level, with an average score of 4.8 out of 5. This was followed by energy security with an average score of 4 out of 5, while climate change and poverty reduction were both ranked as 'not very important' with average scores of 2.2 out of 5 and 2 out of 5, respectively (Interviews with managers from NGOs, 2011). NGO respondents had the most consistent responses of all interviewees as most respondents were in agreement about the scores, although they did not know the scores of other respondents. The perceived key motives of NGOs might reflect the prevailing perception of government and firm activities as well as perceptions of the media and wider public, which seem to be mainly preoccupied with economic growth rather than environmental or social concerns. It is striking that NGOs perceive climate change mitigation only as a marginal motive for wind energy innovation.

Regarding the averaged and individual results per group of respondents, the following observations were made. On average, the respondent group found energy security the most important motive for expanding the Chinese wind energy sector and wind energy innovation at industrial level in China and scored it 4.5 points out of 5, followed by economic growth which scored an average of 4.3 points out of 5, followed by climate change mitigation which scored an average of 3.8 points out of 5 and finally followed by poverty reduction which scored an average of only 2.3 points out of 5 (Interviews with government, industry, research institutions and NGOs, 2011). Figure 2 shows the averaged results as a spider diagram. It has to be stressed once again that this study does not attempt to be representative for the entire wind energy sector in China, but is only representative for the motives of the 33 respondents involved in this study.

The respondents were given the opportunity to mention other motives in addition. Other motives that were mentioned were mainly related to economic competitiveness, such as access to new markets and first mover advantages. Firms further mentioned that high carbon firms will become less competitive in the future due to carbon trading, global environmental standards and the international climate change regime, hence moving towards low carbon development is crucial for the competitiveness of energy firms (Interviews with energy firms, 2011).

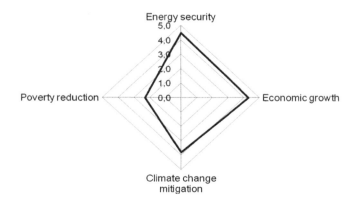

Figure 2.   Averaged motives for wind energy innovation in China for this study: energy security, economic growth, climate change mitigation, poverty reduction. Source: Representatives of government, industry, research institutions and NGOs, 2011.

These findings are in line with assumptions that form the basis of other research such as Berger et al. (2011); Liu and Kokko (2010); Lewis and Wiser (2007), nevertheless the motivations of different actors for driving wind energy innovation have not been laid out explicitly and discussed in much depth before. The international research community, and particularly the research community in the climate change field, tends to predominantly use a climate change discourse to justify the key motivation for wind energy developments. This is broadly in line with the discourse of Chinese government authorities such as NDRC, EPA and the State Council (e.g. NDRC, 2006; NDRC, 2007a; NDRC, 2007b; National People's Congress of China, 2005; CCICED, 2009; State Council, 2011). Our findings however make it clear that while climate change seems to be a driving concern, energy security, economic growth and firm competitiveness seem to be even more important driving concerns of wind energy innovation at the industrial level.

4.3 *Actor analysis*

This section discusses the actors that influence the wind energy sector in China, at the international, national and local level and at the policy/government and firm/industry level. Actor analysis can provide an improved, politically-informed understanding of who drives wind energy innovation in China and why. This is important for understanding the political context of policy-making and technological trajectories for the wind energy sector.

This section draws primarily on the interviews conducted with representatives from government, industry, research organisations and NGOs. The interactions between government authorities, their policies, and firms and other organisations involved in the wind energy sector are dynamic and interactive. There is a two-way flow of influence: (1) the influence of government and policy on wind energy industry and other organisations; (2) the influence of wind energy industry and other organisations on government and policy. In addition, wind energy innovation involves multi-level governance in China. A range of international, national and provincial authorities are engaged in wind energy policy-making and promoting innovation.

The international level provides a general global policy framework for climate change and renewable energy which creates opportunities for new funding for firms and rules that the industry has to follow, such as under the UN Framework Convention on Climate Change and the World Trade Organisation. Nevertheless, most interviewees indicated that the international level plays only a minor role in Chinese wind energy innovation.

The role of the national government is to create demand and supply side policies, strategies, guidelines and financing for wind energy which is geared towards the benefit and appliance of the wind industry. Their role is further to approve and oversee wind energy projects and programmes. National government tends to be more concerned about environmental issues such as climate change, while provincial governments tend to be more concerned about economic growth, tax income and employment opportunities (Richerzhagen and Scholz, 2008). The national government was considered by all interviewees to be the most influential player.

The role of the provincial government is to create incentives for local production of local wind firms and to create provincial policies and targets for wind energy, to enforce national plans and decisions, to approve, oversee and manage wind energy projects and programmes. The provincial government was considered by interviewees to be the second most influential player in relation to wind energy innovation. National government is more influential, but provincial governments have the power to actively or reluctantly implement national wind policies and targets (Interviews with government, energy firms and wind energy experts, 2011).

The role of wind energy firms is to manufacture wind energy technology equipment, operate wind farms, install wind turbines, manage wind farm concessions, implement wind energy plans and projects, engage in R&D and innovation (Interviews with wind energy firms and business associations, 2011). At the same time, large energy SOEs are (indirectly) involved in the complex policy-making process through their 'discourse influence' and their strategic importance (Interview with manager from energy firm, 2011). In addition, wind energy firms provide expertise and consultation to the national and the provincial government and can thereby influence wind energy policies. Firms can also influence technology roadmaps as they are developing and deploying latest technology and have expertise about technological trajectories. Besides the key wind players like Sinovel and Goldwind and provincial firms, a number of new players in the market are important, such as SOEs Huaneng Group, the Datang Corporation and the Guodian Corporation (Interviews with managers from energy firms and energy experts, 2011).

Research organisations can play a key role by providing consultation to the national government, such as the National People's Congress, the State Council and the ministries, and the provincial/local government. Some university-based research labs conduct R&D and run demonstration projects for wind technology innovation. Relationships between leading universities and national and provincial governments are usually well developed in the wind energy field (Interviews with energy experts, 2011).

NGOs such as WWF or Greenpeace are reported to have only limited influence in China for driving low carbon development and wind energy innovation in particular. This is partly because

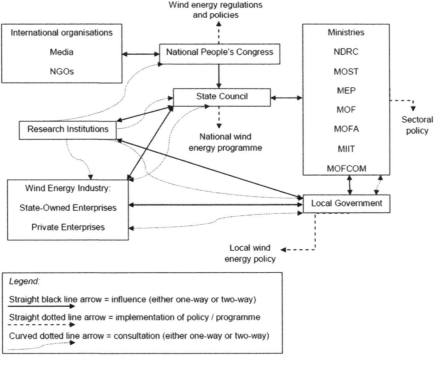

Figure 3. Actor mapping for the policy-industry interactions in the wind energy sector and relationships and influence. Key players are the National Development and Reform Commission NDRC, the Ministry of Science and Technology MOST, the Ministry of Environmental Protection MEP, the Ministry of Finance MOF, the Ministry of Industry and Information Technology MIIT, the Ministry of Commerce MOFCOM. Data source: Interviews with government, industry, research institutions and NGOs, 2011.

NGOs tend to be under-represented and with limited power in China and secondly because their remit is not directly geared towards wind energy innovation (Interviews with government, energy firms, research institutions and NGOs, 2011).

Figure 3 indicates a stakeholder map of the various actors engaged in the wind energy sector in China as well as their relationships and influence.[5] For this particular task the interviewees were asked to draw a stakeholder map of the relevant key government authorities at national and provincial level, firms, research institutions and NGOs and to explain the links and relationships between different actors.

5. Discussion

This section discusses the implications of the findings of this study. There is agreement between the interviewees that the key actors identified play a key role in influencing the direction, speed, development and impact of the Chinese wind energy sector, both in terms of wind energy innovation and in terms of wind energy policy.

This study finds there is a link between the motives and the actors. Research institutions seem to mention energy security and climate change mitigation as the key motives due to their alignment with the UN climate change negotiations and their advisory role for the government's climate and energy policies. Firms tend to be mainly interested in economic growth and firm competitiveness, although it is interesting that energy security seems to be a higher priority than economic growth for Chinese energy firms – which can partly be explained due to their close financial and political relations with the government. It is striking that NGOs perceive climate change mitigation only as a marginal motive for wind energy innovation. NGOs seem to suggest that the government's key driving motivation is economic growth rather than other concerns related to environmental or social issues, which tends to reflect to some extent the reservations and maybe also the disillusionment NGOs might have towards government policy. The government's motives seem to be first energy security, followed by economic growth and climate change. With a population of 1.3 billion and a booming economy predominantly based on industrial activities it is understandable that energy security is at the heart of the government's concerns.

While the motives for specific actors have been elaborated, the link between specific actors, their motives and wind energy policies will be addressed here. As mentioned before, the actors and their motives influence policy-making for wind energy. Energy security has been identified as the key motive for wind energy innovation, followed by economic growth. This is in line with key policies for wind energy (see section 4.1) such as the wind energy targets of the Five-Year Plans, the Mid and Long Term Plan on Renewable Energy by NDRC, the Renewable Energy Law and specific economic and industrial policy such as the local content requirement and the Ride the Wind programme which encouraged indigenous innovation. Climate change mitigation was named as third important key motive, which is in line with the perceived priority of climate policies such as China's Climate Change Programme and the White Papers on Climate Change. In line with the perceived marginal importance of poverty reduction, no interviewee has mentioned policies and incentives which link poverty reduction and wind energy.

The link between actors' motives and policies has been elaborated above. The link between actors' motives and implications for technological trajectories for wind energy innovation will be addressed here:

1. Leading foreign firms tend to focus on larger (offshore) turbines, whereas Chinese firms seem to focus predominantly on technological issues related to grid integration and long-distance transport of electricity. This influences the direction, development and implementation of technological trajectories for wind energy innovation in China,

particularly in relation to building onshore turbines which are more suited for Chinese conditions. This also influences government policy in relation to primarily incentivising onshore turbines.

2. There are potential challenges regarding larger turbines as the Chinese government aims to attract foreign firms for developing larger turbines of more than 1.5MW in China, whereas foreign firms prefer to produce larger turbines in their home markets due to critical IPR issues. This, again, influences the direction, development and implementation of technological trajectories for wind energy innovation in China, particularly in relation to attracting foreign R&D and technology for large wind turbines rather than developing indigenous large turbines. This also influences government policy by encouraging foreign firms to build large turbines in China.

3. There is domestic competition in the small and medium segment of the Chinese wind energy sector as firms – including SOEs – seem to run the risk of crowding each other out of the market. This influences government policies in the wind sector, for example, by announcing that China's wind firms will expand overseas in the future.

4. There is an entry of new smaller-sized and often provincial Chinese firms which acquire foreign technology and licenses as they are new to the wind turbine market. This, again, influences the direction, development and implementation of technological trajectories for wind energy innovation in China, as well as the speed of the technological trajectories. It means that Chinese wind firms can catch up much quicker than established Western firms did due to licensing and technology acquisition.

5. There are different opinions about the extent and the role of indigenous innovation versus the extent and role of licensing and technology acquisition. This influences government policy in relation to content requirements, licensing, IPR and incentives for wind innovation.

These issues related to technological trajectories are linked to the actors and their motives. As the government's key priority is to increase energy security, it aims to promote wind energy innovation which can enable optimum grid integration and enable long-distance transport of electricity to the urban centres along China's coastal areas which are far away from the areas where the electricity is generated. The government further aims to foster innovation for larger megawatt-sized turbines to increase energy security. At the same time, the government aims to create economic growth and firm competitiveness, hence the push for SOEs, provincial firms and indigenous innovation in the wind sector (Interviews with energy experts, 2011).

Regarding the firms' key motive of economic growth a clear trend can be seen both for Chinese and foreign firms. A large number of Chinese firms – large, medium and small-sized, state-owned and private, national and provincial – have recently entered the Chinese wind market. Their key motive is to generate profits; hence they influence the provincial and national government along these lines. Foreign firms' key motive is also to generate profits; hence they enter the Chinese market. Nevertheless foreign firms prefer to conduct R&D for larger, offshore turbines at home rather than in China to reduce potential competition and conflicts in relation to infringements of IPRs (Interviews with energy experts, 2011).

The motives of research institutions and NGOs are less clearly presented in these issues relevant to technological trajectories as they influence policy and wind innovation more indirectly. This is due to the fact that research institutions and NGOs do not have the attributes of policymakers or energy firms.

The findings further indicate that climate change mitigation seems not to be the most important motive for wind energy innovation in China compared to energy security and economic competitiveness, despite the prevailing climate change discourse in policy documents. This is an interesting finding as these results are different from what the recent theoretical and policy debates seem to suggest. This finding can be partly explained by China's status as the most populous country in the world with a rapidly growing economy, which needs large amounts of energy to fuel its growth and increase its development status (IEA, 2011). Hence, energy security and economic growth are at the forefront of government and firm priorities, even though environmental concerns are becoming increasingly important.

6. Conclusion

This paper aims to assess the role of the key actors in the Chinese wind energy sector and their motives for driving wind energy innovation and the paper aims to elaborate the potential implications for wind energy policy and technological trajectories.

This paper highlights key actors and their motivations in the Chinese wind energy sector. A range of international, national and provincial government authorities are engaged in wind energy policy-making and in promoting wind energy innovation in China. In addition, there are a range of state-owned, private and foreign firms engaged in wind energy innovation. Policy-making and conducting research, development, manufacturing and implementation of wind energy technology in the Chinese wind power sector requires working at several scales and levels with a wide range of different authorities, players and interest groups. The direction, speed, development and implementation of wind energy policies and technological trajectories for wind energy innovation depend on the actors identified in this research, particularly national and provincial governments.

The paper finds that key motives behind the development of wind energy innovation are mainly related to energy security and economic competitiveness, despite a growing climate change discourse. The academic debate often seems to be about climate change mitigation as one of the key drivers for renewable energy (e.g. Li, 2010; Liao et al., 2010; Chen, 2011; Climate Policy Initiative Tsinghua, 2010), while the economic and political aspects behind the growth of the renewable energy industry can tend to be downplayed to some extent. Poverty reduction is another motive which is mentioned by interviewees, but seems to have marginal importance as the key emphasis is on creating competitive domestic wind firms which can rival international wind firms, create economic growth and ensure domestic energy security.

The authors suggest that it is important to understand the key actors engaged in the Chinese wind energy sector and their motives. The actors and their motives influence policy decisions and technology trajectories relevant to wind energy innovation. This approach could potentially be important for addressing complex political issues in the wind energy sector, such as opportunities and barriers for cooperation and competition between domestic and foreign firms, for understanding the drivers behind influential forces at the policy and technological level, and for understanding issues of agreement and conflict in the development of the wind energy sector.

Finally, it is often debated whether China will be able to make the transition from high carbon to low carbon and thereby create a paradigm shift towards low carbon technologies and low carbon production and consumption patterns. This could create a substantial competitive advantage in a world where a price is attached to carbon. Often this approach has been associated with technology transfer and technology cooperation (e.g. Watson et al., 2011) and technological catch up theories related to environmental leapfrogging and the Environmental Kuznets Curve (e.g. Stern, 2004). The interviewees in this study suggested that wind energy as an emerging industry opens up great opportunities for Chinese firms to catch up and build innovative capabilities to compete with international players. However, it has been confirmed by the interviewees that China's rapid growth in the wind energy sector has been mainly due to a strong reliance on technology transfer and cooperation in the first stage of its emergence and a strong reliance on local content requirements to reduce competition from foreign firms in the second stage. Since a few years the reliance on both factors has decreased and a large number of domestic firms have emerged, however under strong state leadership and state financing. It has been noted that the domestic market seems to be nearly saturated (Liu and Kokko, 2010). Hence a new stage of the Chinese wind energy industry may begin, namely an outward orientation towards overseas export markets. This is in line with the key motives of the Chinese government and Chinese wind firms. This new expansion may prove the true capacities and scope of China's wind energy sector and it will determine whether a global paradigm shift towards sustainability-oriented innovation systems can be led by China and its distinct wind energy model rather than by established Western wind energy nations. Analysing the key actors' motives can provide new insights into how the Chinese wind sector will develop in the future – both in terms of policy and in terms of technological trajectories.

Acknowledgement

The authors would like to thank Wang Yu and Shasha Wang for valuable contributions in this field and Anna Pegels for suggesting the methodological approach for the motives section. The authors would like to thank the reviewers of this paper for their helpful suggestions.

Notes

1. Nevertheless the WEC assumes that only about 250 GW of this offshore potential are economically and technically feasible.
2. While such a large amount of idle-standing capacity might enter the statistics as 'installed capacity' and enable firms, provincial and national governments to meet their wind energy targets, it would be economically inefficient. It could therefore be the case that there is a time lag between installing the turbines and connecting them to the grid.
3. This research suggests that evidence regarding the build up of innovation capabilities in the Chinese wind energy sector seems to be divided. Most respondents mentioned the increasing innovation capabilities in the wind energy sector (Interviews with government officials, energy firms, energy experts and NGOs, 2011), whereas a small minority of interviewees – mainly from non-Chinese firms - questioned whether indigenous innovation is happening and rather referred to licensing and technology acquisition (Interviews with wind energy firm, 2011).
4. Governments and firms were chosen for these two specific examples as they are the most important players in relation to wind energy innovation.
5. A similar actor analysis was conducted for climate change in China by Richerzhagen and Scholz (2008). Nevertheless their analysis focused more broadly on climate change and not specifically on the wind energy sector.

References

Altenburg, T. (2008) New global players in innovation? China's and India's technological catch-up and the low carbon economy, *Working paper* Bonn, GDI.

Altenburg, T., and Pegels, A. (2012) Sustainability-oriented innovation systems – Managing the green transformation. *Innovation and Development*, forthcoming 2012.

Altenburg, T., Schmitz, H., and Stamm, A. (2008) Breakthrough? China's and India's transition from production to innovation. *World Development*, 36(23), pp. 325–344.

Barton, J.H. (2007) Intellectual property and access to clean energy technologies in developing countries, *ICTSD Trade and Sustainable Energy Series, Issue Paper No. 2* Geneva, Switzerland, ICTSD.

Berger, A., Fischer, D., Lema, R., Schmitz, H., and Urban, F. (2011) Towards a conceptual framework for analysing cooperation and competition between China and Europe in climate and renewable energy issues. *Journal of Current Chinese Affairs*, invited paper for special issue, submitted.

BTM (2010) World market update 2009. BTM Consulting, Ringkøbing.

CCICED China Council for International Cooperation on Environment and Development (2009) China's pathway towards a low carbon economy. CCICED, Beijing.

Chen, J. (2011) Development of offshore wind power in China. *Renewable and Sustainable Energy Reviews*, 15(9), pp. 5013–5020.

Climate Policy Initiative Tsinghua (2010) Review of low carbon development in China: 2010 report. Tsinghua University, Beijing.

Dai, Y. (2011) Wind energy in China – An overview. Presentation for the workshop 'Technological trajectories for climate change mitigation in China, India, EU'. Tsinghua University, Bonn.

Donson, W., and Safarian, A.E. (2008) The transition from imitation to innovation: An enquiry into China's evolving institutions and firm capabilities. *Journal of Asian Economics*, 19(4), pp. 301–311.

EC European Commission (2011) . European energy programme for recovery, available at: http://ec.europa.eu/energy/eepr/index_en.htm

GDAE Global Development And Environment Institute (2011) Encyclopaedia of the earth. Definition of economic growth, available at: http://www.eoearth.org/article/Economic_growth

Gipe, P. (1995) *Wind Energy Comes Of Age* (New York. John Wiley & Sons.

GWEC Global Wind Energy Council (2011) World wind energy report 2010. (Global wind Energy Council, Brussels.

Hong, L., and Moller, B. (2011) Offshore wind energy potential in China: Under technical, spatial and economic constraints. *Energy*, 36(7), pp. 4482–4491.

ICT4D (2011) . Definition of poverty alleviation, available at: http://www.caricomict4d.org/ict-for-development-topics-mainmenu-132/poverty-alleviation-mainmenu-190/68-definition-of-poverty-alleviation.html

IEA International Energy Agency (2010) World energy outlook 2010. Energy poverty – How to make energy access universal? IEA/OECD, Paris.

IEA International Energy Agency (2011) Statistics, available at: www.iea.org/stats/index.asp

Interviews with key actors from the Chinese wind industry, government authorities, research institutions and NGOs, between April – December 2011.

IPCC Intergovernmental Panel on Climate Change (2001) Third assessment report. Mitigation, Working Group III, available at: http://www.grida.no/publications/other/ipcc_tar/

IPCC Intergovernmental Panel on Climate Change (2007) Fourth assessment report. Synthesis Report, available at: http://www.ipcc.ch/publications_and_data/publications_ipcc_fourth_assessment_report_syn thesis_report.htm

Jingfeng, L., Jinli, S., and Linguan, M. (2006) China: Prospect for renewable energy development. Energy Research Institute, Beijing.

Johnson, A., and Jacobsson, S. (2000) The emergence of a growth industry: A comparative analysis of the German, Dutch and Swedish wind turbine industries. (Gothenburg, Chalmers University of Technology.

Kamp, L.M., Smits, R.H.M., and Andriesse, C.D. (2002) Learning in wind turbine development. A comparison between the Netherlands and Denmark. Utrecht University, Utrecht.

Kowalski, G., and Vilogorac, S. (2008) Energy security risks and risk Mitigation: An overview, available at: http://www.preventionweb.net/files/8066_Pagesfromannualreport2008.pdf.

Lema, R., Berger, A., Schmitz, H., and Hong, S. (2011) Competition and cooperation between Europe and China in the wind power sector. *Journal of Current Chinese Affairs*, invited paper for special issue, submitted.

Lema, A., and Ruby, K. (2007) Between fragmented authoritarianism and policy coordination: Creating a Chinese market for wind energy. *Energy Policy*, 35(4), pp. 3879–3890.

Lewis, J.I. (2011) Building a national wind turbine industry: Experiences from China, India and South Korea. *International Journal of Technology and Globalisation*, 5(3), pp. 281–305.

Lewis, J.I. (2007) Technology acquisition and innovation in the developing world: Wind turbine development in China and India. *Studies in Comparative International Development*, 42(3–4), pp. 208–232.

Lewis, J.I., and Wiser, R.H. (2007) Fostering a renewable energy technology industry: An international comparison of wind industry policy support mechanisms. Lawrence Berkeley National Laboratory, LBNL-59116, available at: http://eetd.lbl.gov/EA/EMP.

Li, J. (2010) Decarbonising power generation in China – Is the answer blowing in the wind? *Renewable and Sustainable Energy Reviews*, 14(4), pp. 1154–1171.

Liao, C., Jochem, E., Zhang, Y., and Farid, N.R. (2010) Wind power development and policies in China. *Renewable Energy*, 35(9), pp. 1879–1886.

Liu, F.C., Simon, D.F., Sun, Y.T., and Cao, C. (2011) China's innovation policies: Evolution, institutional structure and trajectory. *Research Policy*, 40(7), pp. 917–931.

Liu, W.Q., Gan, L., and Zhang, X.L. (2002) Cost-competitive incentives for wind energy development in China: Institutional dynamics and politics. *Energy Policy*, 30(9), pp. 753–765.

Liu, Y., and Kokko, A. (2010) Wind power in China: Policy and development. *Energy Policy*, 38(10), pp. 5520–5529.

National Development and Reform Commission of China NDRC (2006 11th Five Year Plan, available at: http://www.gov.cn/english/special/115y_index.htm

National Development and Reform Commission of China NDRC (2007a) China's national climate change programme, available at: http://en.ndrc.gov.cn/newsrelease/P020070604561191006823.pdf

National Development and Reform Commission of China NDRC (2007b) Medium and long-term development plan for renewable energy in China (abbreviated version, English draft), available at: http://www.martinot.info/China_RE_Plan_to_2020_Sep-2007.pdf

National People's Congress of China (2005) The renewable energy law of the People's Republic of China, available at: http://www.martinot.info/China_RE_Law_Beijing_Review.pdf

Pegels, A., Altenburg, T., and Fischer, D. (2011) Low carbon energy policies in China, India and South Africa – The dynamics of policy making, Presentation given at the 9th international conference of the European Society of Ecological Economics (ESEE), Istanbul, 15 June 2011.

Ockwell, D., Watson, J., MacKerron, G., Pal, P., Yamin, F., Vasudevan, N., and Mohanty, P. (2007) UK-India collaboration to identify the barriers to the transfer of low carbon energy technology. DEFRA, London.

Richerzhagen, C., and Scholz, I. (2008) China's capacities for mitigating climate change. *World Development*, 36(2), pp. 308–324.

Rogers, E.M. (2003) *Diffusion of Innovations*. 5th Edition New York, Free Press.

State Council of the People's Republic of China (2008) China's policies and actions for addressing climate change. State Council, Beijing.

State Council (2011) The 12th Five Year Plan (2011–2015), available at: http://pamlin.net/blog/China%2012th%20FIVE%20year%20plan.pdf

Stern, D.I. (2004) The rise and fall of the Environmental Kuznets Curve. *World Development*, 32(8), pp. 1419–1439.

Sun, Y. and Du, D. (2010) Determinants of industrial innovation in China: Evidence from its recent economic census. *Technovation*, 30(9–10), pp. 540–550.

UNFCCC (2010) China's nationally appropriate mitigation actions (NAMAs), available at: http://unfccc.int/files/meetings/application/pdf/chinacphaccord_app2.pdf

Van de Ven, A.H., Harold, L., and Poole, M.S. (1989) *Research on the Management of Innovation* New York, Harper and Row.

Wang, F., Yin, H., and Li, S. (2010) China's renewable energy policy: Commitments and challenges. *Energy Policy*, 38(4), pp. 1872–1878.

Wang, Q. (2010) Effective policies for renewable energy – The example of China's wind power – Lessons for China's photovoltaic power. *Renewable and Sustainable Energy Reviews*, 14(2), pp. 702–712.

Wang, Z., Jiang, C., Ai, Q., and Wang, C. (2009) The key technology of offshore wind farm and its new development in China. *Renewable and Sustainable Energy Reviews*, 13(1), pp. 216–222.

Watson, J. (2002) Cleaner coal technology transfer to China: A win win opportunity for sustainable development? *International Journal of Technology Transfer and Commercialisation*, 1(4), pp. 347–372.

Watson, J. (2008) Setting priorities in energy innovation policy: Lessons for the UK. ETIP Discussion Paper. Belfer Center for Science and International Affairs, Kennedy School of Government. Harvard University, MA, Cambridge.

Watson, J., Byrne, R., Stua, M., Ockwell, D., Xiliang, Z., Zhang, D., Zhang Xiaofeng, Ou Xunmin, and Mallet, A. (2011) UK-China collaborative study on low carbon technology transfer, available at: https://www.sussex.ac.uk/webteam/gateway/file.php?name=uk-china-final-report-april-2011.pdf&site=264

WWEA (World Wind Energy Association) (2011) Wind Energy International 201172012 Yearbook. WWEA, Bonn.

Xu, J., He, D., and Zhao, X. (2010) Status and prospects of Chinese wind energy. *Energy*, 35(11), pp. 4439–4444.

Yu, J., and Zheng, J. (2011) Offshore wind development in China and its future with the existing renewable policy. *Energy Policy*, 39(12), pp. 7917–7921.

Yu, X., and Qu, H. (2010) Wind power in China – Opportunity goes with challenge. *Renewable and Sustainable Energy Reviews*, 14(8), pp. 2232–2237.

Zhang, D., Zhang, X., Jiankun, H., and Qimin, C. (2011) Offshore wind energy development in China: Current status and future perspective. *Renewable and Sustainable Energy Reviews*, doi:10.1016/j.rser.2011.07.084

Zhao, Z.Y., Hu, C., and Zuo, J. (2009) Performance of wind power industry development in China: A diamond model study. *Renewable Energy*, 34(12), pp. 2883–2891.

Zhou, Y., Gu, X., Minshall, T., and Su, J. (2011) A policy dimension required for technology roadmapping: Learning from the development of emerging wind energy industry in China. PICMET, Portland.

Challenges of low carbon technology diffusion: insights from shifts in China's photovoltaic industry development

Doris Fischer

German Development Institute, Deutsches Institut für Entwicklungspolitik (DIE), Bonn, Germany

Large scale diffusion of low carbon technologies (LCTs) is an important element of strategies to mitigate climate change. However, diffusion of LCTs faces a number of barriers especially in developing and emerging countries. The Chinese photovoltaic (PV) paradox is an illustrative example of this dilemma: China is the largest producer of PV cells and modules in the world. However, until recently China did not have considerable PV energy installations. The paper analyses barriers related to technology, policy and politics that hindered solar PV energy use before 2009, and factors that since helped to overcome these barriers. Based on the Chinese solar PV experience the paper argues that diffusion of LCTs in developing and emerging countries demands a holistic approach and can sometimes be triggered by developments largely unrelated to climate change considerations.

1. Introduction

Large scale diffusion of low carbon technologies (LCTs) is an important element of strategies to mitigate climate change, and diffusion of renewable energies for electricity generation potentially plays an important role within such strategies. However, diffusion of LCTs in general and renewable energies specifically face a number of barriers as they often are not competitive with traditional technologies that rely on fossil fuels, at least not in the short run.

Against this background the development of photovoltaics in China is of special interest as it highlights the barriers to LCT diffusion and their interrelations. China has been successfully producing PV cells and modules for exports for years, however, before 2009 a significant local market for PV installations did not emerge. Quite the contrary, until 2009 China's long time targets for PV installations remained far below the already existing annual production capacities of the industry. This led to the paradox situation that a low carbon technology produced and available in China in large quantities was actually rarely applied in the home market.

More recently, the Chinese situation has changed. Since 2009, a local market for PV installations is emerging and currently the market for PV installations in China is expected to grow faster than in Europe or the US. What hampered PV installation and energy use before 2009? What factors have triggered the change in 2009? What are lessons learned from the Chinese PV sector development in terms of factors necessary to accelerate LCT diffusion in developing and emerging countries?

The Chinese PV industry example is interesting from a number of perspectives. First, in the context of the international climate negotiations, the Chinese government likes to argue that the lack of access to (cheap) LCTs is the major reason why China and other developing countries are reluctant to undertake more climate change mitigation efforts and to accelerate LCT diffusion (Lewis, 2007). The Chinese PV industry example suggests that a more holistic understanding of LCT diffusion is important. Second, the Chinese example highlights the fact that support for PV diffusion was, not or at least not only, triggered by long-term climate change considerations but by immediate economic policy considerations.

The paper analyses the Chinese PV sector development with respect to factors that first restricted and later triggered the technology diffusion. Section 1 develops a conceptual framework based on literature relevant to the topic. Section 2 shortly explains the value chain of solar PV as a background for the analysis of the Chinese PV sector development presented in section 3. Section 4 analyses the different barriers to PV diffusion in China while section 5 documents how these barriers were overcome after 2009. Based on the Chinese solar PV experience the paper argues that diffusion of LCTs in developing and emerging countries demands a holistic approach and can sometimes be triggered by developments largely unrelated to climate change considerations. The paper contributes to the argument forwarded by the sustainability-oriented innovation system concept that government support for the diffusion of LCTs is crucial. The paper also contributes to a deeper understanding of China's strategies towards climate change mitigation and renewable energies as well as innovation and development.

2. Barriers to LCT diffusion

A number of factors can hinder the use and larger scale diffusion of LCTs even if they are available in developing countries as will be highlighted by the Chinese PV sector example. From relevant literature three major barriers for the diffusion of LCTs can be identified: First, the lack of an enabling technical, business and knowledge environment. Second, the lack of adequate supportive policies to compensate for higher prices associated with LCTs, especially renewable energies. The aforementioned barriers may hinder LCT diffusion even if there is a political will to expand it. A third barrier to LCT diffusion arises from competing strategic policy considerations as well as vested interests that work against the diffusion of the relevant new technology.

This first barrier is explained by insights developed in the innovation system literature. This literature has shown the complex interrelations between enterprises, public and private actors in science, technology development and innovation. Technological development and innovation have to be understood as a complex, messy, non-linear process related to and embedded in economic, social and political developments (Saviotti, 2005). As a consequence, it is to be expected that technologies developed in one society, once 'transferred', have to be adapted to and embedded into the environment of the receiving country if they are to be applied and used in this country. For this, the existence or creation of a suitable knowledge base is as necessary as an enabling business environment (World Bank, 2010, Byrne et al., 2011). The support for capacity building and knowledge development is therefore integrated into international strategies for technological transfer and cooperation with regard to clean energy use in developing countries (Benioff et al., 2010).

Following these insights from the innovation system literature, the discrepancy between China's success in production and export of PV cells and modules on the one hand and the subdued development of PV installations on the other hand could be a result of a missing business environment and knowledge base for larger scale use and diffusion of PV energy. While it obviously has been possible for China to produce PV cells and modules for export markets based on its experience and expertise in modular value chain production and export processing

(Steinfeld, 2010), establishing the necessary environment in China for PV energy and electricity production is a different matter that needs different know-how and capacities. While the former requires the ability to produce according to international standards and specific production know-how, the latter requires a supportive energy sector, electricity infrastructure and maintenance capacities. If the lack of an enabling technical, business and knowledge environment were the main barrier of low PV installation rates in China prior to 2009, the increase of PV installations after 2009 would presumably be the result of important changes or breakthroughs in the knowledge base and business environment around that year.

Explanations for the second barrier, lack of supportive policies, are also related to innovation system research. A special line of research in innovation systems is sectoral innovation systems (Malerba, 2004) which explore the characteristics of innovation systems related to a specific sector. The reference points of such analyses are the specific knowledge, technologies, inputs and demand, as well as policies related to a specific sector. These features may translate into specific actor constellations and institutions. Different from national innovation systems, sectoral innovation systems do not necessarily end at the national borders, depending on the characteristics of the sector and the involved production value chain (Grimpe et al., 2008, p. 4).

Studies on renewable energy and low carbon development related sectors emphasise the importance of policy and regulation as the 'single most important driver for innovation in the energy area' (Borup et al., 2008, p.73). Similarly, Foster et al. (2010, p. 249) stress that 'without proper institutional and market frameworks to operate and maintain renewable systems long term, they eventually fail' (see also IEA, 2008). Altenburg and Pegels in this volume include this idea into the concept of sustainability-oriented innovation system. For example, the PV power development in Germany thrived due to the 'feed-in law' for renewable energies which triggered market development as well as advances in PV cell and grid connection technologies (Savin and Flavin, 2004). Kirkegaard et al. (2010) integrate this perspective into an analysis of global integration along the production value chain in the solar PV sector.

Following the argument that supportive policies are of crucial importance for LCTs use and diffusion, it would be more important for developing countries to 'transfer' successful policies of other countries than merely transferring technology artefacts. In this line of reasoning, any attempt to copy the success of PV technology in Germany would rely less on transferring the technology as such, but more on copying the respective regulatory framework. However, policies, laws and regulations have to be compatible with the economic situation and institutional environment of the respective country, thus simple copying of the German feed-in law would probably not be sufficient. In the course of such a transfer, policies would have to be adapted to the specific situation and institutional environment of the receiving country.

If a country specific institutional framework is crucial for the diffusion of LCTs in general and renewable energy technologies specifically, an explanation of the Chinese PV paradox could be the lack of relevant national policies and legislation before 2009. Accordingly, we would expect that the shift since 2009 towards more PV installations was triggered by policy shifts and changes in the institutional framework.

The third barrier to LTC diffusion refers to the political economy aspects of public support for LCTs. It could be argued that the lack of supportive policies as described above is nothing more than a lack of 'political will', implying that governments could easily promulgate the necessary policies and legislation if they were just sufficiently dedicated to the target of climate change mitigation. However two major issues question such a straightforward approach to low carbon technology diffusion, namely competing strategic goals on the side of political decision makers and interests of incumbent economic actors that potentially lose from the diffusion of LTCs. First, competing strategic goals can limit the dedication of a government regarding low carbon development. From a government perspective, political goals such as economic development, social equity, export market development, etc. are not necessarily compatible with low carbon development (Newell et al., 2011). Also, even if low carbon development or mitigation of climate change is an important strategic goal of a government, this does not necessarily translate into equal support for all low carbon technologies. Second, interest of incumbent actors can also limit the dedication of a government to low carbon development. Policy priorities for specific LCTs benefit some actors in the economy but potentially harm others, thereby increasing the economic or political rents available for certain actors in the society but discriminating against others (Helm, 2010). Governments that need the support of their constituency want to balance such competing interests and compensate for losses from policy priority shifts. However, if those actors that potentially lose in the course of policy shifts are more closely linked to the government than the potential winners, the government could refrain from initiating policy shifts in the first place.

In reference to this third type of barrier to LCT diffusion, we would expect that strategic considerations hindered an increased use of PV energy in China. While an export oriented development of the sector fitted into the overall growth strategy, an increased use and diffusion of PV energy in China challenged other political goals and interests. Vested interests that profited from the traditional high carbon development path had worked against expansion of solar energy use. We would expect that the shift in development and policies around 2009 was the result of considerable changes in government priorities and interest constellations.

In the following, the paper will take a closer look at China's PV paradox, looking for the barriers that subdued the national market before 2009 and factors that contributed to the turn taken in 2009. The analysis is based on existing Chinese and foreign literature on China's innovation system, low carbon and renewable energy policies as well as insights from interviews with government officials, experts in academia as well as representatives from Chinese and foreign enterprises in the years 2009 to 2011.

In recent years, legislation and industrial policies as well as the sudden rise of Chinese enterprises as competitors in the global wind and solar power markets have triggered a number of studies on China's renewable energy sector development, including the PV market (see for example The Climate Group, 2011; PV Group, 2011). The majority of these studies either assess the potential of the Chinese market or the thrust of Chinese competition in global markets in terms of technological development and energy mix targets (Marigo, 2006; Liu et al., 2010). Also, Marigo et al. (2007) look into the role and technological know-how of Chinese manufacturers in PV cell production from an innovation system research perspective. An OECD study on China's policies for eco-innovation also touched upon the solar energy sector (OECD, 2009).

There is also a growing body of Chinese language literature on China's renewable energy sector development as well as PV sector development. Again, the majority of this literature is either business oriented market research or shorter reports in popular media reporting on sector developments. These latter type of sources have been of great value for this paper, as these reports reflect rather well the internal discussions in China on policy options and sector problems, sometimes being more open than academic articles on the subject. The number of Chinese academic books and articles reflecting more recent sector developments is not that large and often rather descriptive. A weakness shared by all publication on the PV sector related publications is the scarcity of detailed reliable data. This is naturally true for data regarding the year 2011 for which no official statistics are yet available, but also for earlier data, as renewable energies have for a long time not been part of the official Chinese energy statistics.

Most studies on China's PV power sector – both published in Chinese or in English – fail to highlight the embeddedness of the sector's development in the overall economic policy framework of China. No study known to the author has so far tried to systematically discuss the shift of the sector's development around 2009 and the lessons learned for low carbon development or LCT diffusion.

3. PV technologies and value chain[1]

In order to understand the Chinese PV paradox and the policy shifts at the end of the last decade it is necessary to grasp major characteristics of the solar PV value chain. The core of the PV value chain is the solar cell. Solar cells are composed of various semiconducting materials, but over 95% of all the solar cells produced worldwide are composed of the semiconductor material Silicon (Si). Three cell types are distinguished according to the type of silicon used: monocrystalline, polycrystalline and amorphous silicon cells. These three cell technology types differ in terms of their efficiency in solar energy transformation, the quality and amount of purified silicon needed, production costs as well as application.

The major raw material for solar PV, silicon, is not scarce, but has to be purified for PV cell use. In the early times of solar cell production, purified silicon was taken from scrap that came out of silicon production for chips and integrated circuits in the electronics industry. With growing global demand for polycrystalline silicon for PV use, special production facilities became necessary as the volumes of scrap left over from the electronics industry were no more sufficient. Silicon, once purified is then formed into wafers which are used for producing the solar cells. Finally, solar cells are integrated into modules.

At the upstream end of the production value chain, in the case of crystalline-based technology, the production and processing of silicon and its conversion into wafers requires substantial investment and technical knowledge. As a result, until the end of the last decade the number of enterprises engaged at this level of the production value chain used to be very small and prices were high. Cell and module production on the other hand is less knowledge and investment intensive, hence the number of producers is much larger.

Further down the production value chain, crystalline silicon modules and thin film modules do not differ much. The additional PV systems components (Balance of System components, BoS) such as inverters and battery materials are important components in the value chain of either technology for PV power production. Service and installation of PV systems are usually in the hand of smaller local businesses.

Solar energy produced by PV modules can be used in stand-alone technologies, i.e. cells integrated in electric or electronic products in order to produce the energy needed for this specific product. Small grid applications are also stand-alone solutions as the solar energy is fed into a small local electricity network, but not connected to a larger grid which also relies on input from other energy sources. Current discussions on the use and potential of solar energy often refer to PV power fed into a larger electricity grid. On grid solar PV can be produced in specific (larger) PV power plants or by PV installations connected to existing buildings (on roof tops, etc.). Grid connection of solar PV implies a challenge to traditional grids as PV power input is not produced on demand but depends on solar radiation. Therefore on grid PV power often requires technological upgrading of existing grid infrastructure.

This paper concentrates on grid connected solar PV in China but refers to other aspects of solar energy use necessary for putting PV sector development and energy use into perspective.

4. Genesis of China's PV industry paradox

The roots of the photovoltaic industry in China date back to the 1950s when the first attempts in research were undertaken. Until the end of the 1970s, interest in photovoltaic research was mainly nourished by the potential use of solar PV in space. The 6th Five-Year Plan (FYP) (1980–1985) was the first to include photovoltaic science and technology projects. A 'ground solar collaborative group' was established in 1983, as was the China Optoelectronics Technology Center, the first specialised research centre. Research in crystalline silicon cells and related technologies was then encouraged during the 7th FYP (1986–1990) and the first regional Renewable Energy Association was established in Anhui in 1992.

China's PV industry development accelerated during the 9th FYP (1996–2000). This was backed by a development strategy for renewable energies for the years 1996 to 2010, the China Light Project (1997) and support from the World Bank and the GEF for the commercialisation of renewable energies in China, a project that started in 1999. Industry development was also reflected in the founding of associations for renewable (and new) energy in all major provinces in the years after 1998.

During the 1990s and early in the twenty-first century, the industry's focus was on solar consumer goods production (like garden lamps, for example), mainly for exports, and electrification of remote rural areas. The 2002 state policy 'Send electricity to the village' (送电到乡) spurred progress in off-grid PV power generation, though overall PV power use remained at a still low level. At the end of 2003, China's total energy consumption was about 19000 GW (Pu and Zhong, 2008) to which total PV power generation contributed 50 MW. 36% of PV power was used by telecommunications and industry, 51% was used as electricity in rural and remote areas, 9% by solar powered consumer goods and only 4% were fed into the power grid. Also in 2003, China became the largest producer of solar consumer goods globally (Mu and Liu, 2009, p. 208).

Chinese enterprises entered the PV industry at that level in the global PVC where they possessed the greatest competitive advantage, i.e. the comparatively low cost production of solar cells and module assembly. The PV cell and module industry experienced a rapid take-off in the early 2000s when two major enterprises, Suntech Power and Tianwei Yingli New Energy Resources, started production. Between 1997 and 2005, while global production in PV cells grew at an average annual rate of 36%, production capacity in China nearly grew 70% annually (Marigo 2006). In more recent years (2005–2008), global production growth outside China was about 33% annually, while China's PV cell production still grew about 58%. As a result, China's market share in global PV cell production reached 33% in 2008 and 38% in 2009 (Eurobserv'er, 2010). By 2011, four of the 10 largest PV cell production companies in the world in terms of production capacity were of Chinese origin (Suntech, Yingli Green Energy, JA Solar and Trina Solar) with an aggregate production capacity of more than 11 GW (Eurobserv'er, 2011).

Today, most of the larger Chinese PV enterprises are vertically integrated along the core part of the production value chain, i.e. they produce wafers as well as cells and modules. Some are also engaged in silicon feedstock production. By 2010, more than 100 Chinese cities had developed so-called 'PV industry districts'. Total production capacity for PV cells reached about 20 GW with another 20 GW production capacity in the pipeline (Li and Wang, 2011).

Until the mid 1990s PV cell production in China was mainly for domestic use, but this changed completely afterwards. In the year 2009 around 95% of PV cells were produced for exports (Li, 2010, p. 38). China's growing importance in the global market for PV cells and modules was also reflected by the fact that 11 PV consumer goods producers are listed at foreign stock exchanges. The fast rise of China's solar cell producers as suppliers of cells and modules for markets in Europe and the US recurrently resulted in media headlines of China becoming the world's leading solar cell producer and a 'threat' for other countries' PV industry (Stokes 2010). Already the sector is facing trade disputes with US producers accusing the Chinese government of unduly supporting Chinese producers as well as dumping.

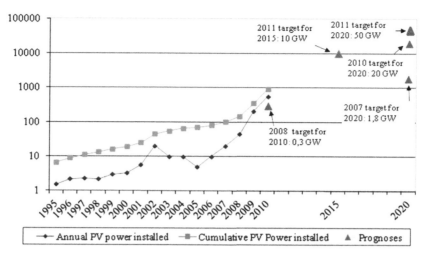

Figure 1.   Annual and cumulative installed PV power in China (in MW).
Source: Yan, 2009; NDRC, 2007; Li and Wang, 2011.

The rapid growth of the PV production and exports seemingly describes an easy to grasp success story of China's photovoltaic sector. However, hidden behind the story is an important paradox of solar energy development in China: while the production of PV cells and modules thrived, PV energy generation lagged behind. As can be seen from Figure 1, annual output of PV cells grew rapidly since 2002, while annual installation only managed to surpass the one time high threshold of 2002 (resulting from the rural electrification policy) again in 2008. As a result, China had a share in global PV cell production of 32.7% in 2008, whereas annual installations only accounted for 0.7% (2008) of global installed PV power (PV Group, 2009; Eurobserv'er, 2010). Until then, the prognoses for future PV power installation in the mainland also remained low: As lately as 2007, the National Development and Reform Commission (NDRC) still envisaged a cumulative PV power installation for 2020 of only 1800 MW (Figure 1). This target roughly equalled the existing Chinese producing capacity for PV cells (see Table 1) in the year 2008. It could hardly pass as ambitious.

Since 2009, annual installations have increased rapidly (see Table 1). While detailed statistics are not yet available for 2011, on grid installations at a minimum increased to 2000 MW according to the EPIA (2012) as well as Chinese newspaper reports.[2] Also since 2009, the official target for cumulative power installation for the year 2020 has been corrected upward by a dramatic degree. In 2010 the less ambitious target discussed was 20 GW installed power for 2020, while a more

Table 1.   Annual output of PV cells and annual PV power installation in China 2002–2010.

	2004	2005	2006	2007	2008	2009	2010
Annual output of PV cells (MWp)	50	200	370	1087	2589	4676	13018
Share in global PV cell production	4,0	11,0	14,6	27,2	32,9	37,6	47,8
Annual PV power installation (MW)	10	8,9	10	20	40	210	559
Off grid installation	8,8	7,4	9	17,8	19	50	84
On grid installation	1,2	1,5	1	2,2	21	160	475

Source: EPIA, 2010; Eurobserv'er, 2010; Li and Wang, 2011, pp. 36 and 40.

daring target of 30 GW was also mentioned. In the first half of 2011, based on the elaborations of the 12th Five-Year Plan (2011–2015), the target for 2020 was upgraded to 50 GW and the 10 GW target was advanced to 2015.[3]

5. Barriers to PV energy diffusion in China

Obviously the development of the Chinese PV sector has been very different in terms of production and export on the one hand and PV energy use on the other hand. This discrepancy between PV industry production and PV energy use was extremely prominent until 2009. Since then a major shift seems to be under way. The main indicator for this shift is rapidly growing PV installation rates in the Chinese market. What has subdued PV energy use before 2009? What has triggered the shift? What are the perspectives for accelerated PV energy use in China? In the following, these questions are discussed based on the framework developed earlier in the paper.

5.1 Barriers to PV diffusion: technology and knowledge base

Though the success story of PV cells and modules produced in China suggests the opposite, Chinese industry experts recurrently complain about the lack of core technologies owned by Chinese enterprise.

Until recently, China did not have the technological know-how for mass production of purified silicon that was suitable for PV cells (Li, 2009). Globally the market for mono- and polycrystalline silicon used to be dominated by seven large firms located mainly in Japan, the US and Europe which also controlled the technological know-how for large scale production. Chinese producers had to import about 95% of the purified silicon used in their PV cell production (Li, 2010, p. 38). With the demand for PV cells and modules growing, prices for purified silicon skyrocketed around 2008. Chinese enterprises feared that PV cells produced in China would not be competitive in the long term due to the dependence on imported silicon feedstock (CAS, 2010).

This situation changed after Chinese firms mastered major technologies for purified polycrystalline silicon production based on a technological cooperation with Russia.[4] Silicon production surged once the technological barriers were taken. Hoping to profit from early mover advantages numerous Chinese enterprises simultaneously started to invest in production lines for crystalline silicon. Statistical data on China's polycrystalline silicon production differ in detail, but they all reflect the same development. In 2005, while national production only amounted to 60 or 80 tonnes, the demand for the PV cell production was above 1600 tonnes. By 2008, the national production had expanded to 4000 to 5000 tonnes but was still lower than the national demand of that year. However production capacity was already said to be around 20,000 tonnes (Zhongguo Dianzi Bao (ZDB), 21.05.2010), indicating a huge growth in production capacity (Li, 2009). At the same time, according to official estimations, production lines were in the pipeline that would add another 100,000 tonnes of production capacity. By mid 2009, with these immense capacities gradually entering the market, overcapacity in crystalline silicon production dominated the local market discourse. Global market prices for purified silicon dropped considerably compared to earlier years challenging earlier business models and contracts. Chinese PV producers still import purified silicon from abroad, though, as only few silicon producers in China are able to meet international quality, efficiency and environmental standards, yet. Local production capacity growth for high quality silicon has not been as fast as PV cell production growth. Hence the lack of ownership of core technologies for the production of polycrystalline silicon is still an issue (Interview information November 2011[5]).

The industry is even more dependent on foreign technologies in other segments of the value chain. As an export-oriented mass production industry, the PV cell and module producing industry did not receive much government attention but was mainly driven by the private sector. Private enterprises in China, especially those in export-oriented industries, tend to be good in cost management, process innovation and production of economies of scale (Breznitz and Murphee, 2011). This has driven the success of the industry in global markets. However, Chinese private enterprises are – generally speaking – not investing much in R&D (OECD, 2008; Orcutt and Shen, 2010). Assessments of China's PV sector with regard to R&D and technology development are also rather pessimistic (Li and Wang 2011; Interview information November 2011). Chinese industry experts complain about a lack of know-how to produce high quality balance of systems components such as power inverters. They also criticise the lack of technological know-how for the production of machinery and assembly lines for PV cell and module production (Interview information April 2009 and November 2011, see also Mu and Liu, 2009, p. 178; Wang et al., 2011).

This in turn means that while Chinese producers are able to import the relevant technology for PV cell and module production, the costs of these imported technologies are deemed too high. Further localisation of production technologies is a major strategy for lowering unit prices of cell and modules as well as – eventually – the price of electricity generated from PV technology (China Medium and Long-term Energy Development Strategy Research Group, 2011).

In sum, due to a still high dependency on imports of foreign technology, China's role in the global PV industry value chain largely remained that of an export-processing PV cell and module producer. As such the PV industry fitted into the popular image of China as 'factory of the world'. From the Chinese perspective the PV sector was just another example of an industry that developed without ownership over the core technological know-how (He, 2010). Breakthroughs in purified silicon production have eased dependence and lowered prices since 2008. This definitely was helpful for diffusion of PV energy after 2009. But as China is still dependent on imports of silicon feedstock and production technology, other factors must have contributed to the shift as well.

5.2 *Barriers to PV energy use: lack of supportive policies*

Though important supporting policies for PV energy use were propagated in 2009, it would be misleading to argue that PV sector development only entered government strategies in 2009. The development of the sector had been supported by government policies even before 2009. Research and international cooperation regarding the production of purified silicon, for example, were supported by related industrial policies formulated in the course of the 10th FYP (NDRC, 2007/4). These policies encouraged the development of expertise on PV power technologies not yet available in China. However, at that time the policy support for the industry was not primarily driven by energy policy strategies. Supporting silicon purification and BoS components technologies fitted well into a major policy strategy that stressed 'indigenous' innovation and technological know-how. Indigenous innovation had become a major target of economic as well as STI policies in the new century in order to increase Chinese ownership in core technologies, including those relevant for export industries (Cao et al., 2006; Gu and Lundvall, 2006).

The promotion of PV for grid connected energy supply in China formally started in 2006 with the Renewable Energy Law (REL 2006). This law was accompanied by 'Provisional Administrative Measures on Pricing and Cost sharing for Renewable Energy Power Generation'. These two regulations established three major principles for PV power installations (Li, 2009; Li, 2010).

- Grid operators should enter into grid connection agreements with legally licensed renewable power generating enterprises, buy the grid-connected power produced from renewable energy within the coverage of their power grid, and provide grid connection services for the generation of power from renewable energies.

- The compensation paid to power generators for solar energy fed into the grid would be defined by the government, with the price level following standards defined by the price authorities of the State Council according to the principle of 'reasonable costs plus reasonable profits'.
- Additional costs occurring from the production and connection of renewable energies would not to be borne by energy producers or grid operators but by all electricity users.

In mid 2007 the National Development and Reform Commission published a 'Long- and medium-term development plan for renewable energies (RE LMDP)' (NDRC 2007) which was followed by an '11th FYP for Renewable Energies' (NDRC 2007/4). The latter revised those parts on the general 11th FYP (2006–2010) relevant to renewable energies based on the policy changes initiated with the promulgation of the Renewable Energy Law and RE LMDP.

Regardless of the progress in legislation and planning, policy support was not sufficient to trigger high rates of PV installations prior to 2009. First of all, the above listed principles for renewable energy purchase by grid operators did not work well. This became obvious by a revision of the REL at the end of 2009 which stressed the duty of grid operators to actually purchase all PV power produced (see also Table 2). Obviously grid operators had been reluctant to do so in

Table 2.   Major PV power installation related regulations, 2009 and 2010.

Date	Name	Focus
March 2009	National subsidy program for building integrated PV (BIPV) applications and rooftop systems (太阳能光电建筑应用财政补助资金管理办法)	Fixed upfront subsidy of 15-20 yuan per watt of installation
July 2009	Rules for model cities in building integrated renewable energy (可再生能源建筑应用城市示范实施方案)	Model cities at district level can receive 50 to 80 million Yuan financial support for large scale installations of building integrated renewable energy On average no more than three cities per province should be supported
July 2009	Golden Sun program (金太阳示范工程财政补助资金管理暂行办法)	Main target areas: – 'User side' grid connected PV power production demonstration projects of large industrial enterprises (BIPV and rooftop) – (Enhanced) electrification of remote and rural areas (off grid) – Integration of wind and PV systems – Large scale on-grid PV power plant projects – Minimum 300 KWp; minimum 20 year use Subsidies of 50 per cent of total investment for on grid projects; 70 per cent of total investment for rural off grid systems; the program was originally limited to support a total of 500 MW in PV installations but later extended to more than 642 MW.
Dec. 2009	REL Revision (in force since April 2010)	Integration of revenues from electricity surcharge and special government funds into the 'renewable energy development fund' Change of 'full purchase (of RE power)' into 'guaranteed full purchase of RE power'

Sources: Wang et al., 2011; Li and Wang, 2011.

the past. Second, as far as targets for renewable energy use were formulated before 2009, these plans focused on wind energy while PV energy related targets were moderate at best. Wind power installations were given policy priority and as a consequence grew much faster than PV installations.

In sum, prior to 2009 and in contrast to the wind energy sector that was supported by additional sector specific preferential policies, the support for PV energy and the PV industry by the central government has not been strong, not well coordinated and lacked comprehensive, systemic administrative rules and fine-tuned policies (He, 2010).

5.3 *Barriers to PV energy use: competing strategies and interests*

The reluctance of the central government to fully support (on grid) PV power installations primarily resulted from a number of competing policy goals and considerations:

- *Energy security.* Until 2009 the dependence of the industry on imports of major input factors (purified silicon) was seen as a weakness of the industry (CAS 2010). As China's energy policies are at least as much driven by concerns of energy security as by concerns of climate change, the dependence on (until 2008) costly imports for the main raw material and major production technologies lessened the attractiveness of PV energy (Hallding et al. 2008). With oil dependence already a major concern in terms of energy security, adding 'silicon dependence' was not a logical thing to do.
- *Low cost energy provision.* The progress in PV technologies notwithstanding, PV power is still expensive compared to fossil-fuel generated power, but also compared to wind power. As Chinese electricity price are not liberalised and low energy prices are still seen as important for social and political stability, PV power was the least welcomed among the renewable energies. Especially wind energy was cheaper than PV energy (Wang et al., 2011).
- *Environmental protection.* PV power production did not enjoy a reputation of being environmentally friendly or energy efficient. Quite the opposite, some scandals exposed weak environmental rules and supervision. Even today, critical assessments of the industry complain about environmental damage created mainly by silicon producers. Some difficulties of environmental problems are attributed to a lack of know-how and the costs of acquiring clean technologies for production processes. In any case, PV energy did not promise progress or reputational gains for governments in terms of environmental protection (Li and Wang, 2011).
- *State guidance for strategic sectors.* Private enterprises dominate the PV manufacturing industry, whereas the energy sector as a strategic sector is under government control. Both sectors follow very different logics, especially in the Chinese economic system. The uneasiness of the state in face of large quantities of smaller and medium-sized private enterprises is discernible in comments that a clean-up of the market is necessary. The uneasiness of the PV industry with state guidance flashes up in discussions about the government trying to crowd out private entrepreneurs (国进民退 (The state enterprises come in and the private enterprises have to step back.)).
- In addition to the challenge PV energy posed for some strategic policy goals, the lack of policy support for PV installations was also the result of investment insecurities. First, PV power production is less locally concentrated than wind production in China. In the long term, the largest potential for PV power is expected from integration of PV energy production into urban areas (building integrated photovoltaics, BIPV). However, the fast changing Chinese urban landscape, the urban electricity system as well as the home ownership system do make investment strategies for urban PV power deployment difficult and risky (OECD 2009). Second, early support of on grid solar PV would have implied a technology

choice. With different PV technologies at hand that differ in terms of energy efficiency as well as production prices (see above), any price for PV energy fed into the grid practically would favour one technology over the other and therefore some enterprises over others.

The principle advantages of PV power in decentralised power generation also dampened the enthusiasm of the big traditional power companies to push for PV power. Even if they did not perceive a challenge to their power as such, the capacity of the Chinese grid to digest larger volumes of PV power in peak times is estimated to be very low.[6] Hence PV energy potentially increased net insecurity and heightens the pressure to improve the net.

6. The shift towards PV use after 2009

Starting from 2009 PV installations started to surge (see Table 1). This surge was the result of three major developments that were important for the industry, namely the international financial crisis, policy changes in the major importing market and shifting government strategies in the context of the Copenhagen climate negotiations.

First, the repercussions of the global financial crisis confronted China's PV industry with the danger of declining exports. Global market prices for polycrystalline silicon had plunged due to the expansion of capacities within and outside China. Lower prices for the main raw material promised higher margin for the industry and led to the expansion of PV cell and module producing capacities. By early 2009, fierce supply competition and falling prices were expected even without the financial crises. In this situation, the global financial crisis additionally dampened perspectives for exports in 2009.

Second, upcoming changes in the German support schemes for PV power installations added speculations about a global market downturn. Together, the high volatility of the market following the silicon production boom and the global financial crisis demonstrated the vulnerability of China's export-oriented PV sector to the Chinese government. It suddenly became obvious that many enterprises and jobs within the PV production chain were in danger. This together with the existing overcapacities meant that a downturn of the industry could create social instability in some regions. While some sector experts saw the crisis as a welcome wave to wash away some of the smaller, more pollutant and less competitive enterprises in the sector, the central government felt obliged to push the local market for PV power installations (Song, 2010).

Third, in the run-up to the Copenhagen summit in 2009 the Chinese government adjusted its attitude regarding the global climate change negotiations. China offered a voluntary commitment as input to the Copenhagen Conference of Parties in 2009 that submitted under the Copenhagen Accord, promising a reduction of carbon intensity of GDP of 40 to 45% until 2020. This ambitious target requires a drastic increase of the share of renewable energy in China's energy mix. Respective objectives have been included in the 12th FYP (Fischer and Chen, 2011). Both the central government and local governments acknowledged that these objectives could only be realised with an increase in the use of solar PV, hence the longer term targets for PV power production were revised accordingly (see Figure 1).

As a result of these developments, PV power suddenly became part of a larger strategy package of the Chinese government to stimulate domestic demand, change the Chinese growth model and promote low carbon development as a remedy against the financial crisis. Two major programmes were published in the first and third quarter of 2009, the BIPV and rooftop subsidy scheme as well as the Golden Sun Project (see Table 2). These were supported by policies for model city experiments and the revision of the Renewable Energy Law.

As can be seen from the Table, the policies provided financial support for PV energy use in addition to the price regulations defined by the earlier renewable energy law. This immediately triggered fast increases in installations as reflected in recent industry statistics (see section 3). In addition, these policies had an important signalling function for the industry and nurtured hopes for a take-off of the Chinese market for PV installations in the near future.

However, with the weakness and volatility of the international markets continuing, the government met increasing pressure in 2011 to formulate more substantial and long-term policies. Hence, in 2011, the government expanded its policy support for the industry by propagating a first national feed-in tariff (FIT) for PV energy in August 2011 (NDRC 2011).

On the one hand, considering past barriers and political concerns regarding support for PV energy use in China explained above, the FIT is a great step ahead towards PV diffusion. On the other hand, the FIT rate is very low. At the current FIT level, only large PV plants located in Western regions of China where sun radiation is good and land prices are low seem to have economic potential.[7] Industry experts expect that the current FIT will only be attractive to state-backed project developers which in return will cooperate with producers of cheap, but comparatively low quality cells and modules. Producers of higher quality and higher price cells and modules will continue to look for export opportunities in markets with more generous policy support for PV energy (Interview information 2011). This may exactly have been the intention of the central government in a situation where it wants to avoid damage to local production and employment from a global market downturn and intends to accelerate grid parity of solar PV simultaneously.

7. Challenges of PV energy use in China: lessons learnt for low carbon development?

The Chinese PV sector example with its specific development paradox underlines the complexity of LCT diffusion. The fact that China already had a large PV manufacturing industry did not trigger solar PV diffusion. Instead, barriers in terms of technology, policies and political priorities dampened PV use for on grid electricity generation before 2009. Referring to the three major potential barriers to LCT diffusion discussed above (section 2) the Chinese PV sector shows that

- Access to LCTs is crucial. The Chinese experience stresses that LCT diffusion depends not merely on the ability to acquire processed raw materials (silicon) or technology (machinery) produced abroad but also on the ability to produce that technology. This approach is in line with the argument of Byrne et al. (2011) as well as Altenburg and Pegels, (2012) that development of a low carbon innovation system is crucial for developing countries progress in low carbon development.
- Policy support for low carbon technology diffusion is important. Policy support and resulting financial incentives for PV installations were insufficient before 2009. Only more dedicated policies and long-term objectives triggered a substantial growth in PV installations. Global negotiations and support for LCT transfer should consequently include support for the development and implementation of diffusion-oriented policies.
- Competing strategic policy objectives can limit LCT diffusion even if technologies are available and supportive policies are nominally in place. With regard to the Chinese PV sector, energy security, social stability and environmental considerations, amongst others, made PV energy a rather unattractive LCT option regardless of the large PV industry existing in the country and a renewable energy law promulgated in 2006.

The PV paradox disappeared only after major technological hurdles were taken, political interests shifted and policies were adjusted accordingly. The shift in solar PV deployment, though eventually beneficial for climate change mitigation, was not only and arguably not even primarily caused by climate policy considerations. Hence, in global negotiations for climate change mitigation and in calls for faster LCT diffusion in developing and emerging countries, the importance of national interests and institutional environments of the involved countries has to be considered seriously. At the same time, the argument that climate change mitigation efforts of developing countries depend on access to technology and hence technology transfer from industrialised countries is only partly true, as availability of LCTs is only a necessary but not sufficient condition of LCT diffusion.

The Chinese solar PV example also shows that LCT diffusion has to be understood in a global market context. Chinese strategies for renewable energy development of recent years always had the importance of renewable energies for future national development in mind, but also aimed at international competitiveness. Similar, while the importance attributed to nationalisation of PV technology was first of all driven by cost considerations, it was also driven by strategic considerations regarding energy security and the international race for technological leadership in green industries.

For the future, with major technical barriers overcome and important policy shifts taken, PV installations in China will continue to grow fast. The Chinese PV paradox will eventually disappear. It can be expected that China will sooner or later become the largest PV industry not only in terms of production but also regarding installations. Foreign producers of cells and modules will probably not gain large stakes in this market as Chinese producers already dominate the world market and have long specialised in low cost production based on economies of scale.

Notes

1. The summary of the technology and PV value chain characteristics is based on Kirkegaard et al., 2010, Foster et al., 2010, PV Group, 2009 and Yang et al., 2003.
2. http://www.solarf.net/html/2011/market/hot-news_12/20309.html.
3. At the end of 2011 the NDRC again accelerated plans, announcing that the target for installation in 2015 was augmented to 15 GW. http://www.solarf.net/html/2011/market/hot-news_12/20309.html.
4. Interview information. See also a news report on the start of this cooperation with an enterprise of Ningxia Autonomous Region on the Siemens process of purified silicon production in 2005. (http://news4888120060323.0595stw.com). Breakthroughs with regard to mastering the technology for mass production of purified silicon were also reported by Sichuan Xingguang Silicon in 2007 (Wei 2007) and Luoyang Zhonggui HighTech in 2009 (Ya 2009).
5. Interviews with researchers and experts in industry associations as well as foreign and Chinese firms were conducted in 2009, 2010 and 2011 in Beijing and Shanghai. The names and institutions of the interview partners are not published in the paper. Especially Chinese interview partners have asked to remain anonymous. Given the nervous state of the industry related to the ongoing trade disputes, also interview partners of foreign firms prefer not to be cited with critical comments.
6. According to one Chinese expert, as of 2011 the grid would face serious trouble as soon as PV energy would exceed 3 GW (interview information November 2011).
7. http://guangfu.bjx.com.cn/news/20110916/310209.shtml

References

Altenburg, T., and Pegels, A. (2012) Sustainability-oriented innovation systems – managing the green transformation, *Innovation and Development*, forthcoming 2012.

Benioff, R., Coninck, H., Dhar, S., Hansen, U., McLaren, J., and Painuly, J. (2010) Strengthening clean energy technology cooperation under the UNFCCC: Steps towards implementation, NREL/T-6A0-48596. Golden, National Renewable Energy Laboratory.

Borup, M., Andersen, P., Jacobbsen, S., and Midttun, A. (2008) Nordic energy innovation systems – Patterns of need integration and cooperation, Nordic Energy Research, November 2008, available at: http://www.nordicenergy.net/publications.cfm?id=3-0&path=10.

Breznitz, D., and Murphee, M. (2011) *The Run of the Red Queen – Government, innovation, globalization and economic growth in China* (New Haven and Londong: Yale University Press).

Byrne, R., Smith, A., Watson, J., and Ockwell, D. (2011) Energy pathways in low-carbon development: From technology transfer to socio-technical transformation. *STEPS Working Paper 46*, Brighton, STEPS Centre.

Cao, C., Suttmeier, R., and Simon, D. (2006) China's 15-year science and technology plan. *Physics Today*, December 2006, pp. 38–43.

CAS (China Academy of Science Sustainable Development Research Group) (2010) China sustainable development strategy report 2010 – Green development and innovation (Chin.). Beijing. Kexue Chubanshe.

China Medium and Long-term Energy Development Strategy Research Group (2011) China medium and longterm (2030, 2050) energy development strategy – Renewable energy volume (Chin.). Beijing, Kexue Chubanshe.

EPIA (European Photovoltaic Industry Association) (2010) Global market outlook for photovoltaics until 2014, Brussels, available at: www.epia.org.

EPIA (European Photovoltaic Industry Association) (2012) Market report 2011, available at: http://www. epia.org/publications/photovoltaic-publications-global-market-outlook.html.

Eurobserv'er (2010) Photovoltaic Barometer, April 2010, available at: http://www.eurobserv-er.org/pdf/baro196.pdf.

Eurobserv'er (2011) Photovoltaic Barometer, April 2010, available at: http://www.eurobser-er.org/pdf/baro202asp

Fischer, D., and Chen, Y. (2011) Climate change governance: A comparison of the EU and China, in: Fues, T., Liu, Y. (eds) *Globl Goverace an and Building a Harmonious World: A comparison of European and Chinese concepts* (Bonn: DIE Studies No. 62), pp. 57–72.

Foster, R., Ghassemi, M., and Cota, A. (2010) *Solar Energy – Renewable energy and the environment* (Boca Raton: Taylor&Francis).

Grimpe, C., Leheyda, N., Rammer, C., Schmiele, A., and Sofka, W. (2008) Sectoral innovation systems in Europe: Monitoring, analysing trends and identifying challenges, Europe Innova Sector Report. Mannheim, ZEW.

Gu, S., and Lundvall, B (2006) China's innovation system and the move toward harmonious growth and endogenous innovation. *DRUID Working Papers 06-07*, available at: http://www3.druid.dk/wp/20060007.pdf.

Hallding, K., Han, G., and Olsson, M. (2009), China's Climate- and Energy-security Dilemma: Shaping a New Path of Economic Growth, *Journal of Current Chinese Affairs*, 38 (3), 119-134.

He, X. (2010) With PV standards in the hand of others, indigenous innovation is the way to break the ice (Chin.), *Science Daily*, 25.1.2010.

Helm, D. (2010) Government failure, rent-seeking, and capture: The design of climate change policy. *Oxford Review of Economic Policy*, 26(2), pp. 182–196, doi:10.1093/oxrep/grq006.

IEA (International Energy Agency) (2008) Deploying renewables – Principles for effective policies. Paris, IEA/OECD.

Kirkegaard, J., Hanemann, T., Weischer, L., and Miller, M. (2010) Toward a funny future? Global integration in the solar PV industry, Peterson Institute for International Economics Working Paper Series, WP 10–6, Washington.

Lewis, J. (2007) China's strategic priorities in international climate change negotiations. *The Washington Quarterly*, 31(1), 155–174.

Li, D. (2009) The solar power sector in China. London Research International. *LRI Energy Paper*, available at: http://www.doc88.com/p-718479322457.html

Li, L. (2010) Concise analysis of the current state of China's PV industry part II (Chin.). *Yangguang nengyuan* (Solar Energy), 2010(2), pp. 36–39.

Li, J., and Wang, S. (2011) China solar PV outlook 2011 (Chin.). Beijing, Zhongguo Huangjing Kexue Chubanshe.

Liu, L., Wang, Z., Zhang, H., and Xue, Y. (2010) Solar energy development in China – a review, *Renewable and Sustainable Energy Reviews*, 14(1), pp. 301–311.

Malerba, F. (2004), Sectoral Systems of Innovation. Concepts, Issues and Analyses of Six Major Sectors in Europe. Cambridge, Cambridge University Press, 2004.

Marigo, N. (2006) The Chinese silicon photovoltaic industry and market: A critical review of trends and outlook, *Progress in Photovoltaics: Research and Applications*, 15(2), 143–162.

Marigo, N., Foxon, T., and Pearson, P. (2007) Comparing innovation systems for solar photovoltaics in the United Kingdom and in China; available at: http://dspace-unipr.cilea.it/bitstream/1889/871/1/Marigo-Foxon-Pearson.pdf.

Mu, X., and Liu, B. (2009) *Research on the Development and Industrialization of New and Renewable Energies* (Chin.) (Beijing: Petroleum Industry Publishing House).

NDRC (2007) National Development and Reform Commission: Long- and medium-term development plan for renewable energies (Chin.), available at: http://www.ccchina.gov.cn/WebSite/CCChina/UpFile/ 2007/20079583745145.pdf.

NDRC (2007/4) National Development and Reform Commission: The 11th Five Year Development Plan for the energy sector (Chin.), April 2007, available at: http://www.ccchina.gov.cn/WebSite/CCChina/ UpFile/File186.pdf.

NDRC (2011) Notice of the National Development and Reform Commission about enhancing the feed-in pricing strategy for grid integrated PV solar energy (Chin.), NDRC price regulation No. 1594 (2011), 01.08.2011.

Newell, P., Philipps, J., and Mulvaney, D. (2011) Pursuing clean energy equitably, UNDP Human Development Research Paper 2011/03.

OECD (2008) OECD Reviews of innovation policy – China. Paris, OECD.

OECD (2009) Eco-innovation policies in The People's Republic of China. Environment Directorate, OECD.

Orcutt, J. and Shen, J. (2010) Shaping China's innovative future: university technology transfer in transition (Cheltenham: Edward Elgar).

PV Group (2009) PV Group white paper – China's solar future, available at: http://www.pvgroup.org/ AboutPVGroup/index.htm.

PV Group (2011) China's solar future – A recommended China PV policy roadmap 2.0, available at: http://www. pvgroup.org/sites/pvgroup.org/files/cms/groups/public/documents/web_content/2011China_White_Paper_ FINAL.pdf.

Pu, G., and Zhong, F. (2008) Construction of a high efficient electricity system for a clean economy, in: M. Cui (ed.) *Annual Report on China's Energy Development 2008*, pp. 210--256, (Chin.) (Beijing: Social Sciences Academic Press).

Savin, J., and Flavin, C. (2004) National policy instruments – Policy lessons for advancement of renewable energy technologies around the world, Thematic Background Paper, International Conference on Renewable Energies, Bonn 2004, available at: http://www.renewables2004.de/pdf/tbp/TBP03-policies.pdf.

Saviotti, P. (2005) On the co-evolution of technologies and institutions, in: M. Weber and J. Hemmelskamp (eds) *Towards Environment Innovation Systems*, pp. 9–31 (Berlin: Springer).

Song, M. (2010) Government support energizes China's PV market, SEMI PV Group, available at: http:// www.pvgroup.org/NewsArchive/ctr_034481, February 2010.

Steinfeld, E. (2010) *Playing Our Game – Why China's rise doesn't threat the West* (Oxford: Oxford University Press).

Stokes, B. (2010) Emerging green technology poses threat of trade wars, YaleGlobalonline, 14.5.2010, available at: url: http://yaleglobal.yale.edu/print/6336.

The Climate Group (2011) China's clean revolution IV: Financing China's low carbon growth (Chin.). Beijing, The Climate Group, November 2011.

The World Bank (2010) World development report 2010 – Development and climate change, Washington.

Wang, Z., Ren, D., and Gao, L. (2011) The renewable energy industrial report 2010 (Chin.). (Beijing: Huaxue gongye chubanshe).

Wei, Z. (2007) Xingguang Silicon in advance in mastering the great struggle of producing poly-christalline silicon (chin.), *Guangfu Zhuankan*, available at: http://www.pvall.com/html/news/2007-03/info21366-546htm

Ya, D. (2009) A production lane of 2000 tons annual production of poly-chrystalline silicon is already in use (chin.), *Zhongguo Dianzibao*, available at: http://www.solar.ofweek.com/2009-04/ART-260003-8

Yan, H. (2009) Subsidy policy design for increasing solar photovoltaic installed capacity in China – A system dynamics based study, University of Bergen.

Yang, H., Wang, H., Yu, H., Xi, J., Cui, R., and Chen, G. (2003) Status of photovoltaic industry in China. *Energy Policy*, 31(8), pp. 703–707.

Index

Tables are indicated by page numbers in **bold** and figures are indicated by page numbers in *italics*.

For Product Safety Concerns and Information please contact our EU
representative GPSR@taylorandfrancis.com Taylor & Francis Verlag GmbH,
Kaufingerstraße 24, 80331 München, Germany

Printed and bound by CPI Group (UK) Ltd, Croydon, CR0 4YY
01/05/2025
01858355-0013